MAX IELTS

雅思阅读

高分榜中榜

刘巍巍　编著

世界图书出版公司
广州·上海·西安·北京

图书在版编目(CIP)数据

雅思阅读高分榜中榜/刘巍巍编著.—广州：广东世界图书出版公司，2005.2
ISBN 978-7-5062-6338-2/H·0424

Ⅰ.雅…　Ⅱ.刘…　Ⅲ.英语—阅读教学—高等学校—入学考试. 国外—自学参考资料　Ⅳ.H319.4

中国版本图书馆CIP数据核字(2003)第120315号

雅思阅读高分榜中榜

策　　划：沙去龙　丁春玲
责任编辑：杨敏珊　丁春玲
封面设计：李康道
出版发行：广东世界图书出版公司
（广州市新港西路大江冲25号　邮编：510300）
电　　话：020-84451969
http://www.gdst.com.cn E-mail: pub@gdst.com.cn
经　　销：各地新华书店
印　　刷：惠州报业传媒印务有限公司
版　　次：2005年2月第1版第1次印刷
2013年11月第2版第6次印刷
开　　本：787mm×1092mm　1/16
印　　张：21
印　　数：13 001~15 000册
字　　数：483千
ISBN 978-7-5062-6338-2/H·0424
定　　价：42.80元

谨以此书献给
在雅思备考中追求卓越，挑战极限，
在绝望中寻找希望的广大考生们。
你们的人生终将辉煌！

序

在刘巍巍老师的新书《雅思阅读高分榜中榜》和《雅思词汇速听速记》即将付诸出版之际，他邀请我为他的新书作序。欣然接受之余，我也感觉非常愉快。雅思考试是目前中国国内参加考试人数最多的国外考试之一，雅思培训，也是新东方国外考试部继托福、GRE和GMAT培训之后，推出的又一品牌项目，在学生中享有很高的声誉。新东方的雅思培训以最严格的标准选拔出各个学科的佼佼者，聚集了国内最顶尖的师资，因而每年都吸引了数万学员前来参加培训，和新东方的老师们一起感受新东方的激情，体验新东方的成功。

不断地开拓新的培训项目，为即将奔赴海外的学子们提供更为全面的服务，是新东方不懈的追求。正是这样的追求，激励着新东方人在出国留学之路上取得了一个又一个巨大的成功，鞭策着新东方在教育强国的道路上大步向前进。新东方不仅成功帮助大批学子顺利踏上出国留学的征途，而且还新启动了"彩虹计划"——建设海外留学生人才库，为回国发展的留学生牵线搭桥。然而仅仅有这样的追求，新东方仍不足以取得今天的巨大成功。理想和信念指明了新东方前进的方向，但前进道路上的每一步，都需要每一个新东方人付出扎扎实实的努力。新东方从创立至今，已经有11年的历史，11年来，从最初筚路蓝缕、辛苦创业，到后来脱颖而出、独树旗帜，新东方走过的每一步，都离不开每一位新东方人的付出和努力。在教学一线的新东方教师，是新东方团队中的中流砥柱；强大的师资，是新东方人有胆量实现我们追求的信心保证。新东方不仅拥有一支教学水平卓越的教师队伍，而且能够不断地吸引更多非常优秀的年轻教师加入到新东方的团队当中来，教授雅思的刘巍巍老师就是他们当中的典型代表。

刘巍巍老师曾是新东方最年轻的老师。凭借在雅思、托福考试中的出色成绩和出众的教学能力，他在刚满20岁时就成为了新东方的教师，是在学生"质疑"的目光中登上新东方讲台的。很快刘巍巍老师就凭借雄厚的英语实力和出色的授课方式，征服了广大的雅思学员，迅速成为了新东方最受欢迎的教师之一。在新东方工作的这几年中，刘巍巍老师又多次在各个部门的教学考核中名列前茅，成为了新东方教师队伍中新一代的领军人物，学生们称他为新东方的"天才教师"。然而新东方深知每一位新东方教师的成功都不会是偶然，就像新东方本身的成功，也绝非偶然。刘巍巍老师在新东方工作期间，即使每天授课十个小时，依然坚持在课后记录自己当天的教学心得，把学生的困惑和自己在课堂教学中发现的问题及时记录下来；即使是几百人的大班，他也坚持课下答疑、回复学生的邮件甚至是电话，以非常谦逊坦诚的态度和学生进行交流，了解学生的实际学习情况，没有一点年轻人的浮躁。正是凭着这样的工作热情，刘巍巍老师才能够迅速在学生中创下良好的口碑，成为教学舞台上的明星。

我曾亲自去课堂里听过刘巍巍老师的授课。作为新东方的创始人，我最为关注的，始终是新东方的教学质量，因为我深知教学质量是新东方的生命力所在。刘巍巍老师的授课让人感觉风格很清新，收放自如，既有年轻人的活泼和朝气，也不失教师的稳重和严谨。相信每一位听过刘巍巍老师雅思课程的新东方学生，对此应该更是深有体会。刘巍巍老师的这两本书，也和他的授课一样，思路清晰，而且文笔非常亲切，排版也很精致，很多考生容易忽视的知识点都用“特别提醒”加以注明，完全没有一般教科书的生硬感，是真正适合学生的备考用书。这两本书原本在2002年就已经完稿，到今年已经有两年多的时间。在这两年多的时间中，刘巍巍老师在新东方面授了上万雅思学员，积累了大量的教学经验，加深了对雅思考试的理解，也提高了对中国学生雅思复习过程中所面临的实际困难的认识。如今，刘巍巍老师将修订了十几遍的原稿整理成册，并且加入了最新的雅思考试资讯和自身的教学心得，相信定能助广大雅思考生一臂之力。

特别值得一提的是，《雅思阅读高分榜中榜》是中国第一本配有详细解题说明的雅思阅读用书，算是开创了国内雅思教学的先河。书中绝大多数题目都配有非常详细的讲解，让考生不仅知其然，而且知其所以然。无独有偶，《雅思词汇速听速记》一书也在语言教学法方面有很大的突破，这本书把雅思考试中的核心词汇按照出现的场景精心分类，彻底从词汇书按字母表顺序排列这一传统习惯中解脱出来，例句也多来源于雅思考试中真实出现的例句或国外经典电影的台词，使雅思词汇更加贴近生活，方便考生记忆。这种编写理念，有别于传统的结构教学法，也不完全等同于情景教学法，属于交际——语法教学法的范畴，代表的是国际语言学领域中最先进的语言教学理念。新东方一直鼓励教师在教学方面大胆创新，很多年轻老师在这方面颇有建树，新东方的课堂，也因此呈现出百花齐放的局面。刘巍巍老师的这两本书，是新东方在雅思教学领域的又一突破，势必会对国内的雅思教学起到很好的引导作用！

最后，祝贺《雅思阅读高分榜中榜》和《雅思词汇速听速记》两书的出版，也祝愿刘巍巍老师的雅思教学方面能够更上一层楼。衷心希望大家顺利通过雅思考试，实现自己的人生梦想，从绝望中寻找到希望！

新东方教育科技集团
董事长兼总裁

2004年12月

第一版前言

在新东方工作的这几年，我有幸接触到数万名学员。他们来自社会不同的角落，怀着不同的梦想，身后拖着不同的人生轨迹，却为了一个共同的目的——顺利通过雅思考试，聚集到了我的课堂。雅思考试只是他们出国过程中的一小步，却也是他们庞大的人生规划中的一大步。天生性格使我很愿意倾听这些学员的故事。他们对自己的人生有着怎样的规划？他们有着怎样的彷徨和迷茫？这些都是我感兴趣的事情。同样因为天生性格，我是个很好的倾听者，学员们大多也很愿意和我聊天。很多学员的年纪都比我大，倾听他们的生活感悟和人生规划，对我而言，是件幸福无比而又受益匪浅的事，尽管还是因为天生性格的原因，聊天的过程中我总是听得很多却说得很少。于是，教学的过程，也就因此而变成了我自己人生阅历丰富的过程，甚至成为了结交朋友的过程。常常庆幸自己能够拥有一份这样的工作，也时时提醒自己要懂得珍惜，要更加用心地去教学。

记得若干年前，我曾在一篇文章中读到这样一句话“Teaching is a job one can never be perfect at（教书是一份永远都不可能完美的工作）”。当时我刚登上讲台，原本就年少气盛、血气方刚，偏偏学生对我的教学又评价颇高，所以自然对此很是不屑。当时骨子里的那股狂妄使我在心里默默下决心要让自己的授课做到比最好还要更好——完美。几年的日子悄然过去了，当年的教材已经破烂不堪，教材的内容却已烂熟于心。虽然授课的确还算成功，虽然学员的反馈一如既往地很好，我却再也不敢轻言完美。阅历的增加使得成熟和理智彻底取代了当年的狂妄，很多的事情都已经发生改变，但是有一件事情却从来没有改变过，那就是内心深处对完美的追求，只是这种追求更多体现在行动中。正是为了追求教学方面的完美，我才下决心一定要挤出时间来系统整理自己的雅思教学材料，于是也就有了写这本书的初衷。

如今书写完了，在更加深刻地理解当年读到的那句话的含义的同时，还很想补充一句，那就是“Compiling is also a job one can never be perfect at（写书也是一份永远都不可能完美的工作）”。用心去写一本好书有多么难，相信每位曾经用心去写过书的人都深有体会。这套书原本在2002年就已经全部完稿，两年多中我把几十万字的书稿反复阅读了数十次。每读一次，都会发现一些不足，也都会获得一些新的思路，于是又开始了漫无止境的校稿和修订过程。这样的反反复复，不仅让出版日期一推再推，也耗尽了我原本就非常有限的空余时间。眼睁睁地看着市面上的雅思类出版物从一种变成几十种，再从几十种变成几百种，说心里不着急，未免过于虚伪。但是我却在这个过程中真真实实地体会到了一种快乐。这种快乐，源自心底对完美的追求。每次修订一遍稿件，心里都有一种特别满足的快感。我向新东方的同事自嘲，说这是完美主义的快乐之旅。

本书完整地收集了我的雅思教学材料，体现的是雅思考试的真正特点。我一直反对考生一味地追求押题或猜题，因为大凡是考试，就必定要求考生有扎实的基础。雅思考试作为一项国际范围的英语语言测试，更是要求考生拥有扎实的语言功底作为依托。缺乏英语语言知识，缺乏对考试内容的正确把握，任何的投机取巧都注定了会失败。这本书里没有任何内容涉及到押题或猜题，但是却扎扎实实地重现了近15年来雅思考试的完整风貌。我希望通过这本书，让考生真正地了解雅思这项考试，了解它的特点、规律和考点。例如，书中的大多数阅读试题都配备了解题指导，我使用尽可能浅显而生动的语言来为读者讲解这些试题，目的就是希望读者能够真正用心体会这些解题思路，由点及面，把握雅思考试的正确方向，跳出题海，站在一个较高的高度看待雅思考试。排版结束后，我又仔细阅读了全部稿件，自认为和同类型的其它书籍相比较，这本书有以下几个突出的特点：

1. 内容全面

本书全面介绍了雅思阅读的全部9种题型，每种题型都配有题型分析和例题讲解，既分析题型技巧，也提供大量实战练习，让考生真正把握雅思考试进入中国15年来的变化趋势。

2. 清晰明了

本书以实际考试中出现频率的高低为顺序介绍了雅思阅读的全部9种题型。每种题型都从“题型介绍”入手，逐步过渡到“技巧讲解”和“例题分析”，编排顺序一目了然，清晰明了。

3. 讲练结合

本书所体现的，是我在新东方的课堂上一直推崇的教学模式“题型—技巧—例题—练习”，讲解和练习相辅相成，有讲有练。只有教师的讲解和学生的练习相结合，才能够相得益彰，事半功倍。

4. 授人以渔

本书中的大多数阅读试题不仅给出了正确答案，而且还配有详细的讲解，让考生不仅可以发现自己的错误，而且还能够对比自己和教师解题思路的异同，自己纠正自己的错误，真正达到授人以渔的目的。

5. 适合自学

本书特别考虑了因为种种原因而未能参加雅思面授的考生。以“特别提醒”的方式，重点突出了雅思考试阅读方面的难点和需要注意的事项，非常适合考生自学。

正如前文所述，因为力求完美，这本书前前后后修订了两年多。估计如果再坚持，继续修订20年也并非不可能。如今，我下定决心将它付诸出版。虽然我很有自知之明，深知这本书绝对说不上是完美的作品，但还是坚信自己的作品还算得上是对雅思考生真正有益处的好书。尽管我对书稿不断修订、审定，甚至有点痴迷于此道，但限于个人水平，书中还是难免会出现各种错误和遗漏，望各位考生、同行批评指正。

上个世纪末，在雅思的热潮刚刚开始的时候，我有幸在求学之余登上讲台，成为了国内第一批雅思教师；如今，雅思的热潮席卷全国，我有幸把自己这些年的教学心得整理成册出版。倍感幸福之余，深知有很多人需要感谢。首先要感谢世界图书出版公司的丁春玲女士和杨敏珊小姐，没有她们细致的工作和耐心的等待，本书就不可能顺利出版！感谢新东方的俞敏洪董事长和沙云龙校长，他们对这本书提了很多宝贵意见！感谢Deloitte中国的Golden Xu先生，他给了我很大的支持和鼓励！感谢我的父母，他们在大学任教数十年，教书育人，兢兢业业，向我展现了中国知识分子的淳朴、正直和严谨，为我树立了最好的榜样！最后要感谢6年来我所有的雅思学员们，他们那种大胆改变自己命运、追求自己梦想的勇气和毅力，一直激励着我，鞭策着我！

衷心祝愿所有的雅思考生梦想成真，如愿以偿！

刘巍巍

乙酉年元旦 于广州珠江

第二版前言

《雅思阅读高分榜中榜》出版以来，一直承蒙各方厚爱。

这本书是我在新东方多年来课堂教学经验的总结，能够得到广大考生的认同，自然让我倍感荣幸。但是高兴之余，也难免感到压力倍增。雅思考试本身发展非常快，不断会有一些调整和变化，因此在指导学生备考方面，我也需要有更多创新的思路。

今年，在出版社的再三邀请下，我根据雅思考试的最新变化趋势，对原书的大部分内容进行了修订。在第二版中，增加了一些新的内容，删除了部分过于陈旧的内容，体现了“与时俱进”的特点。

不久前，我在澳大利亚遇到了很多本书第一版的读者。他们虽然已经顺利通过雅思考试，并且成功地开始了在海外的求学生活，但是依然很热心地向我提供了很多宝贵的意见。在第二版即将出版之际，我要特别感谢所有这些曾经通过电子邮件、电话或是面对面交谈等各种途径向我提出过建议的雅思考生。

衷心希望《雅思阅读高分榜中榜(第二版)》能够助广大雅思考生一臂之力，并祝所有的雅思考生梦想成真！

刘巍巍

2007 年底 于广州—九龙 KCR 列车

Contents 目录

Chapter One
Get to Know the IELTS Reading Test
了解雅思阅读考试

内容提示

- 整体介绍风靡全球的雅思考试
- 整体介绍雅思考试的瓶颈部分——阅读
- 分项介绍雅思阅读考试四大难点
- 分项介绍雅思阅读四大难点之对策

特别提醒

- Part 1 介绍雅思考试全球范围内最新考务变化，请区别于你所了解的以往雅思考试的程序
- 就算你对最新的雅思考试阅读部分已经有充分了解，也千万不要忽视本章的学习。Part 3 和 Part 4 介绍的雅思阅读难点和难点突破对策，或许正是你一直苦苦探求的雅思阅读秘诀

Part 1
Introduction to IELTS
雅思考试简介

"知己知彼，方能百战不殆"。在系统地进行雅思考前复习之前，很有必要对雅思考试进行全面的了解，从而把握考试的命脉，确保考试成功!

雅思考试（IELTS）由英国剑桥大学地方考试委员会创办和推行，是全球最著名的英语语言测试之一。全世界每年共计有近30万应试者，在遍布全球的雅思考点参加雅思考试。在中国，每年有近10万人参与到雅思考试当中来。

与TOEFL（托福）等传统的英语测试相比，雅思考试不仅有更为系统的测试体系，而且有更符合语言学原理的科学的命题方法，因而在创立至今不到20年的时间里，就迅速成为全球最流行的英文测试之一。

一、考试名称

雅思考试的英文全称为"International English Language Testing System（国际英语语言测试系统）"，简称"IELTS（雅思）"。

二、主考机构

雅思考试是由英国剑桥大学地方考试委员会、英国文化委员会和澳大利亚教育国际开发署共同管理的国际英语考试。

①剑桥大学地方考试委员会（University of Cambridge Local Examinations Syndicate—UCLES）

剑桥大学地方考试委员会是全球最权威的英语考试机构之一，隶属英国剑桥大学，成立于1858年，业务覆盖领域广泛，包括学术、职业考试以及各种针对国际市场的考试科目，例如英语等级证书考试、商务英语证书考试等著名的考试项目。UCLES主要负责雅思考试的试题编写、题库建立以及相关复习材料的编辑工作。

②英国文化委员会（British Council）

英国文化委员会是为促进英国与其他国家之间的教育、文化和技术合作而建立的非盈利性机构，已在世界上108个国家设立工作机构，旨在建立长期和广泛的友好合作伙伴关系。British Council 主要负责遍布全球的雅思考试中心以及考务人员的管理工作。组织 IELTS 考试，是英国文化委员会海外工作机构最重要的工作任务之一。

③澳大利亚教育国际开发署（IDP Education Australia）

澳大利亚教育国际开发署是澳大利亚的国际教育组织，主要负责学生咨询、教育项目资料的出版发行以及英语教学和考试等教育活动。IDP Education Australia 主要负责 IELTS 考试的考务管理工作。

三、考试性质

IELTS 的全称为“国际英语语言测试系统（International English Language Testing System）”，考试的性质为英语语言考试，考查英语语言知识的掌握情况和实际运用能力。

作为专门的英语语言测试，雅思考试绝对不考查英语语言以外的背景知识。实际考试中，不需要任何语言以外的背景知识，就能够顺利解答全部的 IELTS 考题。

四、考试类型

根据不同的考试对象和成绩用途，IELTS考试分为Academic Module（学术类考试，简称A类考试）和General Training Module（普通培训类考试，简称G类考试）。两类考试的听力和口语部分完全一致，但在阅读和写作部分有所区别，详见下表。

比较项目 \ 考试类型		Academic Module（学术类考试）	General Training Module（普通培训类考试）
考查目的		旨在考查应试者的学术能力（Academic Skills），用于测试和鉴定应试者在英语环境中攻读学士或硕士等学位课程所必需的英语语言能力	旨在考查应试者的基本生存能力（Social Survival Skills），用于评估在英语社会环境中的基本生存所必需的英语语言能力
适用对象		赴英语国家攻读学士或学士以上学位者	赴英语国家定居、就业或完成中等教育、非学历类教育培训者
考查内容	阅读	分为 3 个较大的部分（Section），每个 Section 为 1 篇较长的阅读文章。阅读文章内容涉及除政治、军事等敏感话题以外的各个学术领域，文章难度较大	通常分为 3 个较大的部分（Section），由 6～8 篇小文章组成，难度递增，文章题材多与日常生活相关，或与校园生活、培训课程相关
	写作	Task One（第 1 题），要求对题目中给出的各种图表（包括表格、柱状	Task One（第 1 题）要求就某个假设的场景写 1 封不少于 150 字的书信，

续表

比较项目 \ 考试类型		Academic Module（学术类考试）	General Training Module（普通培训类考试）
考查内容	写作	图、曲线图、扇形图等）加以观察和分析，并根据已知的图表或数据写1篇不少于150字的小短文；Task Two（第2题）要求根据自己的知识或经验就一个现象阐明自己的态度或见解，或就一个观点发表自己赞同或反对的意见并阐述理由	表达自己的意愿和看法；Task Two（第2题）与A类考试的Task Two基本相同

五、考试流程

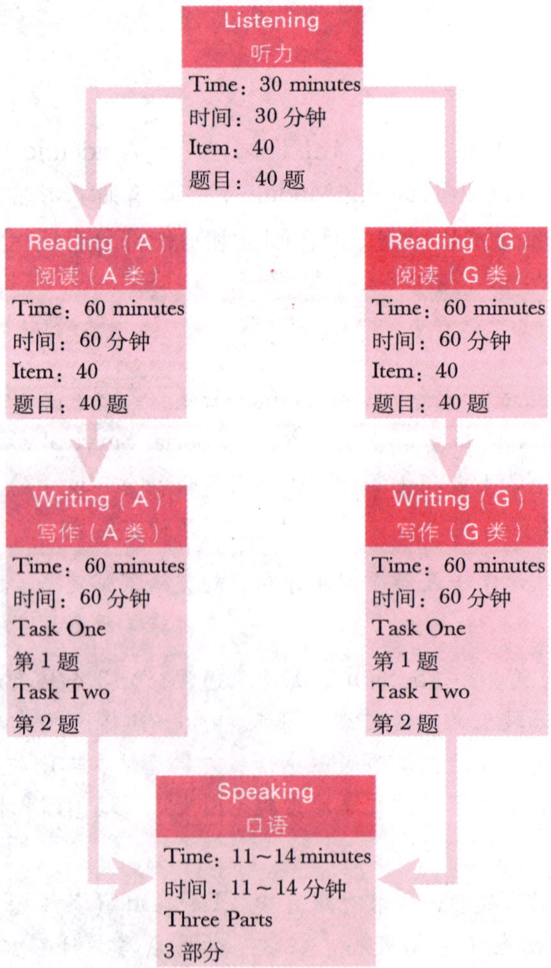

六、IELTS 最新考务变化

British Council（英国文化委员会）于 2006 年下半年，对外公布了全球范围内雅思考试的最新考务变化，内容涉及考前报名、考试现场以及考后成绩领取三方面。主要变化有：

- **取消听力部分填写 Version Number（试题版本号）**
- **逐步取消旧题的重复使用，全球范围内启动一次性试题**

特别提醒……

听力部分取消填写版本号（Version Number），逐步推行一次性试卷，进一步杜绝了在考试前背诵陈题答案的可能性。作为世界级的英语水平考试，IELTS 将不遗余力地把任何企图挑衅考试权威的行为变成 Mission Impossible！

- **笔试入场时间确定为 8:00a.m.～8:30a.m.**
- **取消 8:30a.m. 以后入场考生的笔试资格**
- **取消在指定口语考试时间前 15 分钟尚未入场考生的口试资格**
- **取消阅读部分结束后的 10 分钟休息时间**

特别提醒……

雅思考试当天，一旦进入考场，就意味着在未来近 3 个小时的时间里，你将不能离开考场。因为任何理由离开考场，都将按主动放弃考试处理。请务必在考试当天少喝水，因为考试过程中，是不允许离开考场上厕所的。建议你提前到达考试中心，但是不要过早进入考场，可先在考场外休息片刻，8:30a.m. 左右再进入考场。

Part 2
What is Special about IELTS?
雅思考试的特点是什么？

作为新兴的语言测试，雅思考试之所以能够迅速崛起，在短时间内成为全球最著名的语言测试之一，最重要的原因是雅思考试的三家主考机构能够不断顺应语言测试理论和语言测试技术的发展潮流，适时地对雅思考试进行修改和完善。

在经历了若干次较大规模的调整以后，雅思考试的风格日趋平稳，与之对应的雅思考试的特点也开始保持稳定。

（1）语言国际化

国际化的语言特点，在雅思考试的四个部分中都有所体现。

①口语

雅思口语考试采用考生与考官一对一的对话形式进行。British Council 招募的 1 000 多名口语考官来自世界各地，带有不同的英语口音，而未必是标准的英国口音（British Accent）或美国口音（American Accent）。

雅思考试的口语考官，有来自美国、带有地道美国口音的美籍考官；也有来自英国、带有地道伦敦口音的英籍考官；还有来自南半球、带有浓重澳洲口音的澳大利亚籍或新西兰籍考官。

来自世界各国的口语考官分布到遍布全球的雅思考试中心，用不同口音的英语和参加雅思考试的考生进行口语交流和测试，从而体现了雅思本身所追求的语言国际化的风格。

②听力

作为"国际英语语言测试系统"，雅思听力部分一直采用各种口音混杂的听力语音材料，与听力语音材料完全是美国口音的托福（TOEFL）考试形成鲜明的对比。

在雅思考试的听力部分中，考生不仅能够听到纯正的英国口音、美国口音，而且能够听到带有浓重"地方色彩"的澳大利亚口音，甚至能够听到巴基斯坦人、中国人、日本人等非英语国家人士所说的英语。各种英语口音混杂在一起，形成的雅思听力考试最大特点，也毫无疑问地体现了雅思所追求的国际化特点。

特别提醒……

准备雅思考试时，除了一般的听力资料、BBC 或 VOA 的标准英语外，请务必接触一些口音不那么纯正的英语。请记住，无论是在国际化的雅思考试中，还是在你即将开始的海外生活中，你所听到的英语，都未必总是标准的 BBC 或 VOA 英语。

③阅读

雅思考试的阅读部分取材广泛，阅读文章来自世界各国主要的英文报刊杂志，以及世界各国政府的英文统计报告，而不仅仅是英、美等英语国家的英文出版物。

雅思考试的阅读文章内容可能涉及到世界任何一个国家的文化、经济，内容绝对不局限于有关英语国家的题材，这与阅读文章以美国本土文化为主的托福阅读部分有显著不同，也真正体现了雅思国际化的特点。

④写作

雅思考试中采用的作文题，在真正被雅思考试采纳之前，均经过剑桥大学的语言专家层层筛选和反复考证。最终成为真正雅思考题的作文题，往往是题材开放，并确保世界各地不同种族、不同信仰、不同文化背景的考生都能接受和理解，都能有感而发的国际化的内容。

（2）题型多样化

雅思的各部分都呈现题型多样化特点，与 GRE、TOEFL（托福）等海外考试中，四选一的选择题一统天下的局面形成鲜明对比。

雅思考试中的大多数题目是让人感到陌生的、在别的任何考试中不曾见过的题型。UCLES（剑桥大学地方考试委员会）认为，题型多样化不仅能够体现雅思考试强烈的学术风格，而且能够真正鉴别应试者的实际英语水平。事实上，从语言学理论的角度出发，多样化的题型，毫无疑问是更为科学的考试方式，也更有利于区分不同层次的应试者在语言能力方面的差异。

在实际的 IELTS 考试中，多样化的题型却给考生带来了新的挑战：在备考过程中，不仅要提高英语能力，练好语言基本功，而且要全面系统地了解雅思考试中众多题型的特点，以及每种题型所对应的解题方法，从而避免在考试中，因为缺乏对题型的了解而未能顺利解答试题，痛失展示自己应有英语水平的机会。

特别提醒……

雅思阅读部分有9种题型，除选择题和简答题外，其他7种题型均是别的英文测试中不曾使用过的题型。在准备考试的时候，系统复习这9种题型，是阅读复习的关键所在。或许，多记忆10个英文单词，你的阅读成绩不会有太大改变，但多了解一种雅思阅读题型所对应的解题方法，你的雅思阅读一定会有质的飞跃！

（3）词汇相对简单化

与GRE、TOEFL（托福）等海外考试相比较，雅思考试另外一个显著的特点是词汇考查的相对简单化。

作为“国际英语语言测试系统”，IELTS所关注和考查的，是考生整体运用英语语言的能力，而不仅仅是词汇量大小。实际考试中，考生真正需要全面理解，并且能够达到听、说、读、写“四会”的英语单词，往往集中于以下两类：

①日常生活口语词汇

雅思考试关注和考查的，是考生整体运用英语语言的能力水平，因而在生活当中常见的，如上图书馆还书、上房屋中介公司寻找出租房屋等场景中使用的英语单词，往往成为雅思听力考试中出现频率最高的单词。

这类单词，不外乎英语国家普通百姓日常生活中常用的一些生活化的单词，例如kitchen（厨房）、whiskey（威士忌酒）、physician（内科医师）等。由于这些词语与日常生活息息相关，考生只要留心积累，就肯定能够顺利掌握它们。

②最核心的书面词汇

阅读部分是雅思考试当中，对词汇量要求最大的一个部分。与听力、口语部分中大量出现的口语化、生活化词汇不一样的是，阅读部分考查的单词是英语当中最核心的书面语词汇。

英语当中常见的书面语单词大约有9 000～10 000词，著名的《牛津高级英语词典》仅用了最常见的3 000个英语单词，就能够对所有的英语单词进行释义。在实际的雅思考试中，尽管试题中出现的词语范围相当大，但如果你掌握了英语当中最核心的5 000～6 000个书面语单词，就一定能够顺利解答各个部分的试题。

特别提醒……

词汇学习不等于英语学习的全部，同样，词汇学习，绝对不等于雅思复习的全部。背单词千万不可以走向极端，逢生词必先查后背是雅思阅读复习的大忌，考生只要掌握阅读部分的核心词汇即可。

Part 3
Introduction to IELTS Reading Test
雅思阅读考试简介

阅读被公认为雅思考试当中最难的部分。在考场中，面对文章篇幅长、信息量大、题型众多的雅思阅读试题，考生常常感到困难重重。

在逐一突破雅思阅读的9种题型之前，必须对雅思考试的阅读部分进行全面了解，做到心中有数，从而找到适合自已的复习方法，并且总结归纳出自己的解题策略。

一、考试时间

IELTS阅读部分考试时间为60分钟，切不可在考试时间开始之前解答阅读试题，也不可在阅读考试时间结束之后继续解答阅读试题，否则将被视为舞弊。

与听力部分结束以后专门提供10分钟誊写答案的时间不一样，阅读部分要求考生在60分钟的考试时间之内，不仅解答完全部试题，而且将全部试题答案抄写到答题卡上。

特别提醒……

考官宣布阅读考试开始之前，千万不要把试卷打开，宣布阅读考试结束后，也千万不要继续答题，因为雅思考试只有一种常见处理舞弊的方法——Get out of the room!

二、题目数量

阅读部分共计40道题目，40道题以不同的题型形式出现。

三、试题特点

A类和G类雅思考试的阅读部分均由3个部分（Three Sections）组成，各个部分开始处都有非常明显的提示语言，例如 Section One、Section Two 等。

①A 类考试阅读试卷的特点

三部分各为一篇较长的文章，每篇文章的实际长度为 900～1 000 字，文章均取材于世界著名的报刊杂志以及一些政府的年度发展报告，结构严谨，用词考究，内容涉及到科学领域的各个方面，但是一般不会涉及到专业性太强的题材。

UCLES 的设计意图是 A 类阅读的三篇文章难度递增，即前两篇文章注重文字本身的理解，第三篇则可能会考查对文章内容进行逻辑推理的能力。

实际的雅思考试中，由于中国考生往往擅长逻辑推理，而相对缺乏扎实的英语语言功底，所以一般中国考生很少感觉到三篇文章之间有明显的难度变化。

②G 类考试阅读试卷的特点

Section One 通常为 2～3 篇短的阅读文章，多来源于报刊杂志的启事、广告等，生活化的特点非常明显，主要考查 Social Survival（社会生存）所必需的英语语言能力。

Section Two 通常为 1～2 篇与学校生活或培训课程相关的阅读材料，语法结构和语言表达较 Section One 复杂，主要考查 Training Survival（培训生涯）所必需的英语语言能力。

Section Three 通常为 1 篇结构完整、文体正式的说明文，文章篇幅较长，取材广泛，是三部分中难度最大的，与 A 类的阅读文章难度十分接近。

四、文章体裁

①A 类考试的文章体裁

A类考试中的阅读文章体裁为议论文和说明文。

②G 类考试的文章体裁

G类考试中，前两部分的阅读文章体裁为应用文，最后一篇文章的体裁为说明文或议论文。

五、评分标准

雅思考试中阅读部分的评分标准不是固定的，而是根据考试难度的变化而变化，但基本上历次考试评分标准的变化幅度都控制在下表所给出的范围。

正确题数	9～10	11～12	13～15	16～20	21～23	24～26
分数	4	4.5	5	5.5	6	6.5
正确题数	27～30	31～32	33～35	36～39	40	
分数	7	7.5	8	8.5	9	

Part 4
Guide to Cracking IELTS Reading
雅思阅读难点的突破对策

在充分了解雅思考试的模式和特点之后，很有必要详细了解雅思考试阅读部分的难点所在，从而确定学习方向，明确学习方法，有的放矢地展开复习备考工作，将雅思阅读的难点一网打尽。

- **特点：阅读量较大，时间紧张**

→ **对策：掌握阅读方法，阅读过程中详略得当**

和国内的四、六级考试或托福、GRE 等国外考试的阅读部分相比较，雅思考试阅读部分的阅读量是非常大的。

在 60 分钟的时间里，不仅要阅读完 3 个 Section，近 3 500 单词的阅读文章，而且要完成 40 道题目，并且准确无误地将 40 道题目的答案誊写到答题卡上。这无疑对考生的阅读速度提出了很高的要求。因此，在考试中应该真正做到有详有略、详略结合，仔细阅读一些与考题有关的内容，快速浏览甚至略读一些与考题没有关系的内容。

特别提醒……

对你而言，雅思考试的阅读部分惟一目标就是解答阅读文章后面的全部试题。

精读、略读和跳读相结合，是你在实际雅思考试中能够顺利阅读完全部文章的有效办法。

- **特点：题型多样化**

→ **对策：逐一突破雅思阅读题型**

IELTS 考试阅读部分一个非常显著的特点，就是题型的多样化。实际上，题型的多样化不仅是雅思阅读部分的特点，也是整个雅思考试的显著特点。

题型多样化，导致原本可能已经拥有相当英语语言实力的考生，在考试中因为缺乏对题型的了解，或是被众多题型干扰，不能正常发挥，失去了展示自己原本拥有的英文实力的机会。

准备雅思考试的阅读部分，最重要的一项工作就是逐一突破雅思阅读的题型。

真正把握题型套路和技巧，在雅思阅读考试部分就能更好地展示英语水平，获得考试的成功。

特别提醒……

本书的第 3 章至第 11 章详细分析了雅思阅读考试的 9 种题型的特点，以及这 9 种题型所对应的解题技巧。这几个章节，是全书的精华所在。正在准备雅思考试的你一定要对此高度重视。只要将每种技巧和每道习题真正研究透，就一定能够在雅思的阅读考试中获取令自己满意的成绩！Come on，you can make it！

- **特点：生词比例高**

→ **对策：把握核心单词，跳读生僻单词**

雅思阅读考试的另外一个特点就是生词众多，有些词语相当生僻。

任何一篇内容相对复杂的阅读文章，都不可避免地出现大量生僻词语或是难度相对较大的单词。IELTS 考试所考查的，是实际运用语言的能力，所以雅思考试中，真正需要理解的单词，或是题目中真正考查到的单词，往往是英语阅读中的一些最核心的单词。这些单词虽然数量不多，难度不大，却是必须掌握的。

解决词汇问题的有效途径，就是把握好常见的阅读核心单词。这些单词是英语阅读之根本，也是顺利通过雅思考试的前提条件。扎实掌握这些单词，不仅可以大幅度提高应对雅思阅读考试的能力，而且能够切实有效地提高英语语言水平，为日后的海外生活打下坚实的语言基础。

特别提醒……

雅思阅读考试中，阅读文章里充斥着大量并不需要你认识的单词。或许，你从来没有在阅读中碰见过这些单词，也的确不知道这些单词的意思，但是只要解题方法正确，你就一定能够避开这些单词，顺利解答阅读试题。切记背诵单词的重点一定要放在常见的阅读核心单词上，千万不可以走极端！推荐你使用本书的配套词汇教材：《雅思核心词汇手册》。

- **特点：句型结构复杂**

→ **对策：把握对应语法，逐一突破雅思常考难句**

在雅思考试的阅读部分，还会遇到一个难以突破的障碍，那就是阅读文章中大量充斥着的结构复杂难以把握的难句或复杂句。突破这些阅读难度较大的句子，同样是在雅思考试中获得高分的必要条件。

仔细研究历年 IELTS 考试的阅读试题，不难发现考试中真正构成障碍的难句，不外乎并列复合句、多重复合句、倒装句等几种句式。只要在准备 IELTS 考试时，把握好这几种句式所对应的语法规律，逐一突破这些类型的难句，就能做到心中有数，从而更自信地面对雅思考试的阅读部分。

特别提醒……

本书 Chapter Two 详细解释了雅思考试中常见的难句所涉及到的语法理论，并且分析了大量雅思考试中的实例，值得你仔细阅读。

Chapter Two
Cracking Complex Sentences in IELTS Reading
雅思阅读难句突破

内容提示

- 雅思阅读中难句的类型
- 雅思阅读中各种类型难句的对应阅读策略
- 雅思阅读中经典难句讲解

特别提醒

- 语句理解是篇章理解的基础，请重视本章的学习，突破语句阅读，扫清阅读的第一大障碍
- 难句阅读的关键是与句型相关的语法理论，请留意本章 Part 2 中介绍的句型阅读语法理论

Part 1
Guide to Cracking Complex Sentences
难句阅读的基本方法

雅思考试的阅读部分充斥着大量句型结构复杂、难以理解和把握的复杂句或难句。这些复杂句或难句在很大程度上影响了考生对全文的阅读和理解。

由于这些句子在雅思考试中频繁出现，因此很有必要在IELTS考试前熟悉它们的阅读方法，从而确保在考试当中不会被这些“难句”影响，更加顺利地完成阅读题目。

一、阅读中难句的特点

无论在北半球的英国，还是在南半球的澳大利亚参加雅思考试，你所遇到的阅读试题的风格和难度都是统一的，因为作为目前全世界规模最大的英语水平考试之一，雅思考试一直努力在最大程度上保持试题风格和难度的一致。

每年，在世界各地举行的上千场IELTS考试中，阅读部分出现的难句呈现出这样一些共同的特点：

- **句子冗长，大多数句子由20个以上单词组成，很多句子甚至超过40个单词**
- **结构复杂，频繁使用并列复合句、多重复合句等复杂句式**
- **多为雅思阅读考试的出题点，在阅读试题中常常有所涉及**

特别提醒……

IELTS阅读考试中的难句不仅难，而且经常被作为阅读考试的考点。正在准备雅思阅读考试的你，没有任何理由不用心去体会难句的阅读方法，突破雅思阅读的第一个难关！

二、难句阅读基本方法

在IELTS阅读考试中，如果你发现任何句子结构过于复杂，请果断地开始分析这个句子的句型结构。学会分析句型结构，是提高英语阅读水平的关键。在面对雅思考试里的难句、复杂句时，句型分析的重要性更是不言而喻的。

Part 2
Analysis of Complex Sentences
难句阅读分项突破

特别提醒……

雅思考试阅读部分难度稳定，每次阅读考试中所出现的难句或复杂句不外乎并列复合句、多重复合句等七种类型。如果在考试前，你能够掌握各种句型对应的英语语法知识，再反复体会本节中分析的例句的句型结构，就可以胸有成竹、满怀自信地面对IELTS阅读中的难句了，因为它们绝对不再是你的阅读拦路虎！

句型1 结构复杂的简单句

一、语法分析

如果句子只包含一个主谓结构，而且句子各个成分都只是单词或短语，那么它就是简单句。在实际雅思考试中，简单句可能会以比较复杂的形式出现，句子也可能会很长。

二、突破策略

对于难度较大的简单句，阅读的基本方法是确定句子的主语、谓语和宾语三个基本成分，找出句子的主干，忽略其他成分，将长句变成短句，将句型结构复杂的句子变成句型结构简单的句子。

三、例句分析

例 1：

原文 It involves probing for deeply rooted concerns, devising creative solutions, and making trade-offs and compromises where interest are opposed.（它涉及了探究深层次的关注、想出更有创意的解决方案以及当利益发生冲突的时候，做出交易和妥协。）

分析 这是一个结构稍复杂的简单句。先去掉其他成分，抓住句子主干。句子的主语是 it，谓语是 involves，三个动名词短语 probing for deeply rooted concerns、devising creative solutions 和 making trade-offs and compromises 作宾语。

例 2：

原文 A father accepting responsibility for behaviour problems is linked with positive outcomes.（一个对行为问题负责的父亲是和正面的结果相联系的。）

分析 这个句子的主语是 father，谓语是 is，accepting responsibility for behaviour problems 是现在分词作主语 father 的后置定语。

例 3：

原文 For maximum dung burial in spring, summer and autumn, farmers living in the dry region of the United States require a variety of species with overlapping period of activity.（为了在春、夏和秋三个季节获得最大的粪便埋放量，居住在美国干燥地区的农民需要不同种类的、活跃期重叠的物种。）

分析 这句话的主语是 farmers，living in the dry region of the United States 为修饰主语 farmers 的后置定语，谓语是 require，宾语是 species。

例 4：

原文 A world rise in allergies, particularly asthma, over the past four decades, is now said to be linked with increased air pollution.（据说在过去的 40 年中，世界范围内敏感症，尤其是哮喘病发病率的上升，和加剧的空气污染有关系。）

分析 这句话的主语是 a world rise，基本的句型结构是非常熟悉的“be said to do something”句型。

例 5：

原文 Automated techniques to measure these characteristics and verify a person's identity infallibly are attracting widespread attention in these days of increased use of credit cards and e-mail.（在信用卡和电子邮件越来越多地被使用的今天，用来测量这些特性和确认人的身份的自动技术吸引了广泛的关注。）

分析 这句话的主语是 automated techniques，谓语是 attract，宾语是 attention，in these days of increased use of credit cards and e-mail 在句子里面起时间状语的作用。

例 6：

原文　He was both a free-trade politician and an insurance company officer with some experience of the actual conditions of poverty of working-class people struggling to maintain respectability as the implications of age loomed large in their lives.（他既是支持自由贸易的政客，又是保险公司的员工，而且了解那些年龄问题在生活中很突出、却又努力维持自己受尊敬的状态的工薪阶层人民贫苦的实际情况。）

分析　这句话用词较多，句式也很复杂，仔细分析可以发现，句子的主干为：He is both a politician and an officer，意思为他既是个政客，又是个员工。其他的成分在句子中起的都是修饰的作用，在抓句子主干时，应该先将这些修饰成分去掉。

句型 2　并列句或并列复合句

一、语法分析

如果句子包含两个或更多互不依从的主谓结构，就是并列句。并列句中的分句通常用一个并列连词来连接，最常见的并列连词有 and、or 和 but 。

二、突破策略

如果你在 IELTS 考试中阅读并列句遇到了困难，基本的处理方法是将句子从并列连词处断开，将并列句变成两个或若干个相对短的句子，然后再用处理简单句的方法——抓句子主干，来依次处理每个相对短的句子。

三、例句分析

例 1：

原文　Government has encouraged waste paper collection and sorting schemes and at the same time, the paper industry has responded by developing new recycling technologies that have paved the way for even greater utilization of used fibre.（政府鼓励了废纸的回收和分类计划，同时造纸工业也通过开发新的回收技术作出了反应，这个回收技术为更大程度地利用已经使用过的纤维铺平了道路。）

分析　这是个复合句，从 and 处将句子分成两个相对短的句子：and 前面是一个简单句；and 后面的句子有一个由 that 引导的定语从句，充当 new recycling technologies 的定语。

例 2：

原文 Government regulations limit the oil content allowed to be discharged, and the produced water is treated on the platforms to meet those specifications.（政府的规章制度限制了允许排放的油的含量，而且所产生的水也在平台上处理过，从而达到这些规范要求。）

分析 这是一个非常典型的由 and 连接的并列句，从 and 处将句子分为两个小句子：前面的句子是个简单句，主语是 government regulations；后面的句子是个被动句，主语是 water。

例 3：

原文 Noise generated by traffic on arterial roads and freeways is an increasing problem in Australia and there are growing concerns among highways authorities in Australia about the limitations of some types of noise barriers which have been installed in this country.（在澳大利亚，由主干道和高速道上的交通所产生的噪声是一个日益严重的问题，而且澳大利亚当局的高速公路管理部门也越来越重视已经安装在这个国家的一些噪声屏障的局限性。）

分析 这是一个比较长的并列复合句，并列连词 and 连接了两个句子：前一个句子是简单句，句子的主语是 noise，谓语是 is；后面的句子中有一个由 which 引导的定语从句。

例 4：

原文 The sports that were made by the collision will undoubtedly blow away eventually, but it's much too soon to tell if there will be any permanent changes in Jupiter.（毫无疑问，由碰撞引起的运动将最终消失，但是确认木星是否会有永久的变化还为时过早。）

分析 这是一个由 but 连接的并列句，因而分析句子时应该从 but 处将句子断开，分成两个短句：前一个句子主语为 sports，后面有一个由 that 引导的定语从句修饰主语；后一个句子是由形式主语 it 充当主语的句子。

例 5：

原文 The chamber is then flushed with dry nitrogen gas for five hours to remove the remaining air and DEZ is introduced at a low pressure into the gas stream in order to keep the state of balance.（腔室随后被氮气冲洗了 5 个小时以排除残余的气体，接着 DEZ 在低压的状态下被导入气流中来维持平衡的状态。）

分析 将句子从 and 处断开，分为两个句子：前面的句子是被动句，主语是 chamber；后面的句子也是被动句，主语是 DEZ。

句型3 插入语结构

一、语法分析

插入语一般是对句子的某个成分的解释或补充说明，前后有逗号与其他句子成分分开，比较容易识别。在雅思阅读文章中，插入语的大量出现，往往造成句子理解思路的中断。

二、突破策略

插入语结构处理的基本办法是先略去不读，直接跳过两个逗号之间的内容，使插入语结构前后意思顺畅。

三、例句分析

例1：

原文 In developing countries, where at least 16 cities are expected to have more than 12 million people each by the end of this decade, failing to give priority to public transport would be disastrous.（在发展中国家里，至少有16个城市被认为在这个十年结束的时候，人口将超过1 200万，不优先考虑公共交通，将会导致灾难性的后果。）

分析 在这句话中，两个逗号之间的内容，即 where at least 16 cities are expected to have more than 12 million people each by the end of this decade，充当插入语。阅读句子时，可以先忽略这部分。

例2：

原文 To casual observers, as well as to influential natural scientists and regional planners, the luxuriant forests of Amazonia seem ageless.（对不经意看到的人和有影响力的自然科学家、区域规划者来说，亚马逊地区繁茂的森林似乎是永恒的。）

分析 在这句话中，两个逗号之间的内容，即 as well as to influential natural scientists and regional planners，充当插入语。阅读句子时，可以先忽略这部分。

例3：

原文 Over 120 years ago, the English botanist J.D. Hooker, writing of Australian edible plants, suggested that many of them were 'eatable but not worth eating'.（超过120年前，在写到澳大利亚可食用的植物时，英国植物学家J.D. Hooker就指出它们当中很多可食用，但却不值得食用。）

分析　在这句话中，两个逗号之间的内容，即writing of Australian edible plants，充当插入语。阅读句子时，可以先忽略这部分。

例4：

原文　In relationships of mutual dependence, such as between labour and management or within an organization or a family, the question of who is more powerful turns on who is less dependent on the other.（在相互依赖的关系中，例如劳资关系、组织内部关系、家庭内部关系等，谁更强大的问题就转换为谁更少地依赖对方的问题。）

分析　与上句话一样，在这句话中，such as所引导的结构such as between labour and management or within an organization or a family为插入语。阅读句子时，可以先忽略这部分。

例5：

原文　While wives, chosen for their pedigree, came from suitably upper-class families, geisha were usually working class.（按照血统来挑选，夫人们往往来自上层家庭，而艺妓们往往来自劳工阶层。）

分析　在这句话中，chosen from their pedigree为插入语，阅读句子时，可以先忽略这部分，从而得知came from的主语为wives。

句型4　倒装结构

一、语法分析

在英语当中，主语和谓语有两种顺序：一种和汉语一样，主语在前，称之为自然语序（Natural Order）；另外一种顺序是谓语在主语前面，这种语序就是倒装语序（Inverted Order）。

雅思考试中的绝大多数句子使用的是自然语序，但是某些情况下却需要使用倒装语序。在实际考试中，出现频率较高的倒装结构为以下三种情况：

- **以not only，not until等否定连词引导的句子**
- **以never，seldom，rarely，hardly等否定副词引导的句子**
- **以so，as引导的倒装句式，表示前述的情况同样适合另外一人或事**

二、突破策略

倒装句的基本阅读方法是把倒装句转化为普通语句，把倒装语序还原为自然语序，在自然语序下理解句子。

三、例句分析

例 1：

原文 During the past century, the average air temperature at the surface of the earth has risen, as has the temperature of ocean surface waters.（在过去的百年中，地球表面空气的平均温度上升了，海水表面的温度也一样。）

分析 这是一个非常典型的由 as 引导的倒装句，as 表示“和……一样”。将句子转化成正常的语序为：the temperature of ocean surface has。

例 2：

原文 In a dispute, not only do the interests of one party not coincide with those of the other party, but they are in conflict.（在一个争论中，不仅一方的利益和另外一方不一致，而且它们是相互矛盾的。）

分析 这个句子是由否定连词“not only... but also...”引导的倒装句，意思是“不仅……而且……”。将句子转化成正常的语序为：the interests of one party do not coincide with those of the other party。

例 3：

原文 In a typical example, when viewing photographs of food, hungry subjects experience a much greater increase in pupil diameter than do sated subjects.（在一个典型的例子中，当看到食物照片的时候，饥饿的实验对象比已经吃饱的实验对象的瞳孔直径增加得更大。）

分析 在这句话中，比较状语从句里出现了倒装句式。than 后面的语句转换成自然语序应该为：sated subjects do。

例 4：

原文 A mother's wanting her partner to do more housework and child care is a better predictor of poor family adjustment than is actual time spent by fathers in these tasks.（母亲希望自己的伴侣能做更多的家务活并且能够照顾小孩，而这比父亲们在这些工作上花费的实际时间更能体现家庭关系调整的失败。）

分析 这是一个难度比较大的复杂句，阅读时首先应该抓住主句的主干。than 之前的部分是主句，主句的主语是 a mother's wanting her partner to do more housework and child care。than 后面的比较从句进行了倒装，转化成自然语序为：actual time spent by fathers in these tasks is。在这个比较从句中，主语是 actual time，spent by fathers in these tasks 是过去分词短语作 actual time 的后置定语。

句型 5 强调句式

一、语法分析

在英语中，强调句式的基本句型结构为：It is... that...，表达“……就是……”的意思，被强调的部分只可能是句子的主语、宾语或状语。

- **强调主语：**
  It was Charles Darwin who visited the Galapagos Islands in 1835.
- **强调宾语：**
  It was the Galapagos Islands that Charles Darwin visited in 1835.
- **强调状语：**
  It was in 1835 that Charles Darwin visited the Galapagos Islands.

二、突破策略

强调句的基本阅读方法是先确定被强调部分的句子成分，然后再将强调句还原为普通句式进行阅读。

三、例句分析

例 1：

原文　It is the desire, together with its lack of fulfillment in most families, that brings about stress in the female parent.（就是这种期望以及这种期望在大多数家庭中不能够实现的现实给母亲们带来了压力。）

分析　这是一个典型的强调句，同时句子中还含有插入语成分。先将插入语 together with its lack of fulfillment in most families 省略不读，不难发现句子强调的成分 desire 充当的是主语，将句子还原为普通语句就是：The desire brings about stress in the female parent.

例 2：

原文　It is in market economy that the price of different commodities and services are always changing with respect to each other.（就是在市场经济中，不同的日用品和服务的价格才总因相互影响而发生改变。）

分析 这句话同样是一个典型的强调句，将句子还原为普通语句：In market economy, the price of different commodities and services are always changing with respect to each other. 很容易发现这句话强调的是句子的状语成分 in market economy。

例 3：

原文 It is protein that spiders can make in an environmentally friendly way similar to the way mammals make milk.（蜘蛛能用一种不破坏环境并且和哺乳动物分泌乳汁类似的方法所制造的就是蛋白质。）

分析 这是一个结构稍微复杂的强调句，将句子还原为普通语句：Spiders can make protein in an environmentally friendly way similar to the way mammals make milk. 显而易见，原句强调的是宾语成分 protein。

例 4：

原文 It is his visit to the Galapagos Islands in 1853 that inspired his monumental work on evolution, *The Origin of Species*.（给达尔文带来关于进化的不朽著作——《物种起源》的创作灵感的，就是他在 1853 年对加拉帕戈斯群岛进行的访问。）

分析 这个强调句中的被强调成分稍显复杂，先将句子还原为普通语句：His visit to the Galapagos Islands in 1853 inspired his monumental work on evolution, *The Origin of Species*. 在这个依然有点复杂的句子里，his visit to the Galapagos Islands in 1853 充当的是主语成分，因此前面的强调句中被强调的成分为句子的主语。

句型 6 复合句或多重复合句

一、语法分析

复合句指的是那些含有两个或更多的主谓结构，而且其中有一个或多个主谓结构充当句子的某一成分的句子。

二、突破策略

复合句的基本处理办法是确定句子各层之间的关系，先抓主句的主干，再抓从句的主干，由表及里，层层深入。

三、例句分析

例 1：

原文　Since both rapid and light rail have electric engines, pollution is measured not from the motor exhaust, but from the power plant generating electricity, which is usually located outside the city, where air quality problems are less serious.（因为地铁和轻轨都有电动机，所以污染物不是从车辆尾气中测量，而是从产生电力的发电厂测量，发电厂通常位于城市以外，那里的空气问题不是很严重。）

分析　这个句子中 since 引导了一个原因状语从句，主句包含一个特殊句型"not... but..."，意思是"不是……而是……"，power plant 后面有两个修饰语，一个是由现在分词短语 generating electricity 充当的后置定语，另一个是由 which 引导的定语从句。where 同样也引导了一个定语从句。

例 2：

原文　The challenge now is to develop policies and practices based on a presumption of shared responsibility between men and women, and a presumption that there are potential benefits for men and women, as well as for families and the community, if there is greater gender equality in the responsibilities and pleasures of family life.（现在的挑战在于以如下的假设作为基础开发政策和开展实践；一个假设是男人和女人共同承担责任；另一假设是如果在家庭责任和乐趣上有更大的性别平等，对男人、女人、家庭和社会，都有潜在的好处。）

分析　这是个相对复杂的句子，先抓主句的主干：The challenge now is to develop policies and practices，意为"现在的挑战是开发政策和开展实践"。从 based on 到句子的结尾处是由过去分词短语充当的状语。后一个 presumption 后面有一个由 that 引导的从句，充当 presumption 的同位语。在同位语的后面，是一个由 if 引导的条件状语从句。

例 3：

原文　Since variation in distances and city densities affect the total kilometers of travel, the annual number of trips each person takes by public transport provides a better standard for comparing its importance in various cities.（因为距离和城市密度的不同影响了旅行的总公里数，所以每个人每年乘坐公共交通工具旅行的次数，为比较其在各个城市的重要性提供了一个更好的标准。）

分析　这是一个多重复合句，since 引导一个原因状语从句，主句中有一个省略了 that 的定语从句，each person takes by public transport 充当 the annual number of trip 的定语。

例 4：

原文　The use of gold as the unit of account during the days of the gold standard meant that the price of all other commodities and services would swing up and down with reference to the price of gold, which was not fixed.（在黄金标准时代，使用黄金作为计价单位意味着其他所有日用品、服务的价格都将因为不固定的黄金价格而上下波动。）

分析　阅读这个复合句，应当先抓住主句的主干：use of gold meant that，主句的宾语是 that 以后所有的内容，相对较长。在宾语从句中还出现了一个以 which 引导的定语从句，用来修饰 the price of gold。

例 5：

原文　Despite the significant increase in the number of women with dependent children who are in the paid workforce, Australia research studies over the last 15 years are consistent in showing that divisions of labour for family work are very rigid indeed.（不论有孩子却依然参加工作的妇女的数量如何显著上升，过去 15 年澳大利亚的研究一致表明，家庭工作的劳动分工实际上是固定不变的。）

分析　这个句子由 despite 引导的介词结构作状语，在这个介词结构中还出现了 who 引导的定语从句，用来修饰 woman。主句的主干为：studies are showing that，that 的后面是一个宾语从句。

特别提醒……

难句阅读学习到此完毕，恭喜你！Now you see, you can make it!

突破难句的阅读，不仅能够极大地提高你的雅思阅读整体实力，而且对提高你的写作水平也很有帮助，因为作为语言学习的两个相互联系的部分，阅读和写作本来就是相互制约、互相促进的！

在整个雅思阅读的复习过程中，如果遇到难句，请一定要参考本章的语法讲解，严格按照我们讨论过的方法去处理，日积月累，你的英语阅读水平一定会有很大的飞跃！

Part 3
Exercises of Complex Sentences
难句阅读练习

Instructions:

Read the following sentences and you may turn to the dictionary if you find any words that you are not familiar with. Attentions should be focused on sentence pattern while you are reading them. (请仔细阅读下面的英语句子，句子中或许会包含个别你并不需要认识的生僻词汇，建议查阅字典。阅读句子时，请务必留意句型结构。)

1. Supporting the theory that marijuana was banned to destroy the hemp industry, were two articles written just before the Marijuana Prohibition, claiming that hemp was on the verge of becoming a super crop.
2. Cold water that is from the Poles travels at depth—it is denser than warm water—until it emerges at the surface in another part of the world in the form of a cold current, which people often call massive gyres.
3. It is a dangerous deception to believe that the human-created artifice called economics can keep the indicators rising as the life support systems of the planet continue to decline.
4. Whereas traditional monitoring involves collecting samples of water, gas or soil and sending them for laboratory analysis, which can cost from $100 to $1,000, the new device performs its testing on the site and sends its results via a computer at a collection station to an interactive web site.
5. Gee's outlook rests on a tiny minority of scientists who have faith in the boundless potential of science and technology to overcome the physical constraints of air, water and soil so that a much larger population can be sustained.
6. Finding treatments that match individual gene profiles is the next frontier in drug research and the objective of pharmacogenomics, a new science that combines pharmacological research with the latest advances of genomic studies.
7. The electronic sniffer is a unique monitor that can be put directly underground in groundwater or soil where the humidity reaches nearly 100 percent and detect toxic

chemicals at the site without taking samples to the lab.

8. Rather than just use sticks and stones as levers and hammers, something done by plenty of animals, from chimps to otters to finches, someone had deliberately selected and modified specific raw materials in a sophisticated and consistent way, and with careful intent.

9. A mutual form of ownership would bring this about either by full cooperativization or through supporters' trusts, by which clubs would be administered by a third party responsible to the supporters.

10. Danneel modeled this program after one Sandia initially created to support the US nuclear security mission and that has since been adapted to assess the threat of terrorist attacks on government buildings, air force bases, nuclear power plants, nuclear processing facilities, prisons and federal dams.

Chapter Three
Cracking List of Headings Questions
段落标题题型突破

内容提示

- IELTS 特色题型——List of Headings 题解题技巧
- List of Headings 题实例讲解

特别提醒

- 在 IELTS 阅读考试中，List of Headings 题是你首先需要解答的考题，其重要性由此可见一斑
- 解答 List of Headings 题，你可以了解到整篇阅读文章的行文布局，从而在阅读文章中顺利定位其他阅读题的正确答案

Part 1
Guide to Answering List of Headings Questions
段落标题题解题方法透析

一、题型介绍

List of Headings 题是 IELTS 考试的特色题型之一，它直接考查考生对阅读文章全文结构和主旨的把握。在海外英语语言测试中，IELTS 是惟一直接考查考生对段落主旨把握能力的考试。

如果阅读文章考到 List of Headings 题，那么阅读文章的每个段落往往被标上代码（实际考试中多为英文大写字母）；阅读文章后面附有一张列表（List of Headings），表中列出若干个段落的小标题，每个小标题均被标上代码（实际考试中多为罗马数字）。

List of Headings 题通常以段落的代码作为题目，要求考生对文章中的段落和列表中的段落小标题进行匹配，正确答案就是与段落相对应的小标题的代码。例如：

Questions 5-7

Choose the most suitable heading from the list of headings below for three paragraphs of Reading Passage 1. Write your answers in boxes 5-7 on your Answer Sheet. The first one has been done for you as an example.

List of Headings

ⅰ. Sydney—Location and History
ⅱ. Residential Inner-City Suburbs
ⅲ. Australia—Attractive to International Students
ⅳ. Entertainment for Young and Old
ⅴ. The Harbour and Surrounding Suburbs
ⅵ. The Cultural Climate

Example Paragraph A. ***Answer*** ⅲ

5. Paragraph B.
6. Paragraph C.
7. Paragraph D.

上例中，题目提供了 i -vi共计六个备选的标题，要求考生根据对阅读文章的理解和把握，找出 B、C 和 D 三个段落的标题。

二、题型要求

List of Headings 题所强调的，是题目给出的段落标题和阅读文章的各个段落之间的正确匹配关系。

在实际 IELTS 考试中，List of Headings 题型通常以较大的题量出现（如果考这种题型，一般每次考 1~2 组，每组约 5 道题）。由于题目前面附带的说明文字往往过于冗长，因此考生很容易产生畏难情绪，并且错误理解题目的要求。

三、题型地位

List of Headings 题型是 IELTS 考试阅读部分最重要的题型之一。无论是准备 A 类考试，还是准备 G 类考试，都必须认真学习 List of Headings 题型的解题方法。

特别提醒……

你一定想知道为什么 List of Headings 题是 IELTS 阅读中最重要的题型。事实上，这是因为

- **List of Headings 题出题频率高，涉及到的题量大**

在 A 类考试中，List of Headings 题型几乎每次考试都会出现，并且题目数量也比较大，一般每次考 1~2 组，每组约 5 道题。

在 G 类考试中，由于文章在大多数情况下带有小标题，所以 List of Headings 题出现的频率要低一些，但是一旦考到，也是至少考 1 组，约 5 道题。

在 2003 年下半年的一场 IELTS 考试中，由于整套阅读试题仅仅涉及到 List of Headings 和 True / False / Not Given 两种题型，所以整套阅读考题竟出现了近 15 道 List of Headings 题。

- **优先解答 List of Headings 题，将极大地方便其他题型的解答**

在解答完 List of Headings 题之后，你会对整篇文章的体裁和结构有充分的了解，这对快速定位其他题目的正确答案，顺利解题，无疑是很有帮助的。

四、破题原则

在 IELTS 考试中，考生能否顺利解答 List of Headings 题，在很大程度上取决于考生是否真正明确 List of Headings 题型的两个破题原则：

（1）主旨原则

List of Headings 题所强调的，是段落小标题和段落之间的匹配关系，而段落小标题是一个段落的大意、中心思想或主要内容，因此“把握主旨”是本题型的破题原则之一。

把握主旨意味着可以“抛弃细节”。因为 List of Headings 题只要求考生指出段落的主旨，因此段落当中的细节是绝对可以忽略的。

（2）选项不可重复使用原则

由 List of Headings 题的主旨性可以得知，每一段的标题（Heading）应该是这一段的主旨大意，而按照英语的行文习惯，任何两个段落的大意都不可以重复，否则就会被视为累赘或重复，因此，在 List of Headings 题中，任何两个段落的小标题都不相同，即 List of Headings 题具有选项不可重复使用的特点。

值得注意的是，在 List of Headings 题的 Instruction（解题说明）中，每次都会附有这样的两句话：

NB There are more headings than paragraphs so you will not use all of them.
You may use any heading more than once.

请注意，List of Headings 题具有选项不可重复使用的特点，任何一个标题都不可以使用两次，Instruction（解题说明）中出现的这句话，仅仅是 IELTS 考试的陷阱而已。

五、解题步骤

第一步 仔细阅读文章的大标题，理解全文内容

解答 List of Headings 题之前，有必要阅读文章的大标题（Title），从而了解全文的主要内容和整个阅读文章的主旨。仔细阅读文章的大标题，充分了解文章的题材，对顺利解答 List of Headings 题的帮助是不言而喻的。

在正常情况下，如果阅读文章后面带有 List of Headings 题，那么这篇阅读文章往往是有大标题的。尽管在 A 类考试当中，有时也会出现阅读文章不提供大标题的情况，但毕竟仅为少数，在此不加以讨论。

第二步　仔细阅读解题说明，确定解题目标

在 IELTS 考试中，每一组题型相同的题目之前，都会给出一小段英文的解题说明（Instruction）。比较典型的 List of Headings 题的解题说明如下：

Reading Passage 2 has seven paragraphs（A-G）. Choose the most suitable heading for paragraphs B-E and G from the list of headings below. Write the appropriate numbers（i-ix）in boxes 12-16 on your answer sheet.

NB　There are more headings than paragraphs so you will not use all of them. You may use any of the headings more than once.

阅读解题说明，考生可以明确阅读文章到底是哪几个段落需要匹配标题，从而有的放矢地展开文章的阅读。例如在上面这个解题说明里，题目非常明确地指出是 paragraphs B-E and G（B-E 段以及 G 段）需要匹配标题，那么在阅读文章时，考生就可以先不阅读不需要匹配标题的 A 和 F 段。

第三步　划掉 Example 项

List of Headings 题的选项不可重复使用原则决定了，在例子项中已经使用过的选项，绝对不可能再成为其他任何一个段落的小标题，因此考生可以大胆地将这项首先排除掉，或者从备选项中划掉。例如：

Example　Paragraph A　　　　***Answer***　iii

在这道题目的例子项中，与第一段（Paragraph A）相匹配的标题为iii，所以考生在解答这组 List of Headings 题时，首先应该从列表（List of Headings）里将iii选项排除掉。

第四步　仔细阅读给出的小标题，找出关键词

List of Headings 题通常会给出若干个备选的标题（Headings），有时候给出的标题很长，阅读起来困难较大，这个时候考生可以先把复杂的标题用一两个简单的词语来替代，这些词语被称为关键词（Key Word）。

List of Headings 题里的关键词，不一定是 Headings 所表达含义的“核心词”，而是回文章中寻找、定位答案的“定位词”。

选择“定位词”，最重要的标准当然是“易找”，即所选词语在原文中应该很容易被找到。强烈建议考生将以下几类词语划为“关键词”：

- **以人名和地名为代表的表示名称的词语**
- **时间状语等表示时间的词语**

与其他词语相比，表示名称的词语和表示时间的词语最大的优势在于，这些词

语在题目当中表现形式永远一样，极大地方便了考生定位和寻找答案。

- **特殊印刷体：大写字母、斜体字母、粗体字母、阿拉伯数字、特殊符号**

五类特殊印刷体的共同特点是外观与普通英文字母有巨大差异，所以考生可以很轻松地把它们从原文当中搜索出来。

例如，在下面这段文字中，TAFE 四个大写字母就非常显眼，考生很容易把它们找出来：

Most students would agree that having to study a subject more than once is a waste time of time, if the subject has already been passed and is well understood. Fortunately, these days credits for having passed a subject at High School or at a Technical and Further Education (TAFE) College can often be transferred to another course of study to be taken at a different institution.

而在以下这段文字里，最显眼、最容易寻找的，自然是夹杂在英文字母当中的几个阿拉伯数字：

Foul smelling chemicals are often used to irritate the bees and drive them down into the hive's bottom boxes, leaving the honey-filled supers more or less bee free. These can then be pulled off the hive. They are heavy with honey and may weigh up to 90 pounds each. The supers are taken to a warehouse. In the extracting room, the frames are lifted out and lowered into an 'uncapper' where rotating blades shave away the wax that covers each cell. The uncapped frames are put in a carousel that sits on the bottom of a large stainless steel drum. The carousel is filled to capacity with 72 frames. A switch is flipped and the frames begin to whirl at 300 revolutions per minute; centrifugal force throws the honey out of the combs. Finally the honey is poured into barrels for shipment.

随着 IELTS 考试阅读部分题目难度的增加，大写字母在考试当中出现的频率逐渐降低，斜体字母和粗体字母更是罕见，而以引号和破折号（或是小杠）“—”为代表的特殊符号出现的频率却越来越高。这些特殊符号在文章中同样具备容易寻找的特性。以下文为例：

While some students are able to supplement their funds with money from part-time and / or vacation work, such work is not always regular even when available, and this can contribute to anxiety and study problems. In general, it is unrealistic to start a course with insufficient funds in the hope that 'something will turn up'.

考生应该可以很轻松地把有小杠的“part-time”和加引号的“something will turn up”找出来。

在阅读题目给出的小标题时，可能会遇到各种各样的小麻烦，例如碰到很多不认识的单词，影响了对小标题的文字含义的正确把握。从上述的解题步骤说明中可以发现，很多时候，陌生单词只会造成小标题精确意义理解上的偏差，并不会影响到关键词的选择。因此，即使遇到不认识的单词，考生依然可以巧妙地将 List of

Headings 题的正确答案找出来。

第五步 回文章确定段落主旨

特别提醒……

回到文章中阅读各个段落的时候，你的心里一定要非常清楚自己的目标，那就是把这个段落的主题找出来。面对雅思阅读中冗长的段落，你是否会有云山雾罩的感觉呢？如何在最短的时间内把段落的主题找出来？请仔细阅读以下的技巧点拨，很快会拨云见日啦！

带着已经确认的“关键词”，回到原文当中寻找正确答案。面对或长或短、或难或易的雅思阅读段落，如何才能最快地把主旨“找”出来？这里提供四种便捷的途径：

(1) 直接寻找主旨句

在大多数情况下，考生可以根据文章的主旨句（即主题句，Top Sentence）直接找出具体段落的主旨，从而顺利地找到段落的正确标题。一个段落的主旨句通常可以在以下位置找到：

①段落的首末句

英语文章的行文顺序包括演绎法和归纳法。在按演绎法写的段落中，主题句（Top Sentence）往往位于起始处，而在按归纳法写的段落中，主题句往往位于结尾处。正确地把握段落的首尾句，在寻找段落主旨的过程当中起着致关重要的作用。在以往的 IELTS 考试中，有相当数量的 List of Headings 题，可以通过首尾句的阅读来解答。

②段落的第 2、3 句话

如果在首尾句不能找出 Top Sentence，就要留意段落的第 2、3 句话。因为在这种情况下，段落的首句往往与第 2、3 句话成一定的逻辑关系，IELTS 考试中比较常见的逻辑关系为转折和因果关系。如：

Work invariably takes place in the presence and/or under the direction of others, in a particular organizational setting. The individual has to ‘fit’ in with the work environment, with other employees, with the organizational climate, style of work, organization and culture of the organization. Different organizations have different cultures (Cartwright & Copper, 1991; 1992). Working as an engineer at British Aerospace will not necessarily be a similar experience to working in the same capacity at GEC or Plessey.

很明显，这段文字的 2、3 句话成因果关系，在“因为，所以”的结构中，作者所强调的，自然是“所以”，因此这段话的主题句应该是第 2 句话。

（2）留意反复出现的词语

如果考生能够足够重视段落当中反复出现的词语，那么寻找段落主旨的难度将大大地降低。这种方法尤其适用于那些词汇量较小，不能充分理解段落首尾句的考生。

值得注意的是，在一个段落里反复出现的，未必就是该单词本身。常常可以看到，某个单词在段落里仅出现一次，但随后反复出现指代这个单词的单词。这样的情况，同样可以认为该单词在反复出现。

（3）数字较多的段落——留意数字

如果某一段的数字较多，可以先关注该段的数字，分析数字是表示年代还是金钱等等。在这种数字较多的段落里，数字所表示的事物，往往就是段落的主旨。如：

Approximately one-third of the students questioned, were 20 years and under, and almost three-quarter were 25 and under. Only 8% were aged over 30, and fewer than 3% were over 35. Almost half of all students aged between 31 and 35 were students in Australia on student visas. As expected, a very high proportion (79%) of working holiday visa holder were aged between 21 and 25. Tourist visa holders ranged from under 20 to 31.

非常明显，这段文字中，数字出现的频率很高，而且所有的数字都在讲同一个问题——年龄。毫无疑问，此段主旨是学生的年龄状况。

（4）段落主题指示词

在 IELTS 考试中，部分阅读段落会出现一些特殊的词汇，这些词汇本身就具有提示段落主题的作用，把握好文章里出现的这些词汇，有助于顺利寻找段落主题。

例如，在段落的末尾处看到词组 “in a word”（总之），就可以知道这个词组后面的句子为该段主题句。

常见的可以起段落主题提示作用的单词或词组有：

in a word; in summary; in short; in brief	简而言之；总之
eventually; in the end; finally; consequently	最终；终于
thus; therefore; hence	因此
this (these); that (those)	这（些）就是；那（些）就是

第六步 正确填写答案

List of Headings 题的答案均为代码，一般很少有考生将答案误填。

值得注意的是，IELTS 考试当中，阅读部分并不像听力部分那样专门留有 10 分钟时间用于誊写答案，在解答阅读试题时，考生应该直接将答案填写在答题卡（Answer Sheet）上的正确位置，而不是填写在阅读文章所在的试题册上。

Part 2
Analysis of List of Headings Questions
段落标题题实例透析

Reading Passage 1

The Nature of Disputes

To resolve a dispute means to turn opposing positions into a single outcome. The two parties may choose to focus their attention on one or more of three basic factors. They may seek to (1) reconcile their interests, (2) determine who is right, and / or (3) determine who is more powerful.

A Interests are needs, desires, concerns, fears, the things one cares about or wants. They provide the foundation for a person's or an organization's position in a dispute. In dispute, not only do the interests of one party not coincide with those of the other party, but they are in conflict. For example, the director of sales for an electronics company gets into a dispute with the director of manufacturing over the number of TV models to produce. The director of sales wants to produce more models because her interest is in selling TV sets; more models mean more choice for consumers and hence increased sales, The director of manufacturing, however, wants to produce fewer models. His interest is in decreasing manufacturing costs and more models mean higher costs.

B Reconciling such interests is not easy. It involves probing for deeply rooted concerns, evising creative solutions, and making trade-offs and compromises where interests are opposed. The most common procedure for doing this is negotiation; the act of communication intended to reach agreement. Another interests-based procedure is mediation, in which a third party assists the disputes, the two sides in the dispute, in reaching agreement.

C By no means do all negotiations (or mediations) focus on reconciling interests. Some negotiations focus on determining who is right, such as when two lawyers argue about whose case has the greater merit. Other negotiations focus on determin ing who is more powerful, such as when quarrelling neighbors or nations exchange threats and counter threats. Often negotiations involve a mix of all three—some attempts to satisfy interests, some discussion of rights, and some references to relative power.

D It is often complicated to attempt to determine who is right in a dispute. Although it is usually straightforward where rights are formalized in law, other rights take the form of unwritten but socially accepted standards of behavior, such as reciprocity, precedent, equality, and seniority.

There are often different—and sometimes contradictory—standards that apply to rights. Reaching agreement on rights, where the outcome will determine who gets what, can often be so difficult that the parties frequently turn to a third party to determine who is right. The most typical rights procedure is adjudication, in which disputants present evidence and arguments to a neutral third party who has the power to make a decision that must be followed by both disputants. (In mediation, by contrast, the third party does not have the power to decide the dispute.) Public adjudication is provided by courts and administrative agencies. Private adjudication is provided by arbitrators.

E A third way to resolve a dispute is on the basis of power. We define power, somewhat narrowly, as the ability to pressure someone to do something he would not otherwise do. Exercising power typically means imposing costs on the other side or threatening to do so. The exercise of power takes two common forms: acts of aggression, such as physical attack, and withholding the benefits that derive from a relationship, as when employees stop working in a strike.

F In relationships of mutual dependence, such as between labor and management or within an organization or a family, the question of who is more powerful turns on who is less dependent on the other. If a company needs the employees' work more than employees need the company's pay, the company is more dependent and hence less powerful. How dependent one is turns on how satisfactory the alternatives are for satisfying one's interests. The better the alternative, the less dependent one is. If it is easier for the company to replace striking employees than it is for striking employees to find new jobs, the company is less depen-dent and thereby more powerful. Determining who is the more powerful party without a decisive and potentially destructive power contest is difficult because power is ultimately a matter of perceptions.

Glossary
Disputant: one of the parties in a dispute

Questions 1-5

The reading passage has 6 sections. Choose the most suitable heading for each section from the list of headings (i-xii) below. Write the appropriate numbers (i-xii) in boxes 1-5 on your answer sheet.

NB There are more headings than sections so you will not use all of them.

List of Headings

i. The cost of adjudication
ii. Handling rights-based disputes
iii. Punishing acts of aggression
iv. The role of dependence in disputes
v. The role of arbitrators
vi. Methods of settling conflicting interests
vii. Ensuring choice for consumers
viii. Fulfilling employee's needs
ix. The use of negotiation for different dispute types
x. Advantages of negotiation over mediation
xi. The role of power in settling disagreements
xii. Disagreement of interests

1. Paragraph A ______
2. Paragraph B ______

Example Paragraph C **Answer** ix

3. Paragraph D ______
4. Paragraph E ______
5. Paragraph F ______

答案透析

Question 1

答案 xii

分析 阅读A段的首句：Interests are needs，desires，concerns，fears—the things one cares about or wants. 意思为"利益是人的需要、欲望、关心和担心，即人们在乎或想要得到的一切东西。"很明显，这句话给出了interest（利益）的定义。由此可以得出，段落的主题一定和interest有关。

在List of Headings给出的标题中，只有vi、xii两个选项和interest（利益）有关，因此正确答案必定为vi、xii两个选项中的某一项。

Question 2

答案 vi

分析 阅读B段的首句：Reconciling such interests is not easy. 意思为"调和这样的利益并不容易。"显然这段的其他文字是在讲述应该如何调和这样的利益，段落的主题依然和interest（利益）有关，正确答案也必定为vi、xii两个选项中的某一项。

因为B段所讲述的是应该如何调和这样的利益，即调和利益的方法，因此B段的标题应该为：Methods of settling conflicting interests（解决冲突的利益的方法），正确答案为vi。

由于A段的标题必定为vi、xii两个选项中的某一项，而vi项是B段的标题，所以A段的标题必定为xii。

特别提醒……

做这组题时，我们先确认了B段的标题，然后才能够确认A段的标题。在IELTS考试中，遇到难度相对较大的题目时，一定要果断放弃。说不定解答完下一道题目，再回头看看先前留下的题目，就会像解答这组题一样，有一种"柳暗花明又一村"的感觉呢！

Question 3

答案 ii

分析 阅读D段的首句：It is often complicated to attempt to determine who is right in a dispute. 意思为“确认争辩中谁是正确的一方往往比较复杂。”显然这段文字的主题应该和 who is right（谁是正确的）有关，正确答案为：Handling rights-based disputes（处理以正误作为基础的争辩）。

Question 4

答案　xi

分析　阅读E段的首句：A third way to resolve a dispute is on the basis of power. 意思为“第3种解决争辩的方法是以权势作为基础。”显然后面的文字应该是具体介绍这种解决争辩的方法，因此正确答案为：The role of power in settling disagreements（权势在解决分歧中所发挥的作用）。

Question 5

答案　iv

分析　阅读F段的首句：In relationships of mutual dependence, such as between labor and management or within an organization or a family, the question of who is more powerful turns on who is less dependent on the other. 这句话中含有一个 such as 结构，such as 引导的必定为具体列举的事物，属于细节性内容，可以跳读。

跳读 such as 所引导的部分以后，这句话的意思为“在相互依赖的关系中，谁更强大的问题转变为谁对对方的依赖相对少一些的问题”显然这段文字是围绕着 dependence（依赖）这个主题词展开的，因此正确答案为：The role of dependence in disputes（依赖在争辩中所发挥的作用）。

Reading Passage 2

When Did Man and the Apes Part Company?

A Even people who accept the fact that man is just another type of animal still believe that we are special because we are the only animal of which there is only one species; all other animals exist in several—sometimes hundreds of—species. But scientists have long known that the evolution of a successful animal species almost always involves trial and error, false starts and failed experiment. The human race is no exception. At just about any given moment in prehistorying, our family tree included several species of hominids-erecting, upright-walking primates. All were competitors in an evolutionary struggle from which only one would ultimately emerge. While we would find it bizarre to share the world with another human species, the fact that we have been alone since the Neanderthals vanished some 30,000 years ago is an evolutionary aberration.

B Experts have identified several key transitions in our evolutionary chronicle. The first, which tool place around the time we diverged from the apes, between six million and four million years ago, was the development of bipedalism-two-legged walking rather than locomotion using the arms, leg and tail, which characterizes the monkey. The second, which occurred perhaps 2.5 million years ago, was the invention of tool-making—the purposeful crafting of stone implements rather than just picking up handy rocks. This led to the transition to meat eating, as tools made it easier to kill and slice up game. Then, sometime between two million and one million ago, came the dramatic growth of the brain and our ancestors' first emergence from Africa. Finally, just a few tens of thousands of years ago, our own species learned to use that powerful organ for abstract thought, which quick-ly led to art, music, language and all the other skills that have enthroned humans as the unchallenged rulers of their planet.

C Scientists have calculated that the great apes and hominids branched from a common ancestor between six million and four million years ago. The technique the experts used was to measure the differences between human and chimpanzee DNA, then averaging the rate of genetic change over time and counting backwards. This, however, remained speculation until the mid-1990s, because it was only then that actual fossils of hominids dating the period of the split were discovered, in Ethiopia and Kenya. Teams working in these countries announced that they had each found a new species of hominid, and both discoveries smashed the four-million-year barrier. All told, the scientists excavated the bones and teeth of 17 individuals. Given their age, no one was surprised that they showed a mix of chimpanzee-like and human traits. But the finds clearly show that these creatures were hominids and not apes, as they display evidence of the first two primary advances that mark the emergence of man from the animal kingdom.

D Palaeoanthropologists identify bipedalism as the first significant modification separating humans from the great apes. Our ancestors learned to walk upright long before they acquired other human traits. Bipedalism gave them enormous advantages over other species. Standing and walking upright enabled them to scan the horizon for enemies and animals to prey on. It exposed less body surface to the scorching equatorial sun and more to the cooling wind. In addition, it freed the hands for carrying food and tools.

E Animal bones dating from the same period show signs of having been butchered with stone flake to remove the animal's tongue. The leg bone of another animal is scarred by cuts, chop marks and signs of hammering, evidence that it was scraped clean of meat and bashed open to expose the nutritious marrow. This is not just tool use: it is the dawn of technology. Rather than just sticks and stones as levers and hammers—something done by plenty of animals, from chimps to otters to finches, someone had deliberately selected and modified specific raw materials in a sophisticated and consistent way, and with careful intent.

F Several species of hominid have been found who seem to have been both bipedal and toolmaking. Why did they die out, instead of evolving together with our own species, homo sapiens? The answer would seem to be that homo sapiens was capable of symbolic thought. This enable our ancestors to develop language and art. Thus they could share thoughts, feelings and ideas. This enabled them to cooperate socially more efficiently than other species; rapid innovation became a way of life.

G The domination of the world by homo sapiens has decreed that no other human species is ever likely to emerge. During prehistory, only the fittest individuals and species survived to reproduce. Now, strong and weak alike have access to food, shelter and medicine. After millions of years, evolution by natural selection, operating blindly and randomly, has produced a creature capable of overturning evolution itself.

Questions 1-4

The reading passage has seven paragraphs, A-G. Choose the most suitable headings for paragraphs B-E from the list of headings below. Write the appropriate numbers (i-viii) in boxes 1-4 on your answer sheet.

NB There are more headings than paragraphs, so you will not use them all.

List of Headings

ⅰ. Out of africa
ⅱ. DNA testing to the rescue
ⅲ. The advantage of bipedalism
ⅳ. The first butchers
ⅴ. Milestones in man's evolution
ⅵ. Evidence of the first humans
ⅶ. The culture of primitive man
ⅷ. The dawn of technology

1. Paragraph B ________
2. Paragraph C ________
3. Paragraph D ________
4. Paragraph E ________

答案透析

Question 1

答案 ⅴ

分析 阅读B段的首句：Experts have identified several key transitions in our evolutionary chronicle. 意思为“专家们已经确定了人类进化编年史中几个关键的转变。”

首句出现了evolutionary chronicle（进化编年史），从第2句话开始，依次出现The second,……，Finally，显然是详细叙述进化编年史中的几个关键的转变。因此相应的标题里必定出现单词evolutionary。回到题目给出的标题当中，发现只有Ⅴ项提到了evolution，故正确答案为Ⅴ。

Question 2

答案 ⅵ

分析 阅读C段的首句：Scientists have calculated that the great apes and hominids branched from a common ancestor between six million and four million years ago. 意思为“科学家们已经计算出巨人猿和原始人类是从400万至600万年前的共同祖先分化出来的。”

首句中出现了common ancestor（共同祖先），显然后文必定会解释和说明

common ancestor（共同祖先）以及巨人猿和人类是如何从共同祖先分化出来的。

阅读C段的末尾句：But the finds clearly show that these creatures were hominids and not apes, as they display evidence of the first two primary advances that mark the emergence of man from the animal kingdom. 意思为"但是这些发现清楚地表明，这些生物是人类，而非猿猴，因为他们展示了人类从动物王国里浮现出来的两个最基本的进步。"

段落的末尾句出现的these creatures（这些生物），指的是首句中提到的common ancestor（共同祖先），即和猿猴分化后的第一批人类，因此答案为vi项：Evidence of the First Humans（第一批人类的迹象）。

Question 3

答案 iii

分析 阅读D段的首句，发现句子中出现了bipedalism。尽管这个单词理解起来有一定的困难，但仔细阅读首句，很容易确认bipedalism这个单词的词性为名词。

在D段中单词bipedalism多次重复出现，部分句子的主语it所指代的内容同样为bipedalism，由此可以确定这个段落属于单词重复出现范畴，主题词为bipedalism。因此正确答案必为含有单词bipedalism的iii项：The Advantages of Bipedalism。

Question 4

答案 viii

分析 阅读E段的首句和末尾句，发现两句话描述的都为具体的细节，均无法成为段落的主题句。

在段落的倒数第2句话里出现了单词this，这个单词在这个语境里起总结前文的作用：This is not just tool use; it is the dawn of technology. 意思为"这不是简单的工具使用，而是科技的来临。"很明显，段落主题和dawn of technology（科技的来临）有关系，答案为含有词组dawn of technology的viii项：The Dawn of Technology（科技的来临）。

Reading Passage 3

Asian Economies Not as Vulnerable as Before

A Central bank governors from the Asia-Pacific region, at a recent meeting warned that the global trade environment is much tougher for their countries now than during the Asian crisis of four years ago. Singapore is in recession, and Korea, Malaysia, Thailand, Indonesia, Taiwan and the Philippines have sharply slowing growth. The only bright spot is China, which has maintained brisk output growth because stronger investment and household spending have more than offset the regional export slowdown.

B However, a new financial crisis does not seem to be looming for the region, as some remarkable changes have taken place over the past four years. These changes mean that the region's economies are likely to experience slower but still positive growth this year, and stronger growth next year. The first change is that the economies of Korea, Thailand and Indonesia can no longer be broken by a stampede of foreign bank lenders. The hot money has already gone. According to the most recent International Monetary Fund statistics, net international bank claims in East Asia have fallen by US $354 billion over the last four years. Loans have been repaid by stronger flows of foreign direct investment, by lending from international institutions and by the re-emergence of a bond market in the first half of last year, as well as through large trade surpluses resulting from imports growing more slowly than exports. In the four years from 1997 to 2000, these economies cumulated current account surpluses of US $239 billion, compared to a cumulative deficit of US $88 billion during the five years from 1992.

C Large current account surpluses have seen not only foreign debt reduced, but also big reserves accumulated. These reserves are seen as a cushion against future financial shocks. The reserves in Southeast Asia have increased by US $214 billion in recent years. The central banks of China, Hong Kong and Taiwan hold most of this sum. Moreover, the central banks of the region have agreed on swap arrangements, which could allow the reserves for one currency to be used in the defense of another in case of the threat of another Asian financial crisis. As noted by a report prepared by the regional central banks, intervention is most effective when coordinated.

D These changes defend against a stampede and contagion, but do not, in themselves, encourage growth. That depends on the regional shift toward more flexible exchange rates. Although far from floating freely, most regional exchange rates are no longer hostage to unhedged US dollar bank debt or to entrenched convictions that exchange rate stability is essential. Managed floats have been adopted in most regional economies. Responding to the stronger US dollar, falling exports and slowing imports, these exchange rates have been depreciating. For example, the Singapore dollar recently reached a ten-year low, while the Taiwan dollar reached a 15-year low.

E Foreign direct investment is slowing, and exports are tumbling, but with room to expand domestic demand there are good reasons to think that the region will get through the most serious global downturn in a decade. Foreign investment flows and domestic reconstruction will maintain China's growth. Even Korea and Singapore—all highly dependent on technology exports to the US—are now buttressed by trade surpluses, huge reserves and flexible exchange rates. All these factors are favorable for expanding domestic demand.

F The perennial problems of the Philippines apart, the economies at the greatest risk are those of Thailand and Malaysia, because they are attempting to sustain pegged exchange rates, and this weakens their ability to respond to sudden strains on their currencies. Although Thailand has sharply reduced its foreign debt, it has pegged its US dollar exchange rate at about 45 baht. Without strong capital controls, the informal peg limits Thailand's freedom to ease interest rates. As for Malaysia, its peg depends on its reserves, which have fallen by US $6 billion during the past year as the country has defended an exchange rate appreciating against those of its neighbors.

Questions 1-5

The reading passage has six paragraphs A-F. Choose the most suitable headings for paragraphs B-F from the list of headings below. Write the appropriate numbers (i-ix) in boxes 1-5 on your answer sheet.

NB There are more headings than paragraphs, so you will not use them all.

List of Headings

ⅰ. Disappearance of hot money
ⅱ. Changes in the region's economies
ⅲ. The role of the US dollar
ⅳ. The region's weak spots
ⅴ. The importance of currency reserves
ⅵ. Swap arrangements
ⅶ. The need for flexible exchange rates
ⅷ. Expanding domestic demand
ⅸ. The Philippines' economic problems

1. Paragraph B ______
2. Paragraph C ______
3. Paragraph D ______
4. Paragraph E ______
5. Paragraph F ______

答案透析

Question 1

答案 ⅱ

分析 阅读B段的首句，发现句子中出现some remarkable changes（一些显著的变化）。段落的第2句话承接第1句话，继续谈these changes。很明显，段落的主题涉及到changes，因此相应的标题里必定出现单词changes。回到题目给出的标题当中，发现只有ⅱ项提到了changes，故正确答案为ⅱ。

Question 2

答案 ⅴ

分析 尽管C段中出现了surplus等，对普通考生而言难度稍大的词汇，但是如果仔细阅读段落的首句，就会发现该句出现了单词reserve，而且在第2句、第3句中都出现这个单词reserve。即使不知道reserve的中文意思，也可以断定这个段落的主题包含 reserve。回到题目给出的标题当中，发现只有 V 项提到 reserve，故正确答案为 V。

Question 3

答案 vii

分析 阅读 D 段的首句，发现句子中出现了 stampede、contagion 等对一般考生来说难度较大的单词，理解起来有一定困难。仔细阅读首句，发现这句话其实是“...but...”的结构，相当于汉语中的“虽然……但是……”。很容易理解，这种结构强调的是 but（但是）后面的部分，因此首句只需要理解 but（但是）后面的部分：do not，in themselves，encourage growth（本身并不能够鼓励增长），这句话似乎和后面的任何一个标题都毫无瓜葛，因此决定阅读段落的最后一句话。

D 段的最后一句话是由词组（for example）引导的，表示“比如说；举例说”。这个短语后面的句子显然是用来说明段落主题的例子，而不可能成为段落的主题，因此从 List of Headings 题型的主旨性可以得知，for example 后面的阅读文字应当忽略不读。

首句、末句都无法提示段落的主题，因此考虑阅读段落的第 2 句话：That depends on the regional shift toward more flexible exchange rates.（那要取决于向更灵活汇率的区域性转换。）段落的首句说变化不能够鼓励增长，第 2 句说，增长要取决于向更灵活汇率的区域性转换，这两句话明显成逻辑关系，由前面讨论过的阅读方法可以得知，这种第 1、2 句话成一定逻辑关系的段落里，第 2 句话才是提示主题的句子。第 2 句话里出现的词组 more flexible exchange rates，是标题 vii 的内容，因此答案为 vii。

Question 4

答案 viii

分析 E 段的首句里同样出现了“...but...”的结构，从前面的讨论可以知道，应当直接跳读到 but 后面的内容：...with room to expand domestic demand there are good reasons to think that the region will get through the most serious global downturn in a decade.（……只要还有扩大内需的空间，就有理由相信这个区域将会摆脱十年来最严重的全球性低迷。）这句话里提到了 expand domestic demand（扩大内需）。

阅读 E 段的最后一句话：All these factors are favorable for expanding domestic demand.（所有的这些因素都有利于扩大内需。）all these factors（所有的这些因素）有总结前文的作用，因此可以推测段落主题与 expand domestic demand（扩大内需）有关。事实上，段落的首句、末尾句中都提到同一概念

expand domestic demand，属于单词重复出现，同样可以推测该段落主题与 expand domestic demand 有关。

在题目给出来的标题中，只有viii项出现了 expand domestic demand，因此正确答案为viii。

Question 5

答案 iv

分析 F 段的首句由 the perennial problems of the Philippines apart 引导，意思是"除了菲律宾的长期问题以外"，很明显，这段的主题不可能和 Philippines（菲律宾）有关的，因此首先排除ix选项。

继续阅读段落的首句：...the economies at the greatest risk are those of Thailand and Malaysia, because they are attempting to sustain pegged exchange rates, and this weakens their ability to respond to sudden strains on their currencies（风险最大的是泰国和马来西亚的经济，因为他们试图维持固定汇率，这削弱了他们对货币流通疲软作出及时反应的能力。）这部分提到了 Thailand and Malaysia（泰国和马来西亚），而题目给出的标题里没有任何一个提到 Thailand and Malaysia。但是首句的最后部分提到了 this weakens their ability（这削弱了他们的能力），this 起总结性的作用，因此题目的答案应该为iv项：The region's weak spots（这个区域的弱点）。

Part 3
Exercises of List of Headings Questions
段落标题题实战练习

Reading Passage 1

People and Organisations: the Selection Issue

A In 1991, according to the Department of Trade and Industry, a record 48,000 British Companies went out of business. When businesses fail, the post-mortem analysis is traditionally undertaken by accountants and market strategists. Unarguably organizations do fail because of undercapitalisation, poor financial management, a diverse market conditions etc. Yet, conversely, organizations with sound financial backing, good product ideas and market acumen often underperform and fail to meet shareholders' expectations. The complexity, degree and sustainment of organizational performance requires an explanation which goes beyond the balance sheet and the 'paper conversion' of financial inputs into profit making outputs. A more complete explanation of 'what went wrong' necessarily must consider the essence of what an organization actually in and that one of the financial inputs, the most important and often the most expensive, is people.

B An organization is only as good as the people it employs. Selecting the right person for the job involves more than identifying the essential or desirable range of skills, educational and professional qualifications necessary to perform the job and then recruiting the candidate who is most likely to possess these skills or at least is perceived to have the ability and predisposition to acquire them. This is a purely person / skills match approach to selection.

C Work invariably takes place in the presence and / or under the direction of others, in a particular organizational setting. The individual has to 'fit' in with the work environment, with other employees, with the organizational climate, style of work, organization and culture of the organization. Different organizations have different cultures (Cartwright & Cooper, 1991; 1992). Working as an engineer at British Aerospace will not necessarily be a similar experience to working in the same capacity at GEC or Plessey.

D Poor selection decisions are expensive. For example, the costs of training a policeman are about £20,000 (approx. US$30,000). The costs of employing an unsuitable technician on an oil rig or in a nuclear plant could, in an emergency, result in millions of pounds of damage or loss of life. The disharmony of a poor person-environment fit (PE-fit) is likely to result in low job satisfaction, lack of organizational commitment and employee stress, which affect organizational outcomes i.e. productivity, high labour turnover and absenteeism, and individual outcomes i.e. physical, psychological and mental well-being.

E However, despite the importance of the recruitment decision and the range of sophisticated and more objective selection techniques available, including the use of psychometric tests, assessment centers etc., many organizations are still prepared to make this decision on the basis of a single 30 to 45 minute unstructured interview. Indeed, research has demonstrated that a selection decision is often made within the first four minutes of the interview. In the remaining time, the interviewer then attends exclusively to information that reinforces the initial 'accept' or 'reject' decision. Research into the validity of selection methods has consistently demonstrated that the unstructured interview, where the interviewer asks any questions he or she likes, is a poor predictor of future job performance and fares little better than more controversial methods like graphology and astrology. In times of high unemployment, recruitment becomes a 'buyer's market' and this was the case in Britain during the 1980s.

F The future, we are told, is likely to be different. Detailed surveys of social and economic trends in the European Community show that Europe's population is falling and getting older. The birth rate in the Community is now only three-quarters of the level needed to ensure replacement of the existing population. By the year 2020, it is predicted that more than one in four Europeans will be aged

60 or more and barely one in five will be under 20. In a five-year period between 1983 and 1988 the Community's female workforce grew by almost six million. As a result, 51% of all women aged 14 to 64 are now economically active in the labour market compared with 78% of men.

G The changing demographics will not only affect selection ratios. They will also make it increasingly important for organizations wishing to maintain their competitive edge to be more responsive and accommodation to the changing needs of their workforce if they are to retain and develop their human resources. More flexible working hours, the opportunity to work from home or job share, the provision of childcare facilities etc., will play a major role in attracting and retaining staff in the future.

Questions 1-5

The reading passage has seven paragraphs A-G. Choose the most suitable headings for paragraphs B-E and G from the list of headings below. Write the appropriate numbers (i-x) in boxes 1-5 on your answer sheet.

NB There are more headings than paragraphs so you will not use all of them. You may use any of the headings more than once. trap

List of Headings

i. The effect of changing demographics on organizations
ii. Future changes in the European workforce
iii. The unstructured interview and its validity.
iv. The person-skills match approach to selection B
v. The implications of a poor person-environment fit
vi. Some poor selection decisions
vii. The validity of selection procedures
viii. The person-environment fit
ix. Past and future demographic changes in Europe
x. Adequate and inadequate explanations of organizational failure

Example Paragraph A	***Answer***	x
1. Paragraph B		
2. Paragraph C		
3. Paragraph D		
4. Paragraph E		
Example Paragraph F	***Answer***	ix
5. Paragraph G		

Reading Passage 2

Conflict: Good or Bad for an Organization?

A We have made considerable progress in the last 25 years toward overcoming the negative stereotype given to conflict. Most behavioural scientists and an increasing number of practicing managers now accept that the goal of effective management is not to eliminate conflict. Rather, it's to create the right intensity of conflict, so as to realize its functional benefits. Since conflict can be good for an organization, it is only logical to acknowledge that there may be times when managers will purposely want to increase its intensity. Let' s briefly review how stimulating conflict can provide benefits for an organization.

B Conflict is a means by which to bring about radical change. It's an effective device by which management can drastically change the existing power structure, current interaction patterns, and entrenched attitudes. Conflict facilitates group cohesiveness. While conflict increases hostility between groups, external threats tend to cause a group to pull together as a unit. Intergroup conflicts raise the extent to which members identify with their group and increase feelings of solidarity, while, at the same time, internal differences and irritations dissolve. Conflict improves group and organizational effectiveness. The stimulation of conflict initiates the search for new means and goals, and clears the way for innovation. The successful solution of a conflict leads to greater effectiveness, to more trust and openness, to greater attraction of members for each other, and to depersonalization for each other. In fact, it has been found that as the number of minor disagreement increases, the number of major clashes decreases. Conflicts brings about a slightly higher, more constructive level of tension. This enhances the chances of solving the conflicts in a way satisfactory to all parties concerned. When the level of tension is very low, the parties are not sufficiently motivated to do something about a conflict.

C Groups or organizations devoid of conflict are likely to suffer from apathy, stagnation, group think, and other debilitating diseases. In fact, more organizations probably fail because they have too little conflict, not because they have too much. Take a look at a list of large organizations that have failed or suffered serious financial setbacks over the past decade or two. You see names like E. F. Hutton, General Motors, Western Union, Gimbel's, K-mart, Morrison Knudsen, Eastern Airlines, Greyhound and Digital Computer. The common thread running through these companies is that they stagnated. Their management became complacent and unable or unwilling to facilitate change. These organizations could have benefited by having had more conflict—the functional kind.

D It may be true that conflict is an inherent part of any group or organization. It may not be possible to eliminate it completely. However, just because conflicts exist is no reason to defy them. Some conflict is dysfunctional, and it is one of management's major responsibilities to keep some kind of conflict intensity as low as humanly possible. The negative consequences of conflict can be devastating. The list of negatives associated with conflict is awesome. The most obvious are increased turnover, decreased employee satisfaction, inefficiencies between work units, sabotage, labour grievances and strikes, and physical aggression.

E The effect it conid have on teamwork. A good manager builds a coordinated team. Conflict works against such an objective. A successful work group is like a successful sports team; each member knows his or her role and supports his or her teammates. When a team works well, the whole becomes greater than the sum of the parts. Management sometimes creates teamwork by minimizing internal conflicts and facilitating internal coordination. Competition is not the same as conflict. Competition and conflict should not be confused with each other. Conflict is behavior directed against another party, whereas competition is behavior aimed at obtaining a goal without interference from another party. Competition is healthy; it's the source of organizational vitality. Conflict, on the other hand, can be destructive.

F Managers who accept and stimulate conflicts sometimes don't survive in the organisations. The whole argument about the value of conflict may be moot if the majority of senior executives in an organisation view conflict traditionally. In the traditional view, any conflict will be seen as bad. Since the evaluation of a manager's performance is made by higher-level executives, those managers who do not succeed in eliminating conflicts are likely to be appraised negatively. This, in turn, will reduce opportunities for advancement. Any manager who aspires to move up in such an environment will be wise to follow the traditional view and eliminate any outward signs of conflict. Failure to follow this advice might result in the premature departure of the manager.

Questions 1-5

The reading passage has six paragraphs. Choose the most suitable headings for paragraph B-F from the list of headings below. Write the appropriate numbers (i-x) in boxes 1-5.

NB There are more headings than paragraphs, so you will not use all of them. You may use any of the headings more than once.

List of Headings

i. The motivating effects of conflict
ii. Our changing views of conflict
iii. The dangers of no conflict
iv. The dangers of conflict to teamwork
v. Career dangers of conflict to a manager
vi. The negative side of conflict
vii. Conflict destroys teamwork
viii. Searching for solution through tension
ix. Conflict and change
x. Benefits of conflict

		Answer	
Example	Paragraph A		ii
1.	Paragraph B		
2.	Paragraph C		
3.	Paragraph D		
4.	Paragraph E		
5.	Paragraph F		

Reading Passage 3

Scientists Discover Appetite-Controlling Gene

A Australian scientists have identified a new gene responsible for controlling appetite in humans—a discovery experts said could lead to the first gene-based drug to treat obesity and diabetes. Greg Collins, a professor of microbiology at Deakin University in Melbourne, discovered the gene while researching diabetes in Israeli desert rats. The gene, which he called Beacon, cranks up the appetite, and the rat version is identical to the human one. Obesity sufferers could have weight reduction drugs available in little more than three years, with a European drug company investing up to $100 million dollars to take the discovery from laboratory to clinical trials and to market. The discovery of the gene, follows more than three years of research by a team of twenty scientists at Deakin University.

B The find, presented on September 19, 2000, at a conference of the European Society for the Study of Diabetes, is the third gene linked to obesity, after leptin and NPy. However, Sir George Alberti, president-elect of the International Diabetes Federation, said a drug based on Beacon could be available sooner than one targeting the other two genes because rat Beacon genes and human Beacon genes are a 100% match. ‘While scientists acknowledge that lifestyle and dietary changes are the best treatment for obesity, taking the Australian data, which is similar to data all around the world, rates of obesity have gone from 8% to 13% to 19% over the last five years. If a pharmaceutical that then would just have a small effect, maybe 5% or 10% on energy intake, it would be a good supplement, a good adjunct, a good addition to a dietary lifestyle change, and, hopefully, when someone tries to change his or her lifestyle, this would give that extra benefit, show effects early on and consolidate the process and hopefully lead to lifestyle changes in the long term.'

C Collins and his team took sand rats from the Negev desert in Israel to a laboratory in Melbourne for diabetes research. On their cactus diet in the desert, the rats were lean and healthy. But placed in a Western environment, where rat food was abundant, some ate a lot, got fat, and developed diabetes; others ate reasonable amount and remained lean. This prompted the researchers to look for genetic differences. They removed the rats' brains, examined every gene to find whether any were more active in the fat rats, and came up with the Beacon gene. Using an Israeli sand rat gave them the opportunity to find the genes, and the unique feature of the Israeli sand rat. One litter from a sand rat might have three or four different young ones. They sit in the same cage so they have exactly the same environment, the same food and the same space to exercise in, but one animal will overeat and develop obesity while one animal will overeat and develop obesity and also diabetes. Because scientists were able to control the environment, it provided an excellent opportunity to look at the genes, because the differences in these animals have to be generated by their genetic differences.

D Genes direct the formation, or expression, of proteins that a cell uses to function, repair, or defend itself, and to divide. In the obese rats, the Beacon gene was working in overdrive, forming too much appetite-stimulating protein. Once they had deciphered the sequence, or unique code, of the rat gene, the scientists searched for a match on an Internet gene databank. They found an 81% match with the earthworm, said Dr. Paul Zimmet, professor of diabetes at Monash University in Caulfield, Australia, who participated in the research. About 800 million years of evolution separate the earthworm from the Israeli sand rat, said Zimmet, adding that a gene which is preserved 81% over 800 million years of evolution must play an important role. Collins then searched the libraries of human genetic information for anything that matched the rat gene sequence. He found the identical gene sequence in human DNA. The Beacon gene produces a protein that stimulates the appetite. NPy does the same thing, whereas leptin switches off the appetite. In some obese people, the body does not respond to leptin.

E Collins then produced the protein from the human Beacon gene and injected it into the brains of lean rats with normal behavior of the gene. They gained about 5% of their own body weight in seven days. When he injected protein from both the Beacon and NPy human genes, the rats ate even more and ballooned by 10% in a week. 'Preliminary studies show that the human gene is the same across various regions and ethnicities,' Collins said.

F 'The important part of this discovery was that we found a gene localised in the hypothalamus, that is the part of the brain that controls food intake. And this gene was isolated originally in our animal model of obesity, and we found that this gene was over-expressed in the obese animals compared to the lean animals. When we looked at the product of this gene, which was the Beacon protein, and we gave it back to the animals, we could control food intake and energy balance. So this provides a brand new target for modelling drugs that control food intake, both increased and decreased food intake. And the exciting thing about this discovery was that the gene in the animal is 100% identical to the gene found in humans.' 'The next step,' he said, 'is to subject the protein to hundreds of chemicals, to see if any can block its action. The hope is that a drug can fix the problem if the gene is pumping out too much of the protein. The proposed drugs would then be tested on rats before being given to humans.'

Questions 1-5

The reading passage has six paragraphs. Choose the most suitable headings for paragraphs B-F from the list of headings below. Write the appropriate numbers (i-x) in boxes 1-5.

NB There are more headings than paragraphs, so you will not use all of them. You may use any of the headings more than once.

List of Headings

ⅰ. Dietary changes in australia
ⅱ. The discovery's importance and opportunities
ⅲ. Research findings and drug development
ⅳ. A worm to confirm
ⅴ. Applying the genes to other greatures
ⅵ. Why obesity occurs

vii. The human gene's effect on rats
viii. Calculations and research methodology
ix. The sand rat link
x. Setting up the research environment

Example Paragraph A	***Answer***	vii
1. Paragraph B		
2. Paragraph C		
3. Paragraph D		
4. Paragraph E		
5. Paragraph F		

Reading Passage 4

Rising Seas

Paragraph 1. Increased temperatures

The average air temperature at the surface of the earth has risen this century, as has the temperature of ocean surface waters. Because water expands as it heats, a warmer ocean means higher sea levels. We cannot say definitely that the temperature rises are due to the greenhouse effect; the heating may be part of a 'natural' variability over a long time-scale that we have not yet recognized in our short 100 years of recording. However, assuming the build up of greenhouse gases is responsible, and that the warming will continue, scientists—and inhabitants of low-lying coastal areas—would like to know the extent of future sea level rises.

Paragraph 2. ____________________

Calculating this is not easy. Models used for the purpose have treated the ocean as passive, stationary and one-dimensional, Scientists have assumed that heat simply diffused into the sea from the atmosphere. Using basic physical laws, they then predict how much a known volume of water would expand for a given increase in temperature. But the oceans are not one-dimensional, and recent work by oceanographers, using a new model which takes into account a number of subtle facets of the sea—including vast and complex ocean currents—suggests that the rise in sea level may be less than some earlier estimates had predicted.

Paragraph 3. ________________

An international forum on climate change, in 1986, produced figures for likely sea-level rises of 20 cm and 1.4 m, corresponding to atmospheric temperature increases of 1.5℃ and 4.5℃ respectively. Some scientists estimate that the ocean warming resulting from those temperature increases by the year 2050 would raise the sea level by between 10 cm and 40 cm. This model only takes into account the temperature effect on the oceans; it does not consider changes in sea level brought about by the melting of ice sheets and glaciers, and changes in ground water storage. When we add on estimates of these, we arrive at figures for total sea-level rises of 15 cm and 70 cm respectively.

Paragraph 4. ________________

It's not easy trying to model accurately the enormous complexities of the ever-changing oceans, with their great volume, massive currents and sensitivity to the influence of land masses and the atmosphere. For example, consider how heat enters the ocean. Does it just 'diffuse' from the warmer air vertically into the water, and heat only the surface layer of the sea? (Warm water is less dense than cold, so it would not spread downwards.) Conventional models of sea-level rise have considered that this is the only method, but measurements have shown that the rate of heat transfer into the ocean by vertical diffusion is far lower in practice than the figures that many modelers have adopted.

Paragraph 5. ________________

Much of the early work, for simplicity, ignored the fact that water in the oceans moves in three dimensions. By movement, of course, scientists don't mean waves, which are too small individually to consider, but rather movement of vast volumes of water in huge currents. To understand the importance of this, we now need to consider another process—advection. Imagine smoke rising from a chimney. On a still day it will slowly spread out in all directions by means of diffusion. With a strong directional wind, however, it will all shift downwind. This process is advection—the transport of properties (notably heat and salinity in the ocean) by the movement of bodies of air or water, rather than by conduction or diffusion.

Paragraph 6. ____________

Massive ocean currents called gyres do the moving. These currents have far more capacity to store heat than does the atmosphere. Indeed, just the top 3 m of the ocean contains more heat than the whole of the atmosphere. The origin of gyres lies in the fact that more heat from the Sun reaches the Equator than the Poles, and naturally heat tends to move from the former to the latter. Warm air rises at the Equator, and draws more air beneath it in the form of winds (the 'Trade Winds') that, together with other air movements, provide the main force driving the ocean currents.

Paragraph 7. ____________

Water itself is heated at the Equator and moves poleward, twisted by the Earth's rotation and affected by the positions of the continents. The resultant broadly circular movements between about 10° and 40° North and South are clockwise in the Northern Hemisphere. and anticlockwise in the Southern Hemisphere. They flow towards the east at mid latitudes in the equatorial region. They then flow towards the Poles, along the eastern sides of continents, as warm currents. When two different masses of water meet, one will move beneath the other, depending on their relative densities in the subduction process. The densities are determined by temperature and salinity. The convergence of water of different densities from the Equator and the Poles deep in the oceans causes continuous subduction. This means that water moves vertically as well as horizontally. Cold water from the Poles travels at depth—it is denser than warm water—until it emerges at the surface in another part of the world in the form of a cold current.

Paragraph 8. How the green house effect will change ocean temperatures

Ocean currents, in three dimensions, form a giant 'conveyor belt', distributing heat from the thin surface layer into the interior of the oceans and around the globe. Water may take decades to circulate in these 3-D gyres in the top kilometer of the ocean, and centuries in the deeper water. With the increased atmospheric temperatures due to the greenhouse effect, the oceans' conveyor belt will carry more heat into the interior. This subduction moves heat around far more effectively than simple diffusion. Because warm water expands more than cold when it is heated, scientists had presumed that the sea level would rise unevenly around the globe. It is now believed that these inequalities cannot persist, as winds will act to continuously spread out the water expansion. Of course, if global warming changes the strength and distribution of the winds, then this 'evening-out' process may not occur and the sea level could rise more in some areas than others.

Questions 1-6

There are 8 paragraphs numbered 1-8 in the reading passage. The first paragraph and the last paragraph have been given headings. From the list below numbered A-I, choose a suitable heading for the remaining 6 paragraphs.

NB There are more headings than paragraphs, so you will not use all the headings.

List of headings

A. The gyre principle
B. The green house effect
C. How ocean waters move
D. Statistical evidence
E. The advection principle
F. Diffusion versus advection
G. Figuring the sea level changes
H. Estimated figures
I. The diffusion model

1. Paragraph 2 ______
2. Paragraph 3 ______
3. Paragraph 4 ______
4. Paragraph 5 ______
5. Paragraph 6 ______
6. Paragraph 7 ______

Reading Passage 5

The Era of Biometrics

A It started with fingerprints, but we all have other body parts with unique characteristics that can be measured. Examples are hand geometry and typing and voice patterns. Automated techniques to measure these characteristics and verify a person's identity infallibly are attracting widespread attention in these days of increased use of credit cards and e-mail. This new science with its focus on increasing security is called biometrics.

B People have always used individual traits for identification. In ancient times, the presence of scars, birthmarks and other unusual features helped minimize mistaken identity. Even today, we use techniques that have been around for centuries, such as passwords and signatures. But passwords are notoriously insecure, and signatures can be forged or ignored. Shop assistants, for example, often don't bother to compare the signature on the back of a credit card with the sample provided by the purchaser. And so the search is on for better ways of proving identity. As computer power has grown, so has the idea that biometrics—the automated capture, measurement and identification of distinctive physiological or behavioral characteristics—could safeguard our identities and therefore our property and privacy, and could also be used to fight crime.

C The best-known biometric of all is the fingerprint. Police forces have used fingerprint identification techniques for over a century, but nowadays ideas for applying them commercially (e.g. to control access to personal computers) are coming thick and fast. Imagine an automatic teller machine that uses a fingerprint instead of a number as a password. The machine confirms your identity by comparing your fingerprint with the 'reference' fingerprint originally encoded into the card. These new potential applications of using fingerprints are being made possible by the development of finger scanning. Up until a few years ago, fingerprints were collected in the way we see in police movies: put the finger on an inkpad, then place it carefully on a sheet of paper. In the last decade or so, electronic scanners have been used to 'digitize' the old paper-based prints to form an electronic database. Now, technologies to scan the finger directly are developing rapidly.

D Optical finger-scanners, which work in a similar way to a photo scanner, have been in use for a decade or so, and are starting to be replaced by other methods. One of these is called capacitive scanning: it measures the electrical charge produced by the contact of the fingertip with an array of tiny capacitors mounted onto a silicon microchip. Since the ridges will make better contact with the capacitors than the valleys, this technique generates an image of the fingerprint that can be processed in the same way as an image produced by optical scanning. Ultrasound finger-scanners are also being developed. Fingerprint verification is already being used on a limited basis so far to control access to personal computers, cell phones and ATMs. A quick search of the Internet reveals a host of companies selling finger scanning devices and citing very low 'false rejection' rates and even lower 'false acceptance' rates. Techno-visionaries predict applications for finger scanning far wider than merely access to the laptop or ATM. They foresee a time when the right finger in the right place will unlock car doors, open briefcases, verify identity over the Internet, facilitate travel across International borders and prevent voter fraud.

E Meanwhile, technology companies continue to invest research dollars in other biometric options. Iris and retina scanning seem to have considerable potential: the patterns in both these parts of the eye are unique to the individual. The retina is the innermost layer of the eyeball, and is criss-crossed by tiny blood vessels. As these vessels develop in the womb, they form a unique pattern that does not change over the individual's lifetime; retina scanning can map, code and compare these blood vessel patterns. The iris, the colored part of the eye, contains about 260 unchangeable characteristics—compared to less than 40 in fingerprints—that can be scanned by video camera, coded by algorithms and, later, compared. The chance of an identical match with a different eye is said to be about 1 in 10 billion, which is a very small chance indeed. Of the two eye-scanning technologies, iris-scanning is more likely to gain in popularity. It can be done at a distance of a metre or so in contrast to retina-scanning, which must be done quite close-up, and is therefore likely to be more acceptable to the public.

F But biometrics-based identification systems must deal With a host of thorny issues if they are to gain widespread acceptance. For some, the prospect of submitting body parts for detailed examination is enough to make them, break out in a sweat, while amputees or the blind may not find certain biometric systems to be particularly userfriendly. Sceptics also point to other potential shortcomings. For example, fingerprinting has criminal connotations that will turn many law-abiding people away, and some consumer resistance seems inevitable. Meanwhile, some people worry that biometric data given for an innocent purpose, such as opening a bank account, will be used for other, more sinister purposes by governments or corporations. A further concern is the potential 'hijacking' of biometric data if transmitted over the Internet, for example—by criminals who would then use it to defraud individuals and institutions. Others worry that it could even provoke a wave of violent 'finger snatching' because possessing someone else's fingerprint could be extremely lucrative.

G Such arguments must be weighed against the fact that the aim of most biometric systems is to increase privacy by requiring a more rigorous proof of identity than has been necessary in the past. If the system is robust enough, criminals will find that beating it is a difficult task. Nevertheless, the technologies pose a potential threat of invasion of privacy, and thus present civil libertarians with many issues that must eventually be addressed. Biometric systems face another crucial question: supposing they do bring about an increase in security, will it be worth the financial cost?

Questions 1-7

The reading passage has seven paragraphs A-G. From the list of headings below, choose the most suitable heading for each paragraph. Write the appropriate numbers (i-ix) in boxes 1-7 on your answer sheet.

NB *There are more headings than paragraphs, so you will not use all of them. You may use any of the headings more than once.*

List of headings

i. The role of credit cards
ii. 'Science of Security'
iii. New horizons for fingerprint techniques
iv. Concern about privacy
v. The finger scanning revolution
vi. 'Eye' dentification
vii. The drawbacks of measuring body parts

viii. Defining biometrics
ix. Fingerprinting now out of date

1. Paragraph A
2. Paragraph B
3. Paragraph C
4. Paragraph D
5. Paragraph E
6. Paragraph F
7. Paragraph G

Reading Passage 6

Industrialisation Brought about by Tea and Beer

A Alan Macfarlane thinks he could rewrite history. The professor of anthropological science at King's College, Cambridge has, like other historians, spent decades trying to understand the enigma of the Industrial Revolution. Why did this particular important event—the world-changing birth of industry—happen in Britain? And why did it happen at the end of the 18th century?

B Macfarlane compares the question to a puzzle. He claims that there were about 20 different factors and all of them needed to be present before the revolution could happen. The chief conditions are to be found in history textbooks. For industry to 'take off', there needed to be the technology and power to drive factories, large urban populations to provide cheap labour, easy transport to move goods around, an affluent middle-class willing to buy mass-produced objects, a market-driven economy, and a political system that allowed this to happen. While this was the case for England, other nations, such as Japan, Holland and France also met some of these criteria. All these factors must have been necessary but not sufficient to cause the revolution. Holland had everything except coal, while China also had many of these factors. Most historians, however, are convinced that one or two missing factors are needed to solve the puzzle.

C The missing factors, he proposes, are to be found in every kitchen cupboard. Tea and beer, two of the nation's favourite drinks, drove the revolution. Tannin, the active ingredient in tea, and hops, used in making beer, both contain antiseptic properties. This, plus the fact that both are made with boiled water, helped prevent epidemics of waterborne diseases, such as dysentery, in densely populated urban areas.

D Historians had noticed one interesting factor around the mid-18th century that required explanation. Between about 1650 and 1740, the population was static. But then there was a burst in population. The infant mortality rate halved in the space of 20 years, and this happened in both rural areas and cities, and across all classes. Four possible causes have been suggested. There could have been a sudden change in the viruses and bacteria present at that time, but this is unlikely. Was there a revolution in medical science? But this was a century before Lister introduced antiseptic surgery. Was there a change in environmental conditions? There were improvements in agriculture that wiped out malaria, but these were small gains. Sanitation did not become widespread until the 19th century. The only option left was food. But the height and weight statistics show a decline. So the food got worse. Efforts to explain this sudden reduction in child deaths appeared to draw a blank.

E This population burst seemed to happen at just the right time to provide labour for the Industrial Revolution. But why? When the Industrial Revolution started, it was economically efficient to have people crowded together forming towns and cities. But with crowded living conditions comes disease, particularly from human waste. Some research in the historical records revealed that there was a change in the incidence of waterborne disease at that time, especially dysentery. Macfarlane deduced that whatever the British were drinking must have been important in controlling disease. They drank beer and ale. For a long time, the

English were protected by the strong antibacterial gent in hops, which were added to make beer last. But in the late 17th century a tax was introduced on malt? The poor turned to water and gin, and in the 1720s the mortality rate began to rise again. Then it suddenly dropped again. What was the cause?

F Macfarlane looked to Japan, which was also developing large cities about the same time, and also had no sanitation. Waterborne diseases in the Japanese population were far fewer than those in Britain. Could it be the prevalence of tea in their culture? That was when Macfarlane thought about the role of tea in Britain. The history of tea in Britain provided an extraordinary coincidence of dates. Tea was relatively expensive until Britain started direct trade with China in the early 18th century. By the 1740s, about the time that infant mortality was falling, the drink was common. Macfartane guesses that the fact that water had to be boiled, together with the stomach-purifying properties of tea so eloquently described in Buddhist texts, meant that the breast milk provided by mothers was healthier than it had ever been. No other European nation drank tea so often as the British, which, by Macfarlane's logic, pushed the other nations out of the race for the Industrial Revolution.

G But, if tea is a factor in the puzzle, why didn't this cause an industrial revolution in Japan? Macfarlane notes that in the 17th century, Japan had large cities, high literacy rates and even a futures market. However, Japan decided against a work-based revolution, by giving up labour-saving devices, even animals, to avoid putting people out of work. Astonishingly, the nation that we now think of as one of the most technologically advanced, entered the 19th century having almost abandoned the wheel. While Britain was undergoing the Industrial Revolution, Macfarlane notes wryly, Japan was undergoing an industrious one.

H The Cambridge academic considers the mystery solved. He adds that he thinks the UN should encourage aid agencies to take tea to the world's trouble-spots, along with rehydration sachets and food rations.

Questions 1-5

The passage has 8 paragraphs A-H. Choose the most suitable headings for paragraphs B-F from the list of heading below. Write the appropriate numbers (i-x)。

NB There are more headings than paragraphs so you will not use all of them.

List of Headings

i . The significance of tea drinking
ii . Possible solution to the puzzle
iii. Industry in Holland and France
iv. Significant population increase
v . The relationship between drinks and disease
vi. Gin drinking and industrialisation
vii. Dysentery prevention in Japan and Holland
viii. Japan's waterborne diseases
ix. Preconditions necessary for industrial revolution
x . Introduction

	Answer
Example Paragraph A	x
1. Paragraph B	
2. Paragraph C	
3. Paragraph D	
4. Paragraph E	
5. Paragraph F	

Chapter Four
Cracking True/False/Not Given Questions
正误判断题题型突破

内容提示

- IELTS 特色题型——True / False / Not Given 题解题技巧点拨
- True / False / Not Given 题实例讲解

特别提醒

- *如果你想在 IELTS 考试中获得阅读高分，请特别重视本章的学习，因为 True / False / Not Given 题曾让无数英语高手在 IELTS 考试中战败而归，它是毫无争议的 IELTS 阅读考试高分瓶颈*
- *True / False / Not Given 题解题过程中或许会涉及到一些和你的思维方法相违背的认识观念，请调整你的思路，以最佳的状态迎接 IELTS 考试中 True / False / Not Given 题所带来的挑战*

Part 1
Guide to Answering True / False / Not Given Questions
正误判断题解题方法透析

一、题型介绍

True / False / Not Given 是雅思考试中最具代表性的题型。对千千万万的中国雅思考生而言，它也是阅读考试中难度最大的题型。

当阅读考试出现 True / False / Not Given 题时，在阅读文章后面就会给出若干句子，要求考生根据对阅读文章的理解和把握，判断句子陈述内容的正误。

与国内考试中常见的判断题答案仅仅存在正确、错误两种可能性不一样，IELTS 考试中的 True / False / Not Given 题，对任何一个需要判断正误的句子都给出了三种可能，分别是 True（正确）、False（错误）以及 Not Given（未提及）。如：

Do the following statements agree with the views of the writer in the Reading Passage? In boxes 1-5 on your answer sheet write

True if the statement agrees with the writer

False if the statement does not agree with the writer

Not Given if there is no information about this in the passage

二、题型要求

True / False / Not Given 题所强调的，是根据阅读文章来判断给出句子的正误。在 IELTS 考试中，True / False / Not Given 题不仅要求考生能够准确快速地在原文中找到题目给出的句子，而且要求考生仔细比较原文中的语句和题目给出的语句之间的差异，从而判断出两句话的意思是否统一。

如果不能在阅读文章中找到题目给出的语句，说明阅读文章中未涉及这个语句的内容，则答案应该是：Not Given（未提及）。

如果在阅读文章中找到了题目给出的语句，并且通过阅读比较后发现两句话的意思一致，则答案应该是：True（正确）。

如果在阅读文章中找到了题目给出的语句，并且通过阅读比较后发现两句话的意思不一致，则答案应该是：False（错误）。

三、题型地位

True / False / Not Given 题是 IELTS 考试的必考题型，在历次 IELTS 考试中都有所涉及。

在中国大陆地区的 IELTS 考试中，曾经有一场 IELTS 考试出现了多达 23 道 True / False / Not Given 题，由此可见 True / False / Not Given 题在 IELTS 中非同寻常的重要性。

特别提醒……

无论是从出题数量来看，还是从出现频率来看，True / False / Not Given 题都是 IELTS 阅读考试最重要的题型之一，请你千万要重视！

四、破题原则

（1）定位准确

解答 True / False / Not Given 题的第一个原则是必须定位准确。只有在原文中正确定位题目所给出的语句，才能够对比阅读文章中相关的语句和题目给出的语句，从而洞察两者之间的差异，得出答案。

在 IELTS 阅读部分中，各个题型都涉及到“定位答案”这个核心步骤。True / False / Not Given 题的定位方法和前面讨论过的其他题型的定位方法一致。值得注意的是，在解答 True / False / Not Given 题时，如果不在阅读文章中找到题目给出的语句，就应该直接确认答案为 Not Given（未提及）。

（2）判断准确

正确解答 IETLS 考试中的 True / False / Not Given 题的另一个原则是判断准确。

在阅读文章中定位题目相关的语句以后，需要仔细阅读，并且仔细比较这些语句和题目中给出的语句，找出两者之间的异同，鉴别题目给出句子的正误。

五、判断标准

True / False / Not Given 题要求仔细阅读题目给出的语句，以及在阅读文章中定位得到的和题目所给出句子相关的语句。

阅读完这些语句以后，你一定会发现题目的语句与文章中语句之间存在的一些区别。这时，如果你有一套严格的判断标准，就可以根据标准来判断题目所给语句的正误情况了。

(1) TRUE

在 IELTS 考试中，只有题目中的语句与文章中的语句思想内容完全一致，才可以判定题目的答案为 True。

例 1：

原文　Women could not take part and were forbidden, on pain of death, even to attend the Games.（妇女不能够参加而且被严禁出席运动会。）

题目　The spectators, as well as participants, of the ancient Olympics, were male.（古代奥运会的观众和参加者都是男性。）

答案　True

分析　这两句话虽然文字不一样，但是却表达了同样的意思，即奥运会的参与者和观众都是男性，因此答案为 True。

例 2：

原文　Frogs are losing the ecological battle for survival, and biologists are at a loss to explain their demise.（在和生态环境的斗争中，青蛙正节节败退，而生物学家们却不能够解释它们的死亡。）

题目　Biologist are unable to explain why frogs are dying.（生物学家们不能够解释为什么青蛙死亡。）

答案　True

分析　这两句话虽然文字不一样，但是却表达了同样的意思，题目中的 unable to 与原文中的 at a loss 为同义词组，dying 和 demise 也是同义词，因此答案为 True。

特别提醒……

两句话的思想内容完全一致，并不意味着两句话的文字完全一致。在 IELTS 考试中，大多数答案为 True 的题目的文字，和阅读原文中的文字相去甚远，但意思却真的达到了完全一致。

(2) FALSE

IELTS 考试中的 False 项，有很多种可能的情况，请你静下心来，好好研究以下几种常见的情况。

①与阅读文章中的内容完全相反

如果题目的语句所表达的意思与阅读文章所表达的意思刚好相反，毫无疑问答案应该为 False。

例 1：

原文 These changes defend against a stampede and contagion, but do not in themselves, encourage growth.（这些变化防止了这种现象的扩散和蔓延，但是它们自身却不能够鼓励增长。）

题目 The changes in the region's economies will accelerate their growth.（这个区域经济的变化将会加速经济增长。）

答案 False

分析 这两句话表达了刚好相反的意思：阅读文章中的原句指出经济变化不能够鼓励增长，而题目中却指出经济变化会加速经济增长，两句话的含义相互矛盾，因此答案为 False。

②在阅读文章中为并列关系，在题目中却出现了 only 结构

例 1：

原文 Since the Winter Games began, 55 out of 56 gold medals in the men's Nordic skiing events have been won by competitors from Scandinavia or the former Soviet Union.（从冬季奥运会开办以来，在男子越野滑雪项目中，56 块金牌中有 55 块是被北欧和前苏联的选手夺得的。）

题目 Only Scandinavians have won gold medals in the men's Nordic skiing events in the Winter Olympics.（只有北欧选手获得冬季奥运会男子越野滑雪项目的金牌。）

答案 False

分析 阅读文章中的原句指出，是北欧和前苏联选手获得了金牌，而且是获得了

56 块金牌中的 55 块，题目中却说只有北欧人获得了金牌，因此答案应该为：False。

③阅读文章中包括条件状语，而题目中却省略了条件成分

如果原文中包含条件状语，例如常见的 if 、unless 或 if not 等结构，而题目中却省略了这些表示条件的成分，答案就应该为 False。

例 1：

原文 The Internet has often been a hazardous tool if they are in the hands of young computer users.（如果是年轻人在使用电脑，那么英特网往往会成为危险的工具。）

题目 The Internet has often been dangerous.（英特网往往是危险的。）

答案 False

分析 从阅读文章中的原句可以得知，英特网是危险的工具有一个前提条件，那就是——是年轻人在使用电脑。题目中省略了这个前提条件，直接指出英特网是危险的，所以答案应该为 False。

特别提醒……

文章中说“如果温度在零度以下，水可以结冰”，若题目直接说“水可以结冰”，那么这道题目的答案就应该是 False，尽管众所周知，水是绝对可以结冰的。这就是 IELTS 中的 True / False / Not Given 题所使用的逻辑。或许这种逻辑和你的思维是完全相反的，但是既然决定参加 IELTS 考试了，就要勇于挑战最难的题型——True / False / Not Given 题，而挑战 True / False / Not Given 题的第一步，就是请你用心体会这些 True / False / Not Given 题使用的古怪的判断标准！

④阅读文章中为人们对某件事物的主观看法或感受，题目中却转化为客观事实

例 1：

原文 During those years, most local people believed that keeping butterflies could make a lot of money.（在那个时候，很多当地的老百姓认为养蝴蝶可以挣很多钱。）

题目 Keeping butterflies was a way of making big money then.（在那个时候，养蝴蝶可以挣很多钱。）

答案 False

分析 从阅读文章中的原句可以得知，“养蝴蝶可以挣很多钱”，仅仅是大多数

当地老百姓（most local people）的主观看法而已。题目中将这个主观看法直接转变为了现实，所以答案应该为 False。

（3）NOT GIVEN

①在阅读文章中没有提及题目所讨论的内容

如果在阅读文章中无法找到和题目内容相关的语句，或阅读文章中没有提及题目讨论的内容，答案就应该为 Not Given（未提及）。

②题目将文章所涉及的事物更加细节化，从而无从考证

例 1：

原文 Japanese government decided to send some officials to business schools in the US to receive the best business education in the world.（日本政府决定派遣数名官员前往美国的商学院接受全球最好的商科教育。）

题目 Two hundred officials were to be sent to US to study business by the Japanese government.（200 名官员将被日本政府派遣到美国学习商科。）

答案 Not Given

分析 从阅读文章中的原句获得的信息是：日本政府将派遣数名官员前往美国，文章中并没有具体指明将有多少名官员被派遣到美国。题目中的表述把原文信息更加具体化，指出将有 200 名官员被派遣到美国。数字 200 是文章中没有出现的信息，也是我们无法根据阅读文章的内容鉴别正误的信息，因此答案为 Not Given。

③在阅读文章中提及若干事物，但是没有做出比较，题目当中对这些事物进行了比较，从而无从考证

如果文章中提到了某几个事物或是某几个人，但是没有进行相互之间的比较，而题目中却出现了比较级，这些比较级属于我们无法根据原文内容鉴别正误的信息，因此这种情况的答案为 Not Given。

④在阅读文章中为人的目标、目的、愿望、誓言等的内容，在题目中成为了现实

如果在阅读文章中发现一件事情为某人的目标、愿望或誓言，那么能确认的，仅仅是此人曾经梦想或发誓要做这件事情，至于此人是否真的做成此事，文章中没有给出相关信息，此事自然也无从确认。这种情况下，如果题目中说此人的梦想或誓言已经成为现实，则答案只能是 Not Given（没有给出相关信息，因为无从考证）。

常见的表示目标、目的、愿望、誓言的词语有：

aim; object; objective; goal; aim at	目标
purpose; motive; intention	目的
hope; wish; desire; dream	愿望
swear; pledge; vow; promise	誓言

例1:

原文　His aim was to bring together, once every four years, athletes from all countries on the friendly fields of amateur sport.（他的目的是每四年把世界各国的运动员聚集到友好的业余运动赛场上来一次。）

题目　Only amateur athletes are allowed to compete in the modern Olympics.（现代奥运会上，只允许业余运动员参加比赛。）

答案　Not Given

分析　从阅读文章中的原句获得的信息是：他有一个目的，即每四年把世界各国的运动员聚集到友好的业余运动赛场上来一次，至于这个目的是否实现，文章中并没有提供任何相关的信息，而题目中将这个目地转化为已经实现的事实，因此答案为：Not Given。

六、解题步骤

第一步　仔细阅读题目，确定关键词

解答 True / False / Not Given 题的第一步，要求仔细阅读题目提供的句子，从句子中找出可以用来定位的关键词。关键词的确定方法，请参考 Chapter Three 中所叙述的原则。例如：

Economists notice that in the 15th century, Japan had large cities, high literacy rates and even a futures market.

判断这句话的正误，首先需要去文章中寻找和这句话相关的语句。这句话中出现的数字 15th century、专有名词Japan 都可以作为定位使用的关键词，在阅读文章中先搜索这两个单词，找到它们，正确答案自然就在眼前了。

第二步　在阅读文章中定位相关语句

阅读完题目提供的句子以后，就要回到阅读文章中定位相关语句。可以使用在第一步里挑选出来的关键词，通过搜索关键词的方法来定位相关语句。

特别提醒……

除了使用 Key Word（关键词）以外，其实还有一种定位相关语句的办法！如果你已经解答了这篇文章的 List of Headings 题，就可以通过已经确定的各段的主题，推测相关语句大致会在文章的哪一段，然后在这段中有的放矢地寻找相关语句！在 IELTS 考试中，这种方法往往和 Key Word 有着异曲同工之妙！

第三步　比较阅读文章中的相关语句和题目中语句，根据 True / False / Not Given 题的判断标准确认题目语句的正误

定位出相关语句以后，认真比较阅读文章中的相关语句和题目中语句的区别，然后根据前面讨论过的 True/False/Not Given 题的判断标准确认题目的正误。

第四步　正确填写答案

特别提醒……

在 IELTS 考试中，或许一不小心，你就会犯一个非常低级的错误：有的时候，题目要求你将正确答案填写为 True，有的时候却要求你填写为 TRUE，甚至填写成 YES，你肯定明白，TRUE≠True≠YES，所以解答 IELTS 考题，不仅需要你有相当的英语水平，而且需要你有足够的细心！

Part 2
Analysis of True / False / Not Given Questions
正误判断题实例透析

Reading Passage 1

Please Hold the Line

A Nearly all of us know what it's like to be put on 'musical hold'. Call almost any customer service number, and you can expect to hear at least a few bars of boring elevator music before an operator picks up. The question is: do you hang up or do you keep holding? That may depend on your gender and what type of music is playing, according to research reported by University of Cincinnati Associate Professor of Marketing, James Kellaris.

B Kellaris, who has studied the effects of music on consumers for more than 12 years, teamed with Sigma Research Management Group to evaluate the effects of 'hold music' for a company that operates a customer service line.

C The researchers tested four types of 'on-hold' music with 71 of the company's clients, 30 of them women. Light jazz, classical, rock and the company's current format of adult alternative (a mix of contemporary styles) were all tested. The sample included individual consumers, small business and large business segments. Participants were asked to imagine calling a customer assistance line and being placed on hold. They were then exposed to 'on-hold' music via headsets and asked to estimate how long it played. Their reactions and comments were also solicited and quantified by the researchers.

D Service providers, of course don't want you to have to wait on hold, but if you do, they want it to be a pleasant experience for you. But Kellaris' conclusions may hold some distressing news for companies. No matter what music was played, the time spent 'on hold' was generally overestimated. The actual wait in the study was 6 minutes, but the average estimate was 7 minutes and 6 seconds.

E He did find some good news for the client who hired him. The kind of music they're playing now, alternative, is probably their best choice. Two things made it a good choice. First, it did not produce significantly more positive or negative reactions in people. Second, males and females were less polarised in their reactions to this type of music.

F Kellaris' other findings, however, make the state of musical hold a little less firm: time spent 'on hold' seemed slightly shorter when light jazz was played, but the effect of music format differed for men and women. Among the males, the wait seemed shortest when classical music was played. Among the females, the wait seemed longest when classical music was played. This may be related to differences in attention levels and musical preferences.

G In general, classical music evoked the most positive reactions among males; light jazz evoked the most positive reactions (and shortest waiting time estimates) among females. Rock was the least proferred accoss both gender groups and produced the longest waiting time estimates. 'The rock music's driving beat kind of aggravates people calling customer assistance with a problem' said Kellaris, 'The more positive the reaction to the music, the shorter the waiting time seemed to be. So maybe time does tend to fly when you're having fun, even if you're on musical hold.' Kellaris joked.

H But unfortunately for companies operating on-hold lines, men and women have different ideas about what music is 'fun'. 'The possible solution,' Kellaris joked, 'might be for the recorded message to say: if you're a male, please press one; if your a female, please press two. If you are in a bad mood, please hang up and try later.'

Questions 1-4

Do the following statements agree with the claims of the writer? Write:

True *if the statement agrees with the claims of the writer*

False *if the statement contradicts the writer*

Not Given *if it is impossible to say what the writer thinks about this*

1. The consumer service company surveyed was playing only classical music. [ ]

2. Advertising is considered a poor alternative to ‘on hold’ music. [ ]

3. In general, light jazz evoked the most positive reactions among male. [ ]

4. No matter what kind of music was played, people tend to overestimate the time spent ‘on hold’. [ ]

答案透析

Question 1

答案 False

分析 阅读题目提供的句子：The consumer service company surveyed was playing only classical music（被调查的消费性劳务公司所播放的音乐仅仅是古典音乐）。选定 consumer service company（消费性劳务公司）作为定位使用的关键词。

在阅读文章中搜索关键词 consumer service company，可以发现阅读文章 B 段中出现了单词 consumer。继续阅读下一句话，即 C 段首句：The researchers tested four types of ‘on hold’ music with 71 of the company's clients, ...（研究人员对该公司的 71 位客户进行了 4 种呼叫等待音乐的测试，……），由此可知，该公司播放的是 4 种音乐，而不仅仅是古典音乐，因此答案为：No。

Question 2

答案 Not Given

分析 阅读题目提供的句子：Advertising is considered a poor alternative to “on hold” music（广告被认为是 on hold 音乐的一个较差的选择），选定 Advertising（广告）作为定位使用的关键词。

在阅读文章中搜索关键词 Advertising，发现文章中并没有出现这个单词，即文章中并没有提及 Advertising，因此答案为：Not Given。

Question 3

答案　False

分析　阅读题目提供的句子：In general，light jazz evoked the most positive reactions among male.（通常轻爵士乐会在男性当中激起最积极的反应。）选定 light jazz（轻爵士乐）作为定位使用的关键词。

在阅读文章中搜索关键词 light jazz，可以发现阅读文章 G 段中出现了单词 light jazz。文章中说：In general，classical music evoked the most positive reactions among males；light jazz evoked the most positive reactions... among female（通常古典音乐会在男性当中激起最积极的反应，轻爵士音乐会在女性当中激起最积极的反应。）显然，题目表达的信息刚好与原文表达的思想内容相反，因此答案为：No。

Question 4

答案　True

分析　阅读题目提的供句子：No matter what kind of music was played，people tend to overestimate the time spent ‘on hold’.（不管播放的是什么音乐，人们往往感觉电话等待的时间比实际时间要长。）选定带有引号的词组“on hold”作为定位使用的关键词。

由于词组“on hold”带有引号，所以先在阅读文章中搜索引号。正确答案位于文章 D 段的倒数第 2 句话：No matter what music was played，the time spent ‘on hold’ was generally overestimated.（通常不管放什么音乐，电话等待的时间总是被人们过高地估计了。）显然，题目表达的信息刚好与原文表达的思想内容相同，因此答案为：Yes。

Reading Passage 2

Global Water Crisis

A According to a report released by the World Water Organization (WWO), two-thirds of the world's population will be facing water shortages by 2025. The report states that the world's water supply is not keeping pace with demands being made upon it—consumption rose six-fold between 1900 and 1995, more than twice the rate of population growth. The report also says that while most wealthy countries will cope with falling water supplies due to efficient water management, poorer countries will suffer on a huge scale, making it even harder for them to escape poverty.

B The WWO says the scale of the crisis is such that the world will increasingly witness a new phenomenon, 'water refugees'—millions of people being forced to leave their homes in search of clean water. Chronic water shortages are already being experienced around the world. Lake Chad in Africa, which provides water to 20 million people in six countries, has shrunk by 95% in the past 38 years. Two-thirds of China's cities are facing severe water shortages and Delhi in India is predicted to run out of groundwater by 2015 at current usage rates.

C The world's water supplies are stretched to the limit due to escalating populations, rising agricultural use, poor management and the effects of global warming. Consequently the WWO is urging governments and institutions to take urgent action by:

1. Giving the water crisis high priority at the World Summit on Sustainable Development in 2002.
2. Increasing investment in water supply sanitation and water resources to ensure that the basic needs of poorer communities are met before the luxury needs of the wealthy.
3. Increasing efforts to meet commitments to reduce greenhouse gas emissions

by 5% by 2012.

4. Reintroducing traditional methods of water conservation in poorer countries. For example, water harvesting could significantly help to meet India's water needs if land was set apart for rainfall collection.

D Water is our most essential and basic requirement. Although water has been successfully harnessed for energy, irrigation and industry we are increasingly paying a high cost for it as people in poorer countries die from lack of a fresh, regular supply. Worldwide water shortages will begin to threaten food production in many countries too. By 2025 the amount of water needed for food production around the world will rise by 50%, due to population growth and higher standards of living. Poorer countries will face having to choose between using water for crop irrigation or domestic and industrial use. Consequently many may be forced to risk the vagaries of international markets by importing food. For the 1.3 billion people who live on $1 a day or less, high grain prices could quickly become life threatening.

E The primary reasons for the water supply crisis are:

1. Lack of water regulation, management and investment by governments in poorer countries.

2. Global warming which causes deserts to expand, rivers to dry up, droughts to intensify and melting of the polar ice caps which may lead to the intrusion of salt water into freshwater supplies.

3. Unsustainable use of groundwater which occurs in every continent except Antarctic.

F According to the WWO, even though water shortages and hosepipe bans exist in the UK, each person still has an average of 150 litres of water a day at their disposal—enough to wash 15 cars. In some of the poorest countries, however, people are surviving on a daily ration of less than a bucket of water.

Questions 1-5

Do the following statements agree with the information in the reading passage? In boxes 1-5 on your answer sheet write:

Yes *if the statement agrees with the information*

No *if the statement contradicts the information*

Not Given *if there is no information on this in the passage*

1. The report states that falling world water supplies won't affect most prosperous countries. ______
2. The WWO is urging governments to educate people on the importance of conserving water. ______
3. Global warming will help to create fresh water by melting the polar ice caps. ______
4. A major reason for the water supply problem in poorer countries is their governments' failure to control water usage. ______
5. Traditional methods of water conservation have contributed to the water crisis in poorer countries. ______

答案透析

Question 1

答案　Yes

分析　阅读题目提供的句子：The report states that falling world water supplies won't affect most prosperous countries.（这篇报道声明说正在下降的世界供水不会影响到繁荣的国家。）选定名词 report 作为定位使用的关键词。

在阅读文章中搜索 report，可以发现 report 位于文章 A 段的第 2 和第 3 句话中。题目相关句为 A 段的第 3 句话：The report also says that while most wealthy countries will cope with falling water supplies...（这个报道同样指出大多数富裕国家能够应对下降的供水……），显而易见，题目中的句子表达的思想含义与阅读文章所表达的思想含义相吻合，因此答案为：Yes。

Question 2

答案　Not Given

分析　阅读题目提供的句子：The WWO is urging governments to educate people on the importance of conserving water.（WWO 正在敦促政府教育人们储水的重要性。）选定大写字母组合 WWO 作为定位使用的关键词。

在阅读文章中搜索 WWO，可以发现和这道题目相关的语句为阅读文章 C 段的第 2 句话：Consequently the WWO is urging governments and institutions to take urgent action by...（因此 WWO 敦促各国政府和公共机构采取紧急措施……）C 段列举的 1、2、3 和 4 这四点紧急措施中，没有出现阅读题目中的

educate people on the importance of conserving water，但也没有文字提示说WWO就一定没有采取这样的措施，因此无法断定WWO是否在敦促政府教育人民储水的重要性，因此答案为：Not Given。

Question 3

答案　No

分析　阅读题目提供的句子：Global warming will help to create fresh water by melting the polar ice caps.（全球变暖将促使极地冰冠融化，从而创造淡水。）选定名词词组global warming作为定位使用的关键词。

在阅读文章中搜索global warming，可以发现global warming位于阅读文章E段中：Global warming which causes deserts to expand，rivers to dry up，droughts to intensify and melting of the polar ice caps which may lead to the intrusion of salt water into freshwater supplies.（全球变暖促使沙漠扩张、河流干涸、干旱加剧、极地冰冠融化，导致咸水入侵淡水供给。）很明显，阅读文章传递的信息是全球变暖导致淡水资源受到破坏，和题目所指的创造淡水刚好相反，因此答案为：No。

Question 4

答案　Yes

分析　阅读题目提供的句子：A major reason for the water supply problem in poorer countries is their governments' failure to control water usage.（较贫穷的国家出现供水问题的一个主要原因是政府在控水方面的失败。）

阅读文章的E段列举1、2、和3三点来解释出现水危机的原因，其中第1条原因为：Lack of water regulation，management and investment by governments in poorer countries.（较贫穷的国家的政府缺乏水的规章、管理和投资。）显然，这个理由和题目所传递的意思一致，因此答案为：Yes。

Question 5

答案　No

分析　阅读题目提供的句子：Traditional methods of water conservation have contributed to the water crisis in poorer countries.（传统的储水方法导致较贫穷国家的水危机。）选定名词词组traditional methods of water conservation（传统的储水方法）作为关键词。

通过定位关键词可以发现与题目相关的语句位于阅读文章C段的第4点：Reintroducing traditional methods of water conservation in poorer countries（在较

贫穷国家再次引入传统的储水方法。）显然，作为 WWO 敦促政府采取的紧急措施之一，traditional methods of water conservation 不可能引发水危机，因此答案为：No。

特别提醒……

在 IELTS 考试中，阅读部分有一项要求你不得不重视的非常重要的能力——猜词！比如这道题目中出现的单词 reintroducing，它是动词 reintroduce 的现在分词形式，而动词 reintroduce 是由动词 introduce（引入）和表示“再次”的前缀 re 组成的，意思为“再次引入”。

Part 3
Exercises of True / False / NOt Given Questions
正误判断题实战练习

Reading Passage 1

Getting Girls on-Line

A When Nancy Leveson, now a computer science professor at the University of Washington, was teaching math at a California high school, her best student also happened to be one of the prettiest and most popular girls around. And when the girl got the highest score on a test, Leveson thought nothing of announcing the achievement while handing back the papers. As soon as the class ended, though, the distraught student approached. She begged her teacher never, ever to embarrass her like that again.

B The incident happened nearly 20 years ago, but Leveson notes that little has changed. Now, as then, too many teenage girls feel uncomfortable and even unwelcome in the realms of math, science and computing. Research shows that girls who are gifted in these subjects in elementary school begin to shy away from them by the seventh grade. Eventually, they convince themselves that these are male domains. 'By saying only men are good at these things, you make the women who are good at them seem like freaks,' says Leveson.

C Increasingly, however, educators are trying to reverse the process by retraining teachers and redirecting students. Funded with more than $1 million by the National Science Foundation (NSF) and seven corporations, Computer Equity Expert Project (CEEP) showed 200 math and computer-science teachers how to recognise and eliminate gender bias in their classrooms. CEEP urged teachers to bring more girls into the world of computers by setting up mentoring programs with older students and having girls-only days at the school computer labs.

D Both public and private schools are trying to close the technology gap. Because girls tend to do better in the sciences without the distraction of boy, three California schools have started girls-only math classes over the last two years with promising results. Other schools are hooking up with colleges for help and inspiration.

E But however wonderful the subject looks in high school, interest often diminishes in college, where women earned only 30% of the undergraduate degrees awarded in computer science in 1991, and 16% in engineering in 1993, as opposed to medical school, where women make up 36% of total enrolment. The proportion shrinks still more at the doctoral level, where women receive only 15% of computer science PhDs and under 10% of engineering PhDs.

F Many college women are turned off by the macho swagger of technojocks at schools like MIT, where staying awake for three days to perfect a piece of software is seen as a test of virility. That kind of attitude 'sets cultural parameters not just for MIT but for the intense nature of the computer culture everywhere,' says Steven Levy, author of *Hackers: Heroes of the Computer Revolution.* As a result, it's hard to find female role models in computer science.

G To keep women interested in the field, Nancy Leveson and a colleague from the University of British Columbia spearheaded a program that will match 20 female undergraduates with faculty mentors around the country this summer, thanks to a $2,400,000 grant from the NSF.

H In Rochester, NY, the Rochester Institute of Technology's Women in Science, Engineering and Math mentoring program aims to spark high school girls' career interests by linking 140 girls and professional women in a computer network. Coordinators, who hope to extend the four-month program to three years, note the intense interest shown by girls and women. 'I can't keep the mentors away,' says Carol O'Leary, who helped set the program up. 'I was looking for 40, and I have 67. Women are anxious to give of themselves.'

I Eventually, these computer educators would like to make gender-specific programs obsolete, but that will happen only when computer-science education becomes more creative, according to Paula Rayman, director of Pathways for Women in the Sciences, a research program at Wellesley College. By way of example, Rayman points to her 9-year-old daughter, Lily, whose fourth-grade class at the Bowman Elementary School in Lexington, Mass., is learning several sciences under the guise of bicycle repair. The kids aren't just fixing bikes but ingesting knowledge about mechanics, scientific history and the physics of motion. They're also using their computers to generate charts, graphs and databases. Children of both sexes are eager to work with computers because the machines are revealed as both entertaining and useful, not just as a source of boring drills or violent games, which girls usually find unappealing.

J 'When it comes to girls and computers,' says Rayman, 'we've found that there are three ingredients for user-friendliness: hands-on experience, teamwork and relevance.' These ingredients, of course, would increase anyone's mastery of computers, as well as the usefulness of the machines. By trying to do a better job of teaching girls, computer scientists may learn quite a lot themselves.

Questions 1-6

Do the following statements agree with the information in the reading passage? In boxes 1-6 on your answer sheet write:

YES *if the statement agrees with the information*
NO *if the statement contradicts the information*
NOT GIVEN *if there is no information on this in the passage*

1. The overwhelmingly male computer culture repels many women.
2. The Rochester Institute of Technology is organizing a three-year mentoring program for girls.
3. Special computer programs are being written for women.
4. Women are often anxious about themselves.
5. Physics and history are two of the main subjects taught at Bowman.
6. Computer scientists are likely to learn a lot from teaching girls.

Reading Passage 2

Mystery of the Mummies

A In 1992, a German scientist made a discovery which was to upset whole areas of scientific study from history and archeology to chemistry and botany. Dr. Svetlana Balabanova, a forensic specialist, was performing tissue tests on an Egyptian mummy, part of a German museum collection. The mummified remains were of a woman named Henut-Taui who had died over 3,000 years ago. Amazingly, the tests revealed that her body contained large quantities of cocaine and nicotine. Dr. Balabanova had regularly used the same testing methods to convict people of drug consumption but she had not expected to find nicotine and coca in an Ancient Egyptian mummy. It is generally accepted that these two plants, native to the Americas did not exist on other continents prior to European exploration.

B Dr. Balabanova repeated the tests then sent out fresh samples to three other labs. When the results came back positive she published a paper with two other scientists. If Balabanova was shocked by the results of her tests she was even more shocked at the hostile response to her publication. She received many insulting letters, accusing her of fraud.

C There were two explanations that came immediately to mind. One was that something in the tests could have given a false result. The second was that the mummies tested were not truly Ancient Egyptian. Perhaps they were relatively modern bodies, containing traces of cocaine. Dr. Balabanova then examined tissue from 134 naturally preserved bodies over a thousand years old discovered in an excavated cemetery in the Sudan. About a third of them tested positive for nicotine or cocaine.

D But something had happened even earlier which should have initiated serious discussion. In 1976 the mummified remains of Ramses II arrived in Paris for repair work. Dr. Michelle Lescot of the Natural History Museum (Paris) was looking at sections of bandages and within the fibres found a plant fragment. When she checked it under a microscope she was amazed to discover that the plant was tobacco. Fearing that she had made some mistake she repeated her tests again and again with the same result every time: a New World plant had been found on an Old World mummy. The results caused a sensation in Europe. Was it possible that a piece ot tobacco had been dropped by chance from the pipe of some forgotten archaeologist? Dr. Lescot responded to this charge of contamination by carefully extracting new samples from the abdomen, with the entire process recorded on film. These samples, which could not be 'droppings', were then tested. Once again they were shown to be tobacco. The discovery of tobacco fragments in the mummified body of Ramses II should have had a profound influence upon our whole understanding of the relationship between Ancient Egypt and America but this piece of evidence was simply ignored. It raised too many questions and was too far outside of commonly accepted scientific views.

E So now the question had returned. Could Ancient Egyptian trade have stretched all the way across the Atlantic Ocean? This was an idea so unbelievable it could only be considered after all the other possibilities had been eliminated. Could Egyptians have obtained imports from a place thousands of miles away, from a continent supposedly not discovered until thousands of years later? Was it possible that coca—a plant from South America—had found its way to Egypt 3,000 years ago? If the cocaine found in mummies could not be explained by contamination, or fake mummies or by Egyptian plants containing it, there appeared to be another interesting possibility: a trade route with links all the way to the Americas.

F The Egyptians did make great efforts to obtain incense and other valuable plants used in religious ceremonies and herbal medicines, but to the majority of archeologists, the idea is hardly worth talking about. Professor John Baines, an Egyptologist from Oxford University states: 'I don't think it is at all likely that there was an ancient trade network that included America. The essential problem with any such idea is that there are no artefacts... found either in Europe or in America.' But other experts aren't so sure. Professor Martin Bernal, an historian, from Cornell University says, 'We're getting more and more evidence of world trade at an earlier stage. You have the Chinese silk definitely arriving in Egypt by 1000 BC. In his opinion, it is arrogance on the part of modern people to believe that a transoceanic trading network could only have been set up in recent times.

G The discoveries in the mummies from Egypt and Sudan have challenged conventional beliefs. It is no longer possible to exclude the hypothesis of transoceanic trade in ancient times. The tale of Henut Taui and the story of Ramses II show that, in science, facts can be rejected if they don't fit with our beliefs, while what is believed to be proven, may actually be uncertain. It is understandable then, how a story of a scientist, a few mummies and some routine tests, could upset whole areas of knowledge we thought we could take for granted.

Questions 1-5

Do the following statements reflect the opinions of the writer in the passage? Write:

Yes *if the statement reflects the opinion of the writer*

No *if the statement contradicts the writer*

Not Given *if it is impossible to say what the writer thinks about this*

1. There is proof that tobacco was grown in Ancient Egypt.
2. Trade routes across the Atlantic Ocean may have existed thousands of years ago.
3. Ancient Egyptians were great ship builders.
4. The scientific community generally rejects the idea of contact between Ancient Egypt and the Americas.
5. The unusual test results could have come from 'qat', a plant native to North Africa.

Reading Passage 3

The World of the Flat-footed Fly

A George Poinar has been fascinated by amber, and the insects embedded in it, since childhood. Now a professor of entomology at the Berkeley Campus of the

University of California, he has successfully combined these interests to produce *Life in Amber*, a scholarly and yet very readable book. In it he tells the story of this curious, almost magical substance and the unique record of fossilized life that became trapped and entombed in the sticky resin as it oozed from the forest trees of the ancient past.

B Amber has been endowed with special worth from prehistoric times. Adornments of amber have been found that date back as far as 35,000 BC, and in 1701, King Frederick Ⅰ of Prussia commissioned an entire room made of amber as a gift for Peter, the Creat of Russia. Historically that probably represented the peak of value for amber. Since then our appreciation of it as a decorative material worth its weight in gold has declined somewhat. In Victorian times amber beads had something of a renaissance as an adornment. It now holds greater value as a potential store of fossil DNA.

C Scientific interest in amber has also fluctuated. The embedded small organisms, particularly insects but also frogs and feathers, have always been part of amber's allure. In the first century AD, Pliny noted that amber was the discharge of a pine-like tree, originated in the north and often contained small insects. It was not until the 19th century that collection of the amber flora and fauna really got under way. The largest hoard was of Baltic origin, amassed by Wilhelm Stantien, an inn-keeper, and Moritz Becker, a merchant. They took their collecting seriously and used mining techniques to extract pieces of amber from clays of Tertiary age that had formed during the Eocene, 38 million years ago, in the Samland peninsula, near Kaliningrad (the former Kbnigsberg) on the Russian Baltic seaboard. Their efforts resulted in about 120,000 amber-embedded animal and plant fossils. These were housed in the Geological Institute Museum at Kbnigsberg University. Unfortunately, despite being dispersed for safety during the Second World War much of this amazing colletion was lost.

D Although the depth of this unique view of the insect life in Baltic forests of Eocene age is sadly no longer available in a single collection, we can see something of it. There are still large collections of Baltic amber in public museums around the world, but even in total, they do not amount to much more than that one unrepeatable collection. The Natural History Museum in London has a 'mere' 25,000 specimens.

E Popular misconceptions about amber exist; for example, suggesting that it is the fossilized resin of coniferous trees from the Baltic region, and that its abundance is the result of some unusual condition of these ancient trees. It is true that an astonishing amount of amber has been recovered from this region. However, the most likely candidate to have produced the Baltic amber is an araucariacean tree similar to the living Agathis from New Zealand, which secretes resin. This could well accumulate in this order of magnitude, given the geological time scale of hundreds of thousands, if not millions of years. And, as Poinar discusses, the Baltic region was only one of many different areas, on a worldwide scale, from the Dominican Republic, which is his own favourite hunting ground, to China and Romania, that produced amber in Tertiary times. Furthermore, amber resin producing trees are shown to have an extended geological history extending back to Cretaceous times, more than 100 million years ago and possibly as far back as the Carboniferous (more than 300 million years ago) . Many of these older ambers have not been rigorously investigated with modern techniques but Poinar has collected all the available published knowledge on their biological content.

F If you want to know about the record of the Mycetophagklae (hairy fungus beetles) or the Platypezidae (flat-footed flies) in amber, this is where to look. Amber does provide a uniquely well-preserved view of the past. And we can see them all in amber from the parasitic wasp larva and its spider host to the flies the spider trapped. Poinar's book is a slightly curious mixture of academic taxonomic treatise on the biology of amber and a fascinating semipopular account of how, where and when amber has been produced. But it is by far the best available, well-written and illustrated by a biologist, who is an active and major contributor in the field.

G As the last chapter on the implications of this type of preservation and the prospects for palaeobiological research intimates, amber is perhaps only just beginning to show its worth.

H Since Poinar wrote Life in Amber, two independent teams of American investigators have extracted and sequenced the oldest known DNA from insects trapped in Dominican amber, more than 30 million years ago. Poinar was one of them.

Questions 1-7

Do the following statements reflect the opinions of the writer in the passage? Write:

Yes *if the statement reflects the opinion of the writer*

No *if the statement contradicts the writer*

Not Given *if it is impossible to say what the writer thinks about this*

1. George Poinar has worked in the Dominican Republic.
2. Almost no amber has been found in New Zealand.
3. Compared with what the Geological Institute Museum at Kbnigsberg University used to house, the Natural History Museum in London has a small collection of amber fossils.
4. *Life in Amber* is a book written in the 18th century.
5. Wilhelm Stantien died earlier than Moritz Becker.
6. Amber was more valuable in Victorian times than in the times of Peter the Great.
7. The Eocene is a geological era that is earlier than Cretaceous times.

Chapter Five
Cracking Summary Questions
摘要题题型突破

内容提示

- IELTS 核心题型——Summary 题解题技巧
- Summary 题实例讲解

特别提醒

- 如果你的解题方法不正确，那么 Summary 题可能会耗费掉大量的解题时间，进而严重影响你解答其他考题，因此请你重视本章的学习
- 顺利解答 Summary 题，需要你有一定的英语语法知识。如果你的英语语法知识存在很多漏洞，请在第一时间补习英语语法，为 IELTS 考试乃至将来的海外生活打下坚实的语言基础

Part 1
Guide to Answering Summary Questions
摘要题解题方法透析

一、题型介绍

Summary 题是雅思考试的特色题型之一，考查考生对阅读文章细节内容的把握，同时也考查最基本的英语语法知识。

特别提醒……

与托福、GMAT 等著名的海外测试中有专门的语法测试部分所不同的是，IELTS 并不直接考查语法，但是这绝不意味着 IELTS 考试不考查语法。相反，IELTS 把语法考查巧妙地糅合到阅读考题中，尤其是在 Summary 题中。复习备考 IELTS 的过程中，请千万记得复习基础的英语语法！

如果阅读文章考到 Summary 题，就会在阅读文章的后面附有一篇阅读文章的摘要（Summary），这篇摘要中存在若干空白，需要考生根据阅读文章的内容在空白处填上正确的单词或词组。如：

Read the reading passage and complete the summary below. Choose **NO MORE THAN THREE WORDS AND/ OR NUMBERS** *from the reading passage for each answer.*

二、题型要求

Summary 题所强调的，是对文章中具体细节的理解以及对英语当中基本语法知识的掌握，因为将某个单词填入 Summary 题的空白处以后，Summary 所表达的含义，应该与原文一致。同时，Summary 题的任何语句，都应该是符合英语语法规律的正确的英语句子。

特别提醒……

在 IELTS 考试中，你很可能仅仅注意到在 Summary 题中填的单词必须能够体现阅读文章所表达的思想内容，却忽视了一旦这个单词被填入 Summary 中，Summary 就应该是一篇完整并且符合语法规则的英语文章。语法知识，是 IELTS 考试中 Summary 题考查的重要内容！

三、题型地位

Summary 题在 IELTS 考试中出现的频率虽然不及 List of Headings 和 True / False / Not Given 题，但是依然属于 IELTS 考试的核心题型，是考试中出现次数最多的几种题型之一。

四、破题原则

（1）顺序一致原则

Summary 题的内容，是阅读文章的摘要，因此，IETLS 考试中的 Summary 题的答案排列顺序，必定与阅读文章的行文顺序一直。换句话说，一组 Summary 题的答案在阅读文章中出现的位置，必定和题目顺序一致。

（2）语法正确原则

完整的 Summary，不仅应该能够体现阅读文章本身所表达的思想含义，而且必须是符合语法规律的英语文章。在 IELTS 考试中，足够的语法知识，将大大方便解答 Summary 题。

五、解题步骤

第一步　仔细阅读空格所在句，推测所缺单词的语法属性

语法知识在解答 Summary 题中发挥了很重要的作用。解答 Summary 题的第一步。是仔细阅读空格所在句，通过对这句话进行语法分析，确定空格处所缺单词可能的语法属性。如果题目所给的备选单词中只有一个满足这种语法属性，那么这道题目的答案就必定为这个单词。如果题目所给的备选单词中有多个属于这种词性，

那么虽然无法根据语法直接挑选出正确答案，但至少能够确定答案大致的形式。

第二步 如不能使用语法直接解题，回阅读文章中定位正确答案

在 IELTS 考试中，很多题目都可以直接运用语法知识推测出正确答案，省去了回到阅读文章中寻找正确答案的麻烦。如果不能直接运用语法知识做题，就需要回到阅读文章中定位正确答案。

常见的定位正确答案的方法有两种：

①从题干中寻找关键词，通过定位关键词来定位正确答案

从题干中寻找关键词，由于关键词往往比较显眼，容易从阅读文章中快速搜索出来，因此通过定位关键词来定位正确答案，是 IELTS 阅读中比较有效的阅读技巧。

②运用在 List of Headings 题中所确认的各段主题来推测正确答案可能出现的段落

在 IELTS 考试中，必须首先解答 List of Headings 题，通过解答 List of Headings 题，可以了解到文章各段的大意。在很多情况下，如果已经了解文章各段的大意，推测正确答案所在的段落，就是一件非常容易的事情了。

第三步 确认答案满足题目要求

IELTS 考试中的 Summary 题有一个非常明显的特点，这也是整个 IELTS 考试区别于其他英语测试的特点，那就是题目本身对答案的形式有所限制，例如下面这道 Summary 题就要求你的答案必须是由 3 个或 3 个以下单词组成。

> *Read the reading passage and complete the summary below. Choose* **NO MORE THAN THREE WORDS** *from the reading passage for each answer.*

Summary 题的这种特点，决定了在解答完 Summary 题后，必须小心翼翼地确认答案是否满足题目本身的要求。

Part 2
Analysis of Summary Questions
摘要题实例透析

Reading Passage 1

Management in Cyberspace

A Virtual reality is often used to mimic hazardous environments—cockpits of combat aircraft, burning oil rigs, the treasure-strewn caves of irritable dragons and so on. Until now, though, it has rarely been deployed to simulate that most hazardous environment of all—the office. But if Sandra Testani of the Franklin Institute in Philadelphia has her way, it will soon be possible to hone the black arts of office politics and corporate survival on a computer before you employ them against your colleagues in the real world. Or, from the boss's point of view, you will be able to practise your skills at 'co-operating' in virtual 'team-building' exercises.

B Dr. Testani's virtual world is called CIMBLE. The acronym stands for CADETT (which in turn stands for Consortium for Advanced Education and Training Technologies) Interactive Multi-user Business Learning Environment. The idea behind CIMBLE is to let people who are unable or unwilling to meet face to face practise collaborating with each other over a computer network.

C To do this, CIMBLE's software creates a virtual world for up to six participants. Each acts via an electronic representative known as an avatar. A participant sees the world (including the other players' avatars, which appear on screen as cartoon-like images of men and women) from his own avatar's point of view. Any other characters that the avatars might interact with are played by a moderator, who also acts as Big Brother, overseeing and monitoring the activities of the group and steering things in a suitable direction.

D The CIMBLE software allows the avatars to walk around and manipulate objects in the virtual world (opening doors, for example) at the click of a mouse. It also lets avatars (and hence the participants) talk to one another. Most conversations are assumed to he in the open, and can be heard by everybody. But true office Machiavellis will be pleased to learn that private chats are also possible, since the software can work out who is within earshot of whom, and will transmit sound only to those who should be able to hear it.

E So far, Dr. Testani and her colleagues have devised two exercises in their new electronic world. One simply brings the partcipants together around a virtual conference table and lets them chew over an agenda provided by the moderator. The second, however, is more sophisticated. The participants are deemed to be working for a civil-engineering firm, and are sent off to the proposed site of a new bridge to settle a dispute with local residents and officials. After a long car ride and a night in a hotel (all depicted in loving detail by CIMBLE's software), they meet the irate local and try to mollify them. A successful outcome, allowing the bridge to go ahead, is greeted by an on-screen display of virtual fireworks.

F At the moment, CIMBLE is being evaluated using the institute's high-speed (100 megabytes a second) local-area network. If it passes muster there, the next stage will be to modify it for use on the public Internet (which works at between a tenth and a hundredth of that speed), so all that will be needed to make the virtual office indistinguishable from a real one are virtual daggers to allow the avatars to stab one another in the back.

Questions 1-4

Complete the following summary of the reading passage. Choose **NO MORE THAN THREE WORDS** *from the passage for each answer.*

Dr. Testani of Franklin Institute designed a software called CIMBLE which ___1___ CADETT Interactiye Multi-user Business Learning Environment. This virtual world is used to mimic the office and has made it possible for

2 people to practise collaborating with others over a computer network. 3 is represented by an avatar, and their activities are monitored by 4 .

1. ______
2. ______
3. ______
4. ______

答案透析

Question 1

答案　stands for

分析　空格所在句中出现大写字母CIMBLE，选定其作为题目的关键词，很快可以定位到阅读文章的B段：Dr. Tesani's virtual world is called CIMBLE. The acronym stands for CADETT (which in turn stands for Consortium for Advanced Education and Training Technologies)...(Tesani博士的虚拟世界被称为CIMBLE。这个只取首字母的缩写词代表CADETT，而CADETT又代表Consortium for Advanced Education and Training Technologies)；显然正确答案为stands for。

Question 2

答案　up to six

分析　空格所在句中出现名词computer network，选定其作为题目的关键词，很快可以定位到阅读文章B段的末尾句，但这句话中并没有出现正确答案。正确答案出现在接下来的一句：CIMBLE's software creates a virtual world for up to six participants (CIMBLE的软件创造了6个人的虚拟空间)；显然正确答案为up to six。

Question 3

答案　each participant

分析　空格所在句中出现名词avatar，选定其作为题目的关键词，很快可以定位到阅读文章C段的第2句话：Each acts via an electronic representative known as an avatar（每位都可以通过一个被称为avatar的电子代表来行动），这里的each指代的是上一句中出现的participants，因此正确答案为each participant。

Question 4

答案 a moderator

分析 空格所在句中出现名词activities，选定其作为题目的关键词，很快可以定位到阅读文章C段的第4句话：Any other characters that the avatars might interact with are played by a moderator，who acts as Big Brothers，overseeing and monitoring the activities of the group（avatars所具备的其他特性都是由一个缓冲器来完成的，而这个缓冲器就好像老大哥一样监视着所有人的行为），显然正确答案为a moderator。

Reading Passage 2

Sleepless in America

A America's adults are increasingly living unhealthy and sometimes antisocial lifestyles. Instead of working to live，they are living to work. They report spending more time working and less time sleeping and engaged in social and leisure activities than they did just five years ago. Most say they suffer from sleep problems and when they go to sleep，many sleep alone even if they are married.

B These are some of the findings of the 2001 Sleep in America poll，which looks at the relationship between Americans' lifestyles，sleep habits and sleep problems. Sleep deprivation continues to be widespread in America. According to the poll，a majority of American adults（63%）does not get the recommended eight hours of sleep needed for good health. In fact，nearly one-third（31%）report sleeping less than seven hours each week night. The poll also shows that more than one-third of Americans say they get less sleep now than five years ago. Seven in ten（69%）say they experience frequent sleep problems and most say they would sleep more if they believed it would benefit their overall health and wellbeing.

C One positive finding was that many people don't want to give up any more sleep in spite of their busy lives. On the downside, however, far too many adults still sacrifice sleep, which is unhealthy and counter productive to their lives. One reason for this is the increasingly fast-paced and competitive world in which live is placing growing pressure on people to perform in their jobs and relationships. Poll coordinators say the greatest difficulty lies in educating Americans that a good night's sleep every night, and not just on weekends or holidays, is essential.

D Today Americans' lifestyles are considerably different compared to just five years ago. Now almost as many adults say they spend more time at work as say they spend less time sleeping (40% vs. 38%). More than one-third (38%) say they are working fifty hours or more a week. These people experience more insomnia than those who spend fewer hours working. Research has shown a direct relationship between hours worked and the negative impact it has on sleep, particularly those who work more than 40 hours a week. A secondary effect of working long hours is the sleepiness people feel during the hours they are awake. Many adults say they spend less time involved in leisure and social activities and sleeping compared to five years ago. One-quarter of people polled (25%) say that if they needed to find more time in their lives they would probably give up leisure activities first. Others say they would give up time with family/friends (19%) while seventeen percent say they would give up sleep.

E Children can be a detriment to a good night's sleep and be a catalyst for sleep-related problems. The poll shows that sleep problems occur more in households with children 18 years of age and younger. Married people with children average less sleep during the week than those without children (6.7 vs. 7.2 hours/night), and single people without children (7.1 hrs.). Adults with children are more likely to report symptoms of insomnia than those without children (58% vs. 46%). They also experience more daytime sleepiness that interferes with daily activities a few days a month or more (50% vs. 32%). More than one in ten married adults (12%) with children reports often sleeping with a child and majority of these adults (81%) reports a sleep problem.

F Although seven in 10 adults (69%) say they experience frequent sleep problems, they are most common among adults with children (76%), those who sleep with a child (81%), those with marital problems (77%), caregivers (76%), and people with certain medical conditions. Health problems play a significant role in the quantity and quality of adults' sleep. Those who report chronic medical conditions including diabetes, cancer, hypertension, heart disease and / or arthritis are most likely to experience sleep problems such as insomnia (trouble falling asleep), and sleep disorders such as sleep apnea, (pauses in breathing during sleep), and restless legs syndrome, (frequent limb movements during sleep).

Questions 1-4

Complete the summary below. Choose your answers from the list below the summary and write them in boxes 1-4 on your answer sheet.

NB There are more words than spaces, so you will not use them all.

Working over 40 hours a week has a __1__ on sleep and leads to __2__ during waking hours. Children can cause __3__ problems and be a __4__ to good sleep.

Word List

unhealthy	detriment	satisfaction	sleepiness
negative impact	leisure activities	benefit	sleep-related

1.
2.
3.
4.

答案透析

Question 1

答案 negative effect

分析 空格所在句中出现数词40，选定其作为题目的关键词，很快可以定位到阅读文章D段的第5句话：Research has shown a direct relationship between the hours worked and the negative impact it has on sleep, particularly those who work more than 40 hours a week（研究显示工作的时间和对睡眠的负面影响之间有直接联系，尤其是对于那些每周工作超过40个小时的人来说），显然正确答案为negative effect。

Question 2

答案　sleepiness

分析　正确答案位于第1题答案所在语句的下一句话：A secondary effect of working long hours is the sleepiness people feel during the hours they are awake（长时间工作的第二个影响是人们在醒着的时候感觉到的困意），显然正确答案为sleepiness。

Question 3

答案　sleep-related

分析　空格所在句中出现名词children，选定其作为题目的关键词，很快可以定位到阅读文章E段的第1句话：Children can be a detriment to a good night's sleep and be a catalyst for sleep-related problems（小孩子可能会损害晚上好的睡眠，而且会成为与睡眠相关的问题的催化剂），显然正确答案为sleep-related。

Question 4

答案　detriment

分析　第4题的答案与第3题的答案出现在同一句话中，由第3题的分析可以知道，第4题的正确答案为detriment。

Reading Passage 3

Human Function of Boral

A The multinational company Boral, which has been in business since 1946, employed its first HR professional just five years ago. Since then, HR director

Stuart Yeoland has been leading a small team in building a strategic HR function from the ground up. The metamorphosis of a major Australian company into a dynamic, people-oriented learning organization is well under way, brought about by a true partnership between HR professionals and line managers.

B Between its incorporation in 1946 as Bitumen and Oil Refineries (Australia) Limited and late 1992, Boral did not employ any human resources staff. This is quite remarkable for a company with 22,000 employees and wide-flung operations in Australia, Asia, the United States, and Europe. Boral was a model of outsourcing, with most corporate functions contracted out as the company focused on its core activities of building products, construction materials, and energy.

C In October 1992, the mananing director decided that more focus was required in the area of human resource management. Stuart Yeoland was appointed to the top HR job. He embarked on a huge program of designing, selling, and introducing HR initiatives and processes into the company. Yeoland identified some immediate problems: salary reviews were ad hoc, there were no performance management systems, there were no coordinated training and development initiatives, and most distressingly, no succession planning. In fact, Yeoland quickly realized that most of the senior managers were due to retire within a short period of time with no identified successors. Yeoland developed a three-year HR strategy to introduce key initiatives into the business. With Tony Berg's appointment as managing director in 1994, the three years quickly became 18 months in order to fit his program of '15 years of change in five'.

D From then on, HR was integral in the development of the company's change program, purpose statement, and corporate values. Other HR initiatives were developed by a small corporate HR team, with an eye always on the contribution of HR activities to the profitability of the business. Today each business has its own dedicated HR team reporting to the group managing directors, supported by a corporate function of 11 HR professionals and trainers.

E New managing director Tony Berg discovered that the company needed a great charter for change, and he chose the Magna Carta as a good metaphor. Boral's Magna Carta describes conceptually what its change program is all about. It comprises five key elements: the purpose statement and the four pillars. Boral's purpose is to be a world leader in building products and construction materials, and a major force in energy in Australia and the Pacific. This will be achieved by:

pursuing focused strategies that create and build on competitive advantage, providing customers with better value and service than our competitors, encouraging and implementing innovation to further improve our processes, products, and services and investing in people so that we have the best in our industries.

F Combined with the pillars are the foundation stones, which describe what has to be done to attain the purpose statement. The values, to use a building and construction analogy, are the mortar that holds the whole program together: leadership, respect, focus, performance, and persistence. Arguably the most important pillar of the Magna Carta is the last one, 'Best people'. This, in effect, is the HR strategy as it defines the strategic direction of human resource management within Boral. It is a clear statement that the board and the senior executive team believe that the success and strength of Boral depend very much on the experience, skills, and quality of its people.

G The best People strategy is founded on six core elements, each of which contains a number of strategies and programs. The strategy is purposely designed in such a way that there are linkages between each of the core elements. No one part of the strategy is mutually exclusive; they are linked and dependent on the other for maximum effect. For instance, outcomes of the performance management system flow directly into the remuneration and incentives and training and development processes.

H Boral's HR function is decentralized in its structure, with the general managers HR Reporting to their respective group managing directors. However, Boral has developed a unique approach to HR reporting relationships with a hybrid of decentralized and centralized routes through the Human Resources Management Committee. This has been established to ensure and facilitate coordination and consistency across the entire Boral Group in matters relating to HR. The committee convenes monthly and holds an annual strategy meeting to set the HR stategic direction for the following year, ensuring Boral maximizes the interrelationships and business effectiveness for what is a large and complex business.

I In addition to their primary accountabilities, each member of the committee can have, at any one time, responsibility for a company-wide project such as graduate recruitment, expatriate management, or human resources information systems.

J Although having only a small number of HR professionals, Boral has introduced many innovative HR processes over a relatively short period of time, without a massive increase in HR staff or costs. Similar-sized companies with up to 700 HR staff often struggle with the issue of re-engineering the function to cut costs and improve processes. Boral doesn't face this issue, and makes it an imperative that HR staff maintains a strategic focus rather than administration support and policy development. Boral cannot afford to con duct 'traditional' HR practices and must remain alert to the needs of the business.

Questions 1-5

Complete the summary below. Choose **NO MORE THAN THREE WORDS** *from the passage for each answer. Write your answers in boxes 1-5 on your answer sheet.*

the strategic direction

The 'Best People' strategy, which defines ___1___ of human resource management within Boral, is based on six key factors which are mutually ___2___ and relied on.

Although the structure of Boral's HR function is decentralized, Boral has developed a unique approach to HR reporting relationships by combining ___3___ routes in order to guarantee and facilitate ___4___ across the entire Boral Group.

Boral has successfully introduced many innovative HR processes into the company with a small number of ___5___. Unlike companies of the similar size, Boral does not face the problem of re-engineering the function to reduce expenses and improve processes.

1. ____________
2. ____________
3. ____________
4. ____________
5. ____________

答案透析

Question 1

答案　the strategic direction

分析　题干中出现了带有引号的名词“Best People”，选定“Best People”作为关键词，可以很快定位到阅读文章的F段，正确答案位于F段第4句话：This, in effect, is the HR strategy as it defines the strategic direction of human resource management within Boral.（事实上，这就是人力资源战略，因为它确定了Boral内部人力资源管理的战略方向。）

特别提醒……

定位带有引号的名词时，你可以先在阅读文章中搜索引号，找到引号后再确认引号内的单词是否为你所寻找的单词。

Question 2

答案　linked

分析　题干中出现了数词“six”，选定“six”作为关键词，可以很快定位到阅读文章的G段，正确答案位于G段第3句话：...；they are linked and dependent on the other for maximum effect.（……；为了发挥最大的作用，它们相互联系并且相互依赖。）

Question 3

答案　decentralized and centralized

分析　由于Summary题具有顺序性，所以Summary中各个题目答案在阅读文章中出现的顺序，与题目顺序一致，因此你需要从第2题出现答案的句子后面寻找第3题的答案。

选定题干中的名词routes作为关键词，在阅读文章中搜索routes可以发现答案位于H段第2句话中：However， Boral has developed a unique approach to HR reporting relationships with a hybrid of decentralized and centralized routes through the Human Resources Management Committee.（然而，Boral发展了一套独特的方法用于报告人力资源关系，这套方法是人力资源管理委员会通过结合集中和分散途径形成的。），显然正确答案为decentralized and centralized。

特别提醒……

大量考查同义词是IELTS阅读考试最鲜明的特点之一。例如在第3题中，名词hybrid的意思为混合物、结合物，与Summary题中出现的动词combine意思相近。

Question 4

答案 coordination and consistency

分析 第4题的答案位于阅读文章中出现第3题答案的语句的下一句：This has been established to ensure and facilitate coordination and consistency across the entire Boral Group in matters relating to HR.（建立这个的目的是，为了确保和推动整个Boral集团，在涉及到人力资源管理的事物方面的协调和一致。），显然正确答案为coordination and consistency。

特别提醒……

请留意第4题中出现的同义词：阅读文章中使用的动词ensure和Summary题中出现的动词guarantee。

Question 5

答案 HR professionals

分析 选定题干中的名词HR processes作为关键词，在阅读文章中搜索HR processes可以发现答案位于J段第1句话中：Although having only a small number of HR professionals，Boral has introduced many innovative HR processes over a relatively short period of time.（尽管人力资源的专业人士很少，Boral在相对较短的时间内引入了很多创新的人力资源方法。）显然正确答案为HR professionals。

Reading Passage 4

Team-Based Learning

A With the globalisation of information technology (IT) and world-wide access to the Internet, people from all areas of learning are finding themselves using some form of information technology in the workplace. The corporate world has seen a boom in the use of IT tools, but conversely, not enough people with IT skills that can enter the workplace and be productive with minimal on the job training.

B A recent issue of the New York Times reports that many companies are looking for smart students who may have a budding interest in IT. Some companies, trying to encourage students to attend interviews, provide good salary packages and challenging work environments. For example, one American IT consulting company offers high salaries, annual bonuses, and immediate stock options to potential recruits. It also brings in 25 to 40 prospective applicants at a time for a two-day visit to the company. This time includes interviews, team exercises and social events. The idea behind the team exercises is that the applicants get to see that they will be working with other smart people doing really interesting things, rather than sitting alone writing code.

C In the past 10 years, employers have seen marked benefits from collaborative projects in product development. Apart from the work environment, there is also a similar body of research indicating that small team-based instruction can lead to different kinds of desirable educational results. In order to prepare IT graduates to meet these workplace requirements, colleges and universities are also beginning to include team-based educational models.

D One of the leaders in promoting team-based education is the American Intercontinental University (AIU), which has campuses world-wide. AIU offers programs in IT with a major portion of the curriculum based on team projects. AIU has a large body of international students and students from different educational backgrounds. This team-based learning gives the students a sense of social and technical support within the group, and allows students firsthand experience of both potential successes and of inherent problems encountered when working with others.

E Team-oriented instruction has not been the common mode of delivery in traditional college settings. However, since most college graduates who choose to go into an IT work environment will encounter some form of teamwork at work, it is to their advantage that they are educated using collaborative learning and that they are taught the tools needed to work with different people in achieving common goals or objectives.

F In team-based learning, students spend a large part of their in-class time working in permanent and heterogeneous teams. Most teams are made up of individuals with different socio-cultural backgrounds and varying skill levels. Team activities concentrate on using rather than just learning concepts, whilst student grades are a combination of overall team performance and peer evaluation of individual team members.

G In a team-based environment, the teacher takes on the role of a facilitator and manager of learning, instead of just providing information to passive students. The facilitator / teacher also guides the team in identifying their goals and establishing standards of team performance. Team exercises then help the students to improve their problem-solving skills by applying theory to simulated real-world situations. Working as a team allows students to adopt new roles and empowers them to control their own learning. Students in teams are taught to use each other as resources and accept the responsibility of managing tasks.

H Team members must also study assigned material individually to ensure their preparation for classes. There are individual assessment tests to measure if students have not only read the assigned material, but also understand the concepts of the module, and can apply them to given problems. Additional team assessment tests present a problem for discussion and require consensus, helping students learn critical communication skills. This also enables them to deal with conflicts between members before they escalate to crises. Team presentations (written or verbal) allow the team to focus and build cohesion, with team members sharing the responsibility for presenting and persuading the audience to accept their viewpoint. Feedback on how the team is functioning with task management, team dynamics and overall work is given by the facilitator. Team exercises that are application-oriented help students experience the practical application of concepts and learn from other students' perspectives.

I Team-based classrooms are especially beneficial in colleges with international students. Since this type of learning encourages people to listen and communicate with others, share problems, resolve personal conflicts, and manage their time and resources, it is a great environment for students who are in a new social situation. Since social interaction plays an important role during teamwork, team learning has an added advantage for students who are not comfortable in traditional classroom settings. It allows students from different cultures to understand their differences and use them productively. This type of learning environment also allows students to express themselves freely in a team context, rather than feeling singled out as when answering questions in a traditional classroom.

J This learning model was designed to better prepare students for today's global workplace. Students are encouraged to explore ideas together, to build communication skills and achieve superior results. It is likely that employers will increasingly seek out students with these skills as we move into the future.

Questions 1-7

Complete the summary below. Choose your answers from the box below the summary. There are more words than you will need to fill the gaps.

Although IT is one of the leading career (Example) made by graduates today, the industry's demand for qualified applicants __1__ the supply of skilled IT personnel. Despite the __2__ widespread use of computer technology in all areas of life, __3__ face difficulties recruiting people whose education has equipped them to commence working productively without further training. Several business organisations now offer income and other __4__ inducements to potential employees. They also include group __5__ in their selection procedures, often inviting up to forty __6__ to their company for the two-day visit. In this way the company can demonstrate the reality of the working __7__ which is more likely to involve challenging co-operative projects than individualised tasks.

List of words

exceeds	extracts	choices	candidates	employees
admiration	previous	financial	employment	regularity
advantages	employers	environment	activities	current

Example

	choices
1.	
2.	
3.	
4.	
5.	
6.	
7.	

答案透析

Question 1

答案 exceeds

分析 这道题目可以直接使用语法规则推测出正确答案。仔细阅读第 1 题所在语句可以发现，该句明显缺少谓语，因此空白处所需单词为谓语动词。句子所使用的时态为一般现在时态，空白处的动词同样应该使用一般现在时态，同时因为句子的主语为 the industry's demand（这个行业的需求），因此空白处的动词应该为第三人称单数。题目给出的单词中仅仅有两个符合条件：exceed（超越）、extract（摘录），后者显然不符合空白处的语境，因此正确答案为 exceeds。

Question 2

答案 current

分析 这道题目同样可以直接使用语法规则推测出正确答案。仔细阅读第 2 题所在语句可以发现，该句已经是一个结构完整的语句，因此空白处所缺单词必定充当修饰成分。纵览题目中给出的单词，能够修饰空格后的 widespread use of computer 的，只能是单词 current，因此正确答案为 current。

Question 3

答案 employers

分析 这道题目也可以直接使用语法规则推测出正确答案。仔细阅读第 3 题所在语句可以发现，该句明显缺少主语，因此空白处所需单词为名词或代词。由于题目所给出的备选单词中并没有代词，正确答案必定为名词。空格所在句的谓语动词 face 使用的是一般现在时态，而且 face 并没有加字母 s，所以空白处的名词应该为复数名词；题目给出的单词中仅仅有三个符合条件：advantages（优势）、employers（雇主）、employees（雇员），而原句中提到了 recruiting people（招聘员工），因此正确答案为 employers。

Question 4

答案　financial

分析　这道题目同样可以直接使用语法规则推测出正确答案。仔细阅读第 4 题所在语句可以发现，该句已经是一个结构完整的语句，因此空白处所缺单词必定充当修饰成分。在题目所给出的单词中，只有单词 financial 能够修饰空格后的 inducement，因此正确答案为 financial。

Question 5

答案　activities

分析　这道题目可以直接使用语法规则推测出正确答案。仔细阅读第 5 题所在语句可以发现，该句空格处的单词在该句中担当宾语，因此答案必定是题目所给出的某一个名词。考虑空格前后的语境，只有单词 activities（活动）能够作为空白处的单词。

Question 6

答案　candidate

分析　这道题目可以直接使用语法推测出正确答案。仔细阅读第 6 题所在语句可以发现，空格处的单词在该句中担当宾语，因此答案必定是题目所给出的某一个名词。考虑空格前后的语境，能够担当动词 invite 的宾语的名词，只能是单词 candidate（候选人）。

Question 7

答案　environment

分析　这道题目可以直接使用语法推测出正确答案。分析空格前后的语境可以得知，空格处所缺少的为名词。空格处的名词前有修饰语 working。在题目所给出的名词中，能够使用修饰语 working 的，只有单词 environment（环境），因此正确答案为 environment。

特别提醒……

这组 Summary 题中所有的题目都可以直接使用语法知识从上下文中推测出正确答案，而不需要回到阅读文章中定位。IELTS 考试中，解答 Summary 题的首选方法是结合上下文语境使用语法规则推测正确答案，只有在使用语法规则不能推测出正确答案的情况下，你才可以考虑回到阅读文章中定位正确答案。

Part 3
Exercises of Summary Questions
摘要题实战练习

Reading Passage 1

Herbal Remedies are Facing Stress

A Herbal shampoo and medicine makers could learn something from American Indians about harvesting medicinal and aromatic plants without endangering some vanishing and valuable species.

B American Indians gathering plants for herbal remedies take only those they need, and utter songs and chants lamenting the sacrifice and affirming that the plants are being harvested to relieve suffering, said Tis Mal Crow of Speedwell, Tenn., a Western Band Cherokee healer.

C 'From any one area we limit the amount taken. They are taken only at certain tines of year,' Crow said. That's in contrast with some commercial harvesters who, he said, 'go in there with bulldozers and clear off whole hillsides.'

D Crow is one of 10 members of a Native American Elder Circle who take part in a U.S. Fish and Wildlife Service Medicinal Plant Working Group discussing ways to protect threatened plants. The group also includes representatives from industry, government, academia and environmental organizations.

E 'Plants that our grandfathers' grandfathers respected and protected for future generations are no longer available to us,' said Crow, author of *Native Plants, Native Healing*. He spoke recently at a symposium the working group helped organize on Industrial Leadership for the Preservation of Medicinal and Aromatic Plants.

F North American environments from alpine tundra to prairie grasslands, coastal salt marshes and tropical rain forests have 20,000 plant species, the working group reported in December 2000. At least 175 species are marketed for use in over-the-counter remedies and supplements in the $3 billion U.S. medicinal herb market. Many plants are collected from the wild in large quantities. For example, about 65 million goldenseal plants and 34 million ginseng plants a year have been harvested from eastern U.S. forests in recent years, according to the report.

G The two-day symposium included pharmaceutical, cosmetic, vitamin and herbal product makers, academics, farmers and government representatives. 'We are interested in creating partnerships with as diverse a group as possible and bringing together as many interest groups as possible,' said Julie Lyke, a U.S. Fish and Wildlife Service biologist.

H 'Some plants are plentiful enough to harvest without concern,' said Michael McGuffin, president of the American Herbal Products Association, a Silver Spring, Md., trade group. 'Saw palmetto is harvested in the wild, but it's estimated that there are 4 million acres of it,' McGuffin said. 'Black cohosh is one we are concerned about. The root is the part used. End of plant.' One presentation involved some successful efforts to cultivate black cohosh, an eight-foot perennial with stems and roots used to treat menstrual and digestive problems and rheumatism.

I 'But plants such as goldenseal root, often used in combination with vitamin C; American ginseng, marketed as an energizer and immune stimulant; and echinacea, also sold as an immune stimulant, are considered at risk of extinction,' Crow and McGuffin said.

J 'Herbal product manufacturers' demand for plants can end up preserving natural habitats, such as rain forests,' said Dominique N. Conseil, president of Aveda, a maker of plant-based shampoos, cleansers and cosmetics.

K Conseil said that can be the result if companies show local people how to harvest herbal products that are more profitable than logging or clearing the land for other uses.

L 'Communities need to have a source of revenue. It's about developing a source of revenue that preserves the wild,' Conseil said. 'If they can make a living from the environment without destroying it, when that works, it's ideal.'

M For some plants, the effort comes too late. Of 200 species discovered by Meriwether Lewis and William Clark on their expedition of 1803 through 1860, it isn't known if 30 percent still exist, said Ara DerMarderosian, a professor of pharmacognosy, the study of drugs from natural sources, at the University of the Sciences in Philadelphia.

N It is therefore a primary goal to catalog American plants, DerMarderosian noted. 'We hope they are still there. There are a lot of places you'll go and find a parking lot.'

Questions 1-7

Below is a srmmary of the reading passage. Complete the summary by choosing words from the box following the summary. Write your answers in boxes 1-7 on your answer sheet.

Note *There are more words than spaces so you will not use them all. You may use any word more than once.*

> Native plants are under threat of extinction. This is because of over harvesting by pharmaceutical companies that want to __1__ these plants for their medicinal quality to help __2__ suffering. While Native American Indians have always harvested native herbal plants by taking just what they needed, commercial harvesters often clear whole __3__ with bulldozers. This has lead to the loss of some species and the threat to many others. The market for herbal __4__, however, continues to grow. Goldenseal and Ginseng are two of the most heavily __5__. To save these species and still support a herbal market, communities need to be __6__ that plants can be a source of revenue without destroying the complete plant community. If action is not taken, __7__ will be more common than the old familiar field of flowers.

List of Words

villages	parking lots	alleviate
manufacture	educated	contribute
landscapes	farms	harvested
supported	utilize	remedies

1. ______
2. ______
3. ______
4. ______
5. ______
6. ______
7. ______

Reading Passage 2

The Era of Biometrics

A It started with fingerprints, but we all have other body parts with unique characteristics that can be measures. Examples are hand geometry and typing and voice patterns. Automated techniques to measure these characteristics and verify a person's identity infallibly are attracting widespread attention in these days of increased use of credit cards and e-mail. This new science with its focus on increasing security is called biometrics.

B People have always used individual traits for identification. In ancient times, the presence of scars, birthmarks and other unusual features helped minimize mistaken identity. Even today, we use techniques that have been around for centuries, such as passwords and signatures. But passwords are notoriously insecure, and signatures can be forged or ignores. Shop assistants, for example, often don't bother to compare the signature on the back of a credit card with the sample provided by the purchaser. And so the search is on for better ways of proving identity. As computer power has grown, so has the idea that biometrics—the automated capture, measurement and identification of distinctive physiological or behavioral characteristics—could safeguard our identities and therefore our property and privacy, and could also be used to fight crime.

C The best-known biometric of all is the fingerprint. Police forces have used fingerprint identification techniques for over a century, but nowadays ideas for applying them commercially (e.g. to control access to personal computers) are coming thick and fast. Imagine an automatic teller machine that uses a fingerprint instead of a number as a password. The machine confirms your identity by comparing your fingerprint with the 'reference' fingerprint originally encoded into the card. These new potential applications of using fingerprints are being made possible by the development of finger scanning. Up until a few years ago, fingerprints were collected in the way we see in police movies: put the finger on an inkpad, then place it carefully on a sheet of paper. In the last decade or so, electronic scanners have been used to 'digitize' the old paper-based prints to form an electronic database. Now, technologies to scan the finger directly are developing rapidly.

D Optical finger-scanners, which work in a similar way to a photo scanner, have been in use for a decade or so, and are starting to be replaced by other methods. One of these is called capacitive scanning: it measures the electrical charge produced by the contact of the fingertip with an array of tiny capacitors mounted onto a silicon microchip. Since the ridges will make better contact with the capacitors than the valleys, this technique generates an image of the fingerprint that can be processed in the same way as an image produced by optical scanning. Ultrasound finger-scanners ars also being developed. Fingerprint verification is already being used on a limited basis so far to control access to personal computers, cell phones and ATMs. A quick search of the Internet reveals a host of companies selling finger scanning devices and citing very low 'false rejection' rates and even lower 'false acceptance' rates. Techno-visionaries predict applications for finger scanning far wider than merely access to the laptop or ATM. They foresee a time when the right finger in the right place will unlock car doors, open briefcases, verify identity over the Internet, facilitate travel across International borders and prevent voter fraud.

E Meanwhile, technology companies continue to invest research dollars in other biometric options. Iris and retina scanning seem to have considerable potential: the patterns in both these parts of the eye are unique to the individual. The retina is the innermost layer of the eyeball, and is criss-crossed by tiny blood vessels. As these vessels develop in the womb, they form a unique pattern that does not change over the individual's lifetime; retina scanning can map, code and compare these blood vessel patterns. The iris, the colored part of the eye, contains about 260 unchangeable characteristics—compared to less than 40 in ringerprints—that can be scanned by video camera, coded by algorithms and, later, compared. The chance of an identical match with a different eye is said to be about 1 in 10 billion, which is a very small chance indeed. Of the two eye-scanning technologies, iris-scanning is more likely to gain in popularity. It can be done at a distance of a metre or so in contrast to retina-scanning, which must be done quite close-up, and is therefore likely to be more acceptable to the public.

F But biometrics-based identification systems must deal with a host of thorny issues if they are to gain widespread acceptance. For some, the prospect of submitting body parts for detailed examination is enough to make them break out in a sweat, while amputees or the blind may not find certain biometric systems to be particularly user-friendly. Sceptics also point to other potential shortcomings. For example, fingerprinting has criminal connotations that will turn many law-abiding people away, and some consumer resistance seems inevitable. Meanwhile, some people worry that biometric data given for an innocent purpose, such as opening a bank account, will be used for other, more sinister purposes by governments or corporations. A further concern is the potential 'hijacking' of biometric data—if transmitted over the Internet, for example—by criminals who would then use it to defraud individuals and institutions. Others worry that it could even provoke a wave of violent 'finger snatching' because possessing someone else's fingerprint could be extremely lucrative.

G Such arguments must be weighed against the fact that the aim of most biometric systems is to increase privacy by requiring a more rigorous proof of identity than has been necessary in the past. If the system is robust enough, criminals will find that beating it is a difficult task. Nevertheless, the technologies pose a potential threat of invasion of privacy, and thus present civil libertarians with many issues that must eventually be addressed. Biometric systems face another crucial question: supposing they do bring about an increase in security, will it be worth the financial cost?

Questions 1-6

Complete the summary below, using words from the box. Write your answer in boxes 1-6 on your answer sheet.

The growing demand for accurate identification of people who use credit cards, e-mail, and other long-distance services has led to the emergence of the new science of __1__. One of the earliest methods of scientific identification of a person using a body part was __2__. Long used by the police, this method is now being developed for use by banks and other __3__ bodies. The technique known as __4__ has made possible new developments in this field. Other body parts which are thought to provide foolproof identification include the __5__ and __6__ of the eye.

List of words

commercial	hand geometry	biometrics	false rejection
iris	passwords	capacitors	retina
Ultrasound	fingerprinting	Internet	civil libertarians
finger scanning			

1.

2.

3.

4.

5.

6.

Reading Passage 3

A Woman's Work is Never Done

A More and more women are now joining the paid labour force world-wide. They represent the majority of the workforce in all the sectors which are expanding as a result of globalisation and trade liberalisation—the informal sector, including subcontracting; export processing or free trade zones; homeworking; and the 'flexible', part-time, temporary, low-paid labour force. Even in countries which have low levels of women paid workers, such as the Arab countries, employment is rising.

B In South-East Asia, women represent up to 80 per cent of the workforce in the export processing zones, working mainly in the labour-intensive textile, toy, shoe and electronic sectors. In Latin America and the Caribbean, 70 per cent of economically active women are employed in services. Many women in South-East Asia are moving from manufacturing into services.

C Long excluded from many paid jobs and thus economically dependent on husbands or fathers, paid employment has undoubtedly brought economic and social gains to many women. For many previously inexperienced young women, the opportunity to gain financial independence, albeit limited and possibly temporary, has helped break down some of the taboos of their societies and prescriptions on women's behaviour.

D Any gains, however, should be seen in a wider context. Declining economic and social conditions throughout the world, in particular declining household incomes, have compelled many women to take any kind of paid work to meet their basic needs and those of their families. The jobs available to them are, in the main, insecure and low-paid with irregular hours, high levels of intensity, little protection from health and safety hazards and few opportunities for promotion.

E Women's high participation in informal employment is partly due to the fact that many jobs in the formal economy are not open to them: they are actively excluded from certain kinds of work or lack access to education and training or have domestic commitments. The increase of women's participation in the informal sector has been most marked in the countries of Sub-Saharan Africa where sharp economic decline and structural adjustment policies have reduced the official job market drastically.

F Job gains for some women have meant losses for others. Female employment in export production is increasing in Bangladesh, Vietnam and El Salvador, for instance, while women in Taiwan and Hong Kong are faced with redundancies as the industries which have relied on their labour for three decades (textile, clothing, shoe and electronics) relocate elsewhere. (In South Korea, industries which tend to employ mensteel, petrochemicals, electricity, automobiles, shipbuilding, machinery, have received government subsidies to stay put.)

G As domestic markets are opened up to international competition and quotas which restricted the quantity of imports from any one country are abandoned, cheap, subsidised foreign imports are threatening the livelihoods of many women small producers and entrepreneurs in 'cottage industries'. In countries such as India and Bangladesh, for instance, more than 90 per cent of economically-active women work in the informal sector at jobs such as hand loom weaving.

H Far from escaping patriarchal control, the industrial setting invariably replicates it, the head of the factory taking the place of husband or father. To attract investors, some Asian countries such as Malaysia and Thailand emphasise the 'dexterity of the small hands of the Oriental women and traditional attitude of submission'. Women workers are particularly exposed to sexual harassment, a form of violence which reflects the subordmation they have to submit to to be allowed to work. Complaints often lead to dismissal.

I In general, women are paid less than men are, and women's jobs pay less than men's jobs. On average, most women earn 50 to 80 per cent of men's pay, but there are considerable variations. In Tanzania, which ranks first in the world for pay equality, women earn 92 per cent of what men earn; in Bangladesh, they earn 42 per cent. Women also have less job security and fewer opportunities for promotion. Higher status jobs, even in industries which employ mostly women, tend to be filled by men.

J In addition, women usually have to continue their unpaid domestic and caring work, such as of children, the sick and the elderly, which is often regarded as women's 'natural' and exclusive responsibility. Even when they have full-time jobs outside the home, women take care of most household tasks, particularly the preparation of meals, cleaning and child care. When women become mothers, they often have no option other than to work part-time or accept home work.

Questions 1-7

Complete the summary. Choose your answers from the words in the box below the summary.

The social and personal __1__ women have made by entering the __2__ must be offset against the losses. While they may have won greater freedom, their high level of __3__ in the __4__ has left them at a disadvantage. They do not have the __5__ of men in full-time employment. __6__, they are further disadvantaged because of their inescapable __7__ obligations.

List of words

domestic	paid labour force	children
trading	official job market	informal labour sector
bargaining power	salaries	losses
obligations	freedom	gains
global market place	nowadays	furthermore
however		

1. ________
2. ________
3. ________
4. ________
5. ________
6. ________
7. ________

Reading Passage 4

Kids and Sports

A Two Italian psychologists, Vincenzo Marte and Giovanni Notarnicola, describe the traditional spontaneous practice of sport by children-climbing trees, riding a bicycle along quiet roads, racing their friends across the fields, as an activity of freedom, a special activity of discovery and learning. In the case of free sporting activity, the child's time is given up entirely to the activity, as can be seen in the endless games of football young children play, which may then be followed by bicycle races and / or a swim in the river, for example.

B Today, however, children's discovery of sport has become very different. It is often parents who take their children, when they are very young, to the swimming pool or to the sports grounds or sports halls. Children's first experience of sport thus takes place as an organised activity, which they see as organisation of their free time. By organising sport for children, and often deciding for them, we unfortunately create an imbalance preventing them from managing their own play / sports time, thus denying them an opportunity of autonomy and independence as was possible in the past.

C A first possible reasom for the imbalance in the practice of sport by children is threfore linked to the urban society we live in today. We need not regret the past; it is rather a question of knowing how to recreate this freedom in our towns and in the country, where sport is increasingly based on organised leisure activities. Doing one sport is now the rule in clubs. Sports grounds are often on the outskirts of cities, and are overcrowded and invariably enclosed, while recreational areas such as parks or hard-packed surfaces, are very few and far between. How can we find the balance of a varied and spontaneous relationship to sport under such conditions?

D Some interesting answers have already been suggested which take into account the need to recreate this freedom. Marte and Notarnicola have shown that children who have experienced such freedom were considered by sports trainers to be more capable when they joined organised sport aged 12-13. Their study concluded that no formal training, no matter how early in life it took place, could replace these first experiences.

E Measures which would reverse this imbalance include: increasing the number of sports facilities which encourage self-organisation by the children, and also setting up unstructured playing areas with little in the way of equipment. Areas where street sport can be practised need to be established and sports clubs which offer multidisciplinary sports training should be supported. Children should be offered pre-school activity where they can the discover different sports.

F For children, sport remains a special kind of discovery and learning, no matter how much adults limit and control the practice of early intensive training. Here is the second example of imbalance in children's sport. Today, sport is practised with early intensive training from the youngest possible age. Sometimes this is even before the age of six and is usually one specific sport within an organised framework. When adult-style competitions are introduced at an early age, the conditions which encourage a balanced development of children through sport are no longer respected.

G Today, early intensive training is much more widely on offer. Many sports organisations claim that they are forced to do this type of training because of what is called 'the golden age' to acquire the physical skills. It is considered unthinkable for a young skater or gymnast to miss this period, because if they did so, they would fall so far behind the best, that they could never hope to catch up. Faced with this demand for early ability, it is important that a safety net is put in place to maximise the benefits and minimise the disadvantages of such intensive training.

H Why do very young children give up sport? The most common reasom for leaving a sport is to change to another sport, which in itself is no bad thing. However, children may leave a sport because they believe that they have received too much criticism and too many negative assessments. We know that young children, up to the age of eleven or twelve, cannot assess their own level of competence. They believe that if they are making an effort, then this in itself is a sign of their competence. We also know that young children are particularly sensitive to criticism from adults or peers. Trainers must therefore pay particular attention to this and avoid excessive criticism. They should also avoid any strategies that discriminate against the child: for example in team sports, naming first choice players and reserves. It should be remembered that primary school children's main desire is to have fun and socialise. The desire to improve and become a good competitor will develop later. This brief example shows that knowledge of child development is indispensable for those who take care of children at this age. It is up to trainers, sports doctors and psychologists to implement the measures necessary to limit this excessive early practice of sport by children.

I A third source of imbalance which threatens children and sport is parental attitudes. The American psychologist, Rainer Martens, emphasises that, 'too often children's joy of sports is destroyed by adults who want glory through victory.' Several studies have shown that parental pressure is high on the list of reasons why children leave sport. The presence of mothers and fathers can prevent children from considering sport as their own, where they can learn to master technical difficulties, manage interpersonal relations, and experience success and failure. As Martens highlights, 'adults are solely to blame if joy and sadness become synonymous, to a child, with victory or defeat.'

J If the children make the decisions, this ensures that they enjoy being a child in sport, and are relaxed with their development as human beings. We need only observe the activity in a school playground, where games are organised on an improvised playing field, to understand that children show genetic traces of the hunter instinct, which naturally leads them to physical activity. Sport is included as something they want, and which they identify both as a means of release and as a form of self-expression. By acting as a route to self-discovery, sport gives children both the opportunity to know their limits, and to acquire tools which will allow them to surpass them. Playing sport is a source of learning, progress and pleasure; an additional way of enriching life.

Qusetions 1-8

Complete the summary below using ***NO MORE THAN TWO WORDS FROM THE PASSAGE.***

Marte & Notarnicola define the spontaneous sporting games of children as activities of __1__. Because today sport is often decided and __2__ by parents, children lose their autonomy. A first imbalance occurs because __3__ are out of the city and often crowded, whilst there are a limited mumber of open recreational areas where children can play spontaneously. Children should discover and learn about sports themselves. The second imbalance occurs because they start early ___4___ training very young and participate in only ___5___ specific activity. Children often give up a sport because of negative ___6___. It is important that trainers avoid excessive criticism of young children, who should have ___7___ at sporting activities. Another reason that children may give up sport is the attitudes of their parents. This third imbalance occurs as parents exert ___8___ on children to win rather than to enjoy sport.

1. ______
2. ______
3. ______
4. ______
5. ______
6. ______
7. ______
8. ______

Reading Passage 5

Crop Circles

A The crop circle phenomenon has puzzled and mystified humanity for many years. The designs just appear, placed carefully in fields of food grains. Some are larger than football fields and highly complex in design and construction. Others are smaller and more primitive. We call them crop circles, but many of them are not circular. Some are elongated abstract designs, a few resemble insects or other known forms, and some are mixtures of lines, circles, and other shapes melded into intricate patterns. Most become visible overnight, though it has been claimed that a few have appeared within a half-hour in broad daylight.

B Crop circles have appeared all over the world. About 10,000 instances from various countries have been reported in recent years. The first modern rash of crop circles appeared in Australia in December of 1937. A strange circular imprint appeared in a wheat field near Wokurna, a community southeast of Adelaide. Soon seven swirled circles up to 14 feet in diameter appeared in an oatfield nearby. In December of 1989, an amazing set of circles, ranging from a few inches to a few feet in diameter appeared in the wheat belt west of Melbourne. As many as 90 crop circles were found. The best documented and largest modern spread of crop circles began in Southern England during the summer of 1980. By the end of 1988, 112 new circles had been formed. At that time circles were being reported worldwide, 305 by the end of 1989. The total grew to an outstanding 1,000 newly-formed circles in 1990. In 1991, 200 to 300 circles were reported. Crop circles have been documented in over 30 countries, including Canada, the former Soviet Union, Japan and the United States.

C Nine out of ten circles remained simple with broken stems flattened to the ground and swirled. The stalks around the circles remained completely erect. But over the years, crop circles have become much more geometrically intricate. Patterns involved multiple circles, bars, triangles, rings, and spurs. Pictorial imagery also appeared. Reliable eyewitnesses have reported seeing unusual lights and hearing unidentifiable sounds while on an early-morning walk in the countryside where a crop circle showed later that day. High-pitched, warbling noises have been recorded at the site of some crop circles. On several occasions a strange glow or a darker colouring has been seen in the sky over a crop circle. And in more than one instance, the electrical power of small planes flying overhead has been cut off abruptly. While the causal energies do not seem to harm animals, or even insects as far as we can tell, wild creatures tend to avoid the circles. Flocks of birds have been seen to split apart and fly around the perimeter rather than go directly over a crop circle formation.

D Researchers have spent a great deal of time investigating different aspects of crop circles. They try to detect traces of human involvement in the circle-making, test the area of the circle itself for geophysical anomalies, and analyze the field's grain both from within and outside the circles, searching for differences.

E Dr. W.C. Levengood of BLT Research in Cambridge, Massachusetts, has analyzed many grain samples and confirmed, time after time, significant changes at the cellular level of crop circle plants. The plants from the circles have elongated cells and blown-out growth nodes. Seeds from the circle plants often show accelerated growth rates when they are sown, and in some instances, quite different-looking plants result, In many instances it appears that a vortex-like energy causes the plants to swirl down, flattening the design into the land. Whatever this energy is, it does not generally inhibit the plants' growth. They continue to show normal response to the sun, raising upward over several days following the appearance of the circle. Michael Chorost of Duke University found occasions of short-lived radionuclides in the top layer of soil in some of the formations. A British government laboratory found diminished nitrogen and decreased nematode populations as well as decreased water content in the soil of a formation. Researchers have discovered other anomalies as well, such as curious embedded magnetic particles and charred tissue. Some of the plant stalks within the circles show evidence of being exposed to rapid microwave heating.

F Scientists have attempted to explain crop circles as a result of natural processes. One popular theory, accepted by many mainstream scientists and academics, is known as 'Plasma Vortex Theory'. Developed by Dr. Terence Mearden, it theorizes that electrified air (plasma), on the side of hills, becomes mini-tornadoes and screws down onto the ground, creating the circles. The theory also holds that the electrified air would cause a light to appear above the circle and therefore account for UFO sightings. Although this theory still has considerable support it has come under fire because of the highly intricate and complex crop circle patterns that have appeared since 1991. Another theory is that the circles are all hoaxes or practical jokes. Major support came to this theory when, on September 9, 1991, two Englishmen claimed to have created approximately 250 crop circles. However, those circles were more ragged than others, and many were already suspect. It is irrational to believe that all crop circles are faked for publicity or other reasons. May crop circles appeared long before the phenomenon gained large recognition from the public and press. Too many circles and patterns are formed each year in too many countries for them to have been hoaxes. Many crop circles show strange mathematical traits when analyzed.

G The crop circle phenomenon is an enigma. Many dollars have been spent by researchers and their associations in an attempt to find a solution to this intriguing puzzle which will continue to haunt humanity until an explanation is found.

Questions 1-4

Complete the summary below. Choose ***NO MORE THAN THREE WORDS FROM THE PASSAGE*** *for each answer.*

Since the early 1970's, over ten thousand crop circles have been reported around the world, the greatest number in __1__, where in a single year, over one hundred circles appeared. Phenomena such as the appearance of strange lights and unusual __2__ sometimes occur around the sites of crop circles. __3__ are not affected but it has been observed that birds __4__ flying over a formation.

1. ________
2. ________
3. ________
4. ________

Chapter Six
Cracking Sentence Completion Questions
完成句子题题型突破

内容提示

- IELTS 阅读最难题型之一——Sentence Completion 题解题技巧点拨
- Sentence Completion 题实例讲解

特别提醒

- 在 IELTS 考试中，Sentence Completion 题是公认的难度最大的题型之一，请你认真学习本章，为夺取 IELTS 阅读的高分甚至满分扫清障碍
- Sentence Completion 题的解题方法与 Summary 题的解题方法相似，请注意体会两者之间的异同

Part 1
Guide to Answering Sentence Completion Questions
完成句子题解题方法透析

一、题型介绍

Sentence Completion 题是 IELTS 阅读考试最传统的题型之一，也是最难的题型之一。

Sentence Completion 题往往提供若干个结构不完整的句子，要求考生根据阅读文章的大意，将这些结构不完整的句子补充成完整的句子，并对答案提出若干限制性的要求。

IELTS 考试中的 Sentence Completion 题分成两类：第一类，要求直接在所给句子的空白处填写单词，把句子补充完整；第二类，要求从题目给出的备选单词或词组中挑选出一项，填入所给句子的空白处，把该句补充完整。例如：

> *Using* **NO MORE THAN THREE WORDS**, *complete the following statements.*
>
> ……
>
> *Choose* **ONE** *phrase from the list of phrases A-J below to complete each of the following sentences.*

二、题型要求

Sentence Completion 题强调的是，补充完整的句子必须表达和阅读文章完全一致的思想内容。

在实际 IELTS 考试中，Sentence Completion 题往往对答案的形式也作出具体的要求，例如“NO MORE THAN THREE WORDS（不能超过 3 个单词）”或“with words taken from the reading passage（使用阅读文章中出现的单词）”等。

三、题型地位

Sentence Completion 题是 A 类 IELTS 考试中出现频率最高的四种题型之一，其他三种出现频率较高的题型分别为：List of Headings、True / False / Not Given 以及 Summary。

在 G 类 IELTS 考试中，Sentence Completion 题出现频率较 A 类考试低，虽然不属于高频出现的题型，但也是必考题型之一。

四、破题原则

Sentence Completion 题的破题原则是——语法正确原则。

补充完整的句子，不仅应该能够体现阅读文章本身所表达的思想含义，而且毫无疑问必须是符合英语语法规律的语句。

特别提醒……

IELTS 阅读考试中，Sentence Completion 题和 Summary 题都必须满足语法正确原则，因此在解答这两类题目时，你的第一选择应该是直接利用语法规则解题，而不是回到阅读文章中搜索正确答案！

五、解题步骤

第一步　仔细阅读解题说明，明确题目对答案的限制性要求

IELTS 考试中，很多题型都对答案的形式提出了明确的要求，Sentence Completion 题也不例外。类似 "NO MORE THAN THREE WORDS（不能超过 3 个单词）" 或 "with words taken from the reading passage（使用阅读文章中出现的单词）" 的限制性要求频繁出现在 Sentence Completion 题的解题说明当中，因此解答 Sentence Completion 题首先要明确题目对答案的限制性要求。

特别提醒……

对答案的形式提出明确的要求，是 IELTS 阅读考试各题型共同的特点。不仅是 Sentence Completion 题，Summary 题、Table 题、Flow Chart 题等 IELTS 题型均有答案形式方面的要求。所以解答完 IELTS 考题后，请务必确认你的答案是否满足题目本身的限制性要求！

第二步 仔细阅读空格前后内容，判断空缺部分的语法属性

通过对空格前后内容的分析，可以推测空缺部分所属的句子成分，进而判断空格部分的语法属性。例如，某个空格后接动词，则可估计空格部分是该句的主语，进而判断空格部分应该为名词结构或代词。在 IELTS 考试中，如果使用语法知识直接推测出正确答案，那么就可以省去在阅读文章中寻找正确答案的麻烦。

第三步 如不能使用语法直接解题，则回阅读文章中定位正确答案

如果不能直接运用语法知识答题，就需要回到阅读文章中定位正确答案。常见的定位正确答案的方法有两种：

- 从题干中寻找关键词，通过定位关键词来定位正确答案
- 利用在 List of Headings 题中确定的各段主题来推测正确答案可能出现的段落

第四步 确认答案是否满足题目要求

特别提醒……

费尽周折找到了题目的正确答案以后，请千万不要仓促地将答案填写到答题卡上。你必须再花一点点时间，确认你的答案是否满足题目的要求，因为只有这样才能确保你真的能够拿下这道 IELTS 考题！

Part 2
Analysis of Sentence Completion Questions
完成句子题实例透析

Reading Passage 1

Confucius's Influence over Science in China

A Confucius (551-479BC), the great Chinese philosopher, had so deep and penetrating a knowledge of human nature that his influence over Chinese history has been immense. One of the great tenets of Confrcianism—the need for each individual to know his or her place in the social hierarchy—contributed much to the continuation of Chinese civilization through the dynasties. But knowing one's place also militates against curiosity and creativity, and I believe that the influence of Confucius explains why China has never been strong in science, especially abstract science.

B The ' Four great inventions' of ancient China, namely, the compass, gunpowder, paper and printing, were all technological innovations. They are undoubtedly of tremendous practical value but are not of great importance to our cognition of the world surrounding us. The Western concept of science began to be introduced into China in the middle of 19th cetury, largely because the rulers of the Qing Dynasty realized that it was not possible to fend off foreign invaders with Confucianism alone. Importing ideas from the West allowed them to consolidate their rule and to enjoy a more pleasant lifestyle, and they concentrated on mastering technological innovations, such as electricity, railways and automobiles, and paid little attention to scientific theory. To accelerate learning from the West, modern universities were established by the beginning of the 20th century, and the Academia Sinica [now generally known as the Chinese Academy of Sciences (CAS)], with its affiliated researh institutes, was founded in the 1930s.

C But old lessons die hard, and even to this day science is virtually always linked to technology. Indeed, the link between science and technology is so intimate that they have merged into one term in the Chinese language, 'keji', which means scitech. Unfortunately, scitech refers mainly, sometimes exclusively, to technology and rarely to science. The National Science Foundation of China (NSFC) was founded to support basic research, but almost all grants are given to projects which emphasize practical applications.

D Given the relative lack of support at government level, and bearing in mind the low salary levels for scientists, a recent questionnaire sent to members of the general public in some of the major cities produced a very surprising finding: Scientists, along with university professors, are the most respected professionals.

E This esteem must be jealously guarded, but it is currently under threat from the inexorable rise of psuedoscience. Recently, some well-established, Western-trained scientists backed a claim that a certain powder, when mixed with water, turns the water into gasoline. Fortunately, in this case the fraud was exposed, but it seems that, at least in the short term, the cause of rational science faces an uphill struggle. It is to be hoped that the high public standing of scientists will emerge unscathed. The isolation of nearly 30 years has left some legacies for the generation of Chinese scientists that graduated from the universities before the Open Door policy and have been used to publishing in 'home' journals. The difficulty lies not so much in following progress in their own fields of interest, but rather in understanding the 'rules of the game' of international science. While I am convinced that the editors of most international journals are reasonably free of prejudice, this is not always true of reviewers. However, perhaps the biggest obstacle for Chinese scientists is their poor English, which can often obscure otherwise good work.

F With the younger generation, there is another problem—the flow of talented young people abroad. For some of the major universities, it is not unusual for half of the students to arrange postgraduate studies abroad even before their graduation. Since China opened its doors to the outside world, I have supervised about 50 postgraduate students. Without exception, all of them have gone abroad after receiving their postgraduate degree, and until now only four have come back to a job in China. This is to be expected, not only because the research facilities in China are not on a level comparable with those overseas, but also because the pay here is only about 2% of that earned in the West.

G In spite of these hardships, there is some cause for optimism. There is a hard core of devoted Chinese scientists working on basic aspects of science, trying to develop good reputations internationally and at the same time trying to improve the infrastructure at home. Will they succeed? I believe that the future of Chinese science hangs in the balance. It depends on two factors: on the higher input of funds from the government (private enterprise is still of minor importance in China), and on the optimal use of those funds to encourage serious research by the most talented scientists.

Questions 1-4

Complete each of the following statements with words taken from the Reading Passage. Write ***NO MORE THAN THREE WORDS*** *for each answer. Write your answers in boxes 1-4 on your answer sheet.*

1. The legacy of Confucius has stifled _____ among the Chinese people.

2. When China started to learn from the West, its rulers were more interested in _____ than in scientific ideas.

3. An example of the present emphasis in China on technology as opposed to pure science is the NSFC, which mainly supports research which _____.

4. A survey found that the general public in China regards scientists as the country's _____.

答案透析

Question 1

答案　curiosity and creativity

分析　第 1 题的题干中出现了含有大写字母的单词 Confucius 以及 Chinese。选定这两个单词作为关键词，题目的正确答案出现于阅读文章A段的第3句话：But knowing one's place also militates against curiosity and creativity，...（但是明确自己的位置，同样妨碍了人的好奇心和创造力，……）因此正确答案为curiosity and creativity。

Question 2

答案 technological innovations

分析 第2题的题干中出现了含有大写字母的词组the West，选定the West作为关键词，在阅读文章中搜索the West，可以发现the West位于阅读文章B段的第4句话：Importing ideas from the West allowed them to consolidate their rule and to enjoy a more pleasant lifestyle，and they concentrated on mastering technological innovations，such as electricity，railways and automobiles，and paid little attention to scientific theory.（引入西方的理念使得他们可以巩固自己的统治，享受更美好的生活方式，因此他们专注于掌握技术创新的内容，例如电、铁路和轿车，却很少关注科学理论。）因此正确答案为technological innovations。

Question 3

答案 emphasizes practical applications

分析 第3题的题干中出现了大写字母组合NSFC，选定NSFC作为关键词，在阅读文章中搜索NSFC，可以发现NSFC位于阅读文章C段的第4句话：The National Science Foundation of China（NSFC）was founded to support basic research，but almost all grants are given to projects which emphasize practical applications.（中国自然科学基金是为了支持基础研究而建立的，但是几乎所有的款项都花在那些强调实际应用的项目上了。）因此正确答案为emphasizes practical applications。

Question 4

答案 most respected professional

分析 第4题的题干中出现了名词scientists，选定scientists作为关键词，在阅读文章中搜索scientist可以发现scientist位于阅读文章的D段的末尾句：Scientists，along with university professors，are the most respected professionals.（和大学教授一样，科学家被认为是最受尊敬的职业。）因此正确答案为most respected professional。

Reading Passage 2

Doctors Divided Over Heart Pills

A A group of drugs now being marketed in the United States under a variety of brand names have been proved to reduce deaths among heart-attack survivors by more than 40% over five years. The drugs are collectively known as statins, and are currently being taken by over 10 million Americans. Doctors are currently wondering if statins will be just as effective in preventing heart attacks in people who do not necessarily fit the profile of a 'highrisk' patient.

B The people the doctors are targeting for possible presription of statins are those whose LDL, or 'bad' cholesterol, is somewhat high, or their HDL, or 'good' cholesterol is a little low. Again, maybe they have diabetes, which commonly leads to cardiovascular disease, but do not yet show symptoms of the latter. A study report in the British Medical Journal concluded that statins could reduce by 30% the risk of dying from a heart attack, even among people with normal cholesterol levels and no signs of cardiovascular disease.

C Leading pharmaceutical companies have gone so far as to petition the US Food and Drug Administration (FDA) to allow consumers to buy some low-dose statins without having to first obtain a physician's prescription, or 'over the counter'.

D Statins work by partly blocking an enzyme, known as HMG, found in the liver that turns some of the food that you eat into cholesterol. The body, in fact, needs some cholesterol to produce hormones and Vitamin D. Excess cholesterol builds up in the arteries, reducing the blood flow and increasing the danger of heart disease. By slowing down the function of the HMG enzyme, statins reduce the amount of cholesterol entering the blood stream, and force the body to draw on the cholesterol already in the arteries to make up the shortfall in its needs.

Thus, there is a regular clearing out of cholesterol from the arteries. Doctors emphasize that statins work best when a person adopts a low-fat diet.

E There are, however, certain drawbacks to statins. Apart from the fact that they are expensive—about $3 per pill, and you would presumably have to take them for the rest of your life—they can cause liver damage or a breakdown of muscle tissue. Anyone taking statins needs to undergo periodic blood tests to check for signs of liver trouble. Most people on the pills report no complaints; those who do commonly list fatigue as the major side-effect.

F Companies manufacturing dietary supplements became interested in statins when it was discovered that Chinese red yeast fermented on rice contains small amount of the same active ingredient found in statins. They then made a dietary supplement containing this ingredient and publicized it as a wonder drug for preventing heart attacks. The FDA banned its sale over the counter, and the two sides are still locked in a lengthy court case.

G In the meantime, another intriguing possibility has convinced doctors that making statins more freely available may be a good thing. Research has shown that taking an aspirin a day can reduce a heart patient's risk of suffering a heart attack. Would combining aspirin with a statin have a powerful effect in preventing heart disease? Similarly, many cardiologists are impressed by the ability of a group of drugs called ACE inhibitors to normalize high blood pressure and reduce the strain on the heart. Do they work better alone, or would a combination of ACE inhibitors and statins enhance their efficacy?

Questions 1-3

Choose one phrase (A-H) from the list of phrases to complete each key point below. Write the appropriate letters (A-H) in boxes 1-3 on your answer sheet. The information in the completed sentences should be an accurate summary of points made by the writer.

NB There are more phrases A-H than sentences, so you will not use them all. You may use any phrase more than once.

List of Phrases

A. a variety of brand names
B. people with low levels of cholesterol
C. breakdown of muscle tissue

D. reduce the amount of cholesterol entering the blood stream
E. a statin ingredient
F. allow statins to be sold over the counter
G. normalize high blood pressure
H. receive regular blood tests to check for signs of liver trouble.

1. Doctors are unsure whether statins can benefit ____.
2. Big pharmaceuticals companies want the US government to ____.
3. Chinese red yeast fermented on rice contains ____.

答案透析

Question 1

答案　B

分析　第1题可以直接运用语法知识解答，不需要回阅读文章中寻找答案。仔细阅读题目给出的句子，不难发现该句缺少动词 benefit 的宾语，因此空白处缺少的是名词结构，而且必定是表示“人”的名词结构（因为动词 benefit 的宾语只能是“人”），由此可以推测出正确答案为B。

Question 2

答案　F

分析　第2题的句子中出现了大写字母US，选定US作为关键词，在阅读文章中搜索US，可以发现US位于阅读文章C段的首句：Leading pharmaceutical companies have gone so far as to petition the US Food and Drug Administration (FDA) to allow consumers to buy some low-dose statins without having to first obtain a physician's prescription, or 'over the counter'.（主要的制药公司一直在请求美国食品和药物管理局批准消费者购买低剂量的 statin 无需先获得医生的处方，即直接在柜台购买。）因此正确答案为F。

Question 3

答案　E

分析　第3题的句子中出现了含有大写字母的单词Chinese，选定Chinese作为关键词，在阅读文章中搜索Chinese，可以发现Chinese位于阅读文章的F段的第

1 句话：Companies manufacturing dietary supplements became interested in statins when it was discovered that Chinese red yeast fermented on rice contains small amount of the same active ingredient found in statin.（当人们发现在稻米上发酵的中国红酵母含有少量和 statin 中一样的活跃成分，生产食物添加剂的公司马上对 statin 产生了兴趣。）显然正确答案为 E。

Reading Passage 3

A New Menace in the Air

A The death of Emma Christofferson, 28, just after flying from Australia to England set alarm bells ringing among frequent airplane passengers, and triggered an avalanche of lawsuits. Christofferson died of a condition known as deep vein thrombosis (DVT), and of all the health fears associated with the skies; it is DVT that has captrued most public attention. Erroneously referred to as 'economy-class syndrome', DVT can strike cramped passengers in any section of an aircraft. In some victims, the effect of the blood clots might be a sharp stabbing pain and swelling in the lower leg. In others, it might be much more serious: Part of the clot may detach itself and travel through the bloodstream to the lungs, where it can cause a pulmonary embolism, an obstruction that can prove fatal. Part of the clot can also lodge in other organs, including the brain, where it can't rigger a stroke.

B Those at greatest risk of developing DVT while travelling, according to experts, are people with an inherited predisposition to blood clots—people who have suffered previous incidents of thrombosis or who have close family members with a history of the disease. But other factors can also increase the likelihood of DVT. Age is important, said Patrick Kesteven, a consultant hematologist at Newcastlec's Freeman Hoppital. A person in his or her mid-20s has a less than one-10,000 chance of developing DVT; by the age of 75, the risk is closer to one-in-1,000. Also at higher risk are people who have suffered or are suffering from cancer, women taking contraceptive pills and women who are pregnant or have recently given birth. And even generally healthy passengers are at some risk if they stay immobile during a long flight. 'There's no doubt that sitting still can be a factor,' said Kesteven.

C The airline companies are being blamed. 'We are talking about a real risk, with real and appreciable harm,' said Paul Henderson, of the Melbourne law firm of Slater and Gordon. 'It's a small risk, and easy to reduce by taking some fairly simple steps, which are not very expensive for airlines to do. And yet, if they do not take them, you might die.' Slater and Gordon have collected 2,300 cases of DVT, of which 120 involved deaths. 'The cases involve just about every airline flying to and from Australia,' said Henderson, 'and we're the top of the iceberg.'

D The airlines' defense rests on lack of conclusive evidence linking flying to dying, or even to getting sick. 'There is no scientifically valid evidence that the cabin environment in commercial aircraft is unhealthy,' declared Dr. Russell Rayman, executive director of the Aerospace Medical Association.

E As for risk, the airlines maintain that so far there is no evidence that suggests that sitting in an aircraft cabin might be more dangerous than sitting still anywhere, whether on a crowded train or bus, or in a car, or even at home. The airlines insist that the passengers are primarily responsible for their own health. After all, cramped conditions can lead to stress, and even disruptive and unruly behavior, but no one blames the airlines for air rage. 'DVT has been around for a long time. It's linked to immobility, not flying,' said Patrick Garrett of Cathay Pacific. According to Yoshie Otaka of Japan Airlines, 'Basically, it's a matter of primary self-care.'

F But in Asia, risk awarenesss is thin, and no pan—Asian transport body exists to call upon the air carriers to take precautionary measures, as the European Commission has done. During the Moslem pilgrimage season, when tens of thousands of the faithful go to Mecca, Pakistan International Airways routinely refits aircraft in order to cram as many passengers in as possible. Li Ru, spokeswoman for Air China, dismissed the danger of DVT on her company's carrier, saying, 'We are shorter and smaller than Westerners, so we are less uncomfortable in airplane seats.'

G Doctors suggest that if you have a proven predisposition to thrombosis, you should consider an injection of anti-coagulant within 24 hours prior to flying. Though taking aspirin may ward off clots for some people, pregnant women (among others) should not take aspirin. Once inside the plane, make sure you have enough room to move your legs as possible, and even consider wearing support stockings, which can improve the blood flow in the veins of the legs. While some doctors recommend moving around the cabin every half hour or so, the airline companies prefer passengers to do gentle exercises in their seats—both for safety reasons and to avoid getting in the way of the cabin crew.

Questions 1-4

Complete the notes below. Choose ***ONE OR TWO WORDS*** *from the passage for each answer. Write your answers in boxes 1-4 on your answer sheet.*

1. Following the death of Emma Christofferson, airline companies faced a sudden onslaught of ______ accusing them of endangering passengers' health and lives.
2. Blood clots can form in the leg of a long-distance airplane passenger. Part of a clot may become detached and cause a ______ in the lungs.
3. The number of cases of DVT involving Australian airlines is described etaphorically in the passage as the top part of an ______.
4. ______ can assist the blood to flow in the lower limbs.

答案透析

Question 1

答案 lawsuits

分析 第1题的句子中出现了人名Emma Christofferson，选定Emma Christofferson作为关键词，在阅读文章中搜索Emma Christofferson，可以发现Emma Christofferson位于阅读文章A段的首句：The death of Emma Christofferson, 28, just after flying from Australia to England set alarm bells ringing among frequent airplane passengers, and triggered an avalanche of lawsuits.（28岁的Emma Christofferson刚刚结束澳大利亚到英格兰的飞行便去世了，这给经常乘

坐飞机出行的乘客敲响了警钟，也使得大量的诉讼纷至沓来。）因此正确答案为 lawsuits。

Question 2

答案 pulmonary embolism

分析 第 2 题的句子中出现了名词 lung，选定 lung 作为关键词，在阅读文章中搜索 lung，可以发现 lung 位于阅读文章 A 段的倒数第 2 句话：Part of the clot may detach itself and travel through the bloodstream to the lungs, where it can cause a pulmonary embolism, ...（这些凝块的一部分可能会脱离凝块，并且通过血流进入到肺当中，在那里它们会引发肺部栓塞，……）因此正确答案为 pulmonary embolism。

Question 3

答案 iceberg

分析 第 3 题的句子中出现了含有大写字母的单词 Australian 和大写字母组合 DVT，选定 Australian 和 DVT 作为关键词，在阅读文章中搜索 Australian 和 DVT，可以发现正确答案出现于阅读文章 C 段的尾句：'The case involve just about every airline flying to and from Australia,' said Henderson, ' and we're the top of the iceberg.'（Henderson 说："这种情况涉及到任何飞往或来自澳大利亚的航班，我们只不过是冰山一角而已。"）显然正确答案为 iceberg。

Question 4

答案 support stockings

分析 第 4 题的句子中出现了名词 blood，选定 blood 作为关键词，在阅读文章中搜索 blood，可以发现正确答案出现于阅读文章 G 段的第 3 句话：Once inside the plane, make sure you have enough room to move your legs as possible, and even consider wearing support stockings, which can improve the blood flow in the veins of the legs.（进入机舱以后，应确保你有足够的空间移动你的腿，你甚至可以考虑穿能够改善腿部血管内血液流动的保护袜，因为它可以改善大腿内部的血流。）因此正确答案为 support stockings。

Part 3
Exercises of Sentence Completion
完成句子题实战练习

Reading Passage 1

Short Shift

A The benefits of employing part-time staff are well known, but little has been done to improve the quality of, or access to part-time work.

B The long awaited consultation document on part-time work had the potential to tackle the long hours culture, underpin the government's family friendly stance and encourage flexibility in the labour market, but the reality is disappointing. Opting for a light touch, the regulations fail to improve the quality of part-time work or to aid the development of part-time work on a voluntary basis.

C More than six million people (a quarter of the workforce) work part-time, including nearly one million men. Two categories-wholesale, retail and motor trade, and health and social work account for 45 percent of part-time jobs, with many more in the hospitality industry. The increase in part-time work has been a major feature of employment trends in the past decade, but most jobs remain low-paid and low in status.

D Many employers already acknowledge the key role that part-time work plays in employment strategies. Tesco, for example, is on record as describing its part-time workforce—which makes up 65% of the total—as the 'lifeblood' of the organisation. Labour supplies can be tailored to trading peaks and demand for ever longer trading hours.

E Furthermore, specialist jobs do not always require full-time cover, particularly in smaller organisations. Christine Pointer, a chief executive with a local authority who works with limited budgets, finds it better to employ a more senior professional on a part-time basis, rather than a less qualified person full-time. Part-time work at senior levels also helps to retain key staff who might otherwise leave the organisation.

F Unfortunately, not all employers recognise these potential benefits. In the health service for example, where few such opportunities exist, many doctors leave, despite the high cost to the state of training them. And the insurance sector has lower levels of part-time working than any other area of financial services.

G Sadly the widespread view that part-time work is primarily attractive to women with caring responsibilities is reinforced both by legislature and organisational culture. The growing trend for men to seek a better work / home balance is being ignored. Women have managed to negotiate limited access to part-time work at senior levels on the back of equal opportunities legislation. But the assumption remains that there is something odd about men who want to work part-time—they lack ambition and commitment to their employer.

H Disabled employees represent a large proportion of the workforce that could benefit from part-time work. The labour force identifies over two million economically active people with a long term health problem or disability. It also shows that nearly fifteen million people of working age judge themselves to be covered by the Disabilities Discriminations Act's definition of disability. This includes almost one million who are not working but would like to. For many of them, part-time work is the simplest 'reasonable adjustment' that an employer can make.

I On access to training for part-timers, the consultation document again disappoints. While placing an obligation on employers not to exclude part-timers in principle, there is no legal requirement to structure training to accommodate them. New technologies can and do provide flexible access to training-making this omission inexcusable. Ironically, the government is on record as saying that competitiveness depends on the UK making the best use of the talents of as many people as possible and that the larger the number of people to which business can look, the better. However, little is done to encourage the development of these talents in the workforce.

J Similarly nothing has been done to alter the perception that part-time work is a 'Woman's issue'. A recent press release states 'the new measures will simplify the legal position for part-timers—80% of whom are women—who will no longer have to go down the indirect route of claiming discrimination under the sex discrimination act'. Wonderful! But occupational segregation is still maintained by gender.

Questions 1-6

Choose one phrase (A-L) from the box to complete each of the following key points. Write the appropriate letters (A-L) in boxes 1 to 6 on your answer sheet.

NB There are more phrases than key points, so you will not use all of them. You may use any of the headings more than once.

List of phrases

A. many of them are voluntary
B. most of them are poorly paid
C. they don't have to provide training at appropriate times
D. if they want to work part-time
E. if they can't work part-time
F. would like to work
G. part-time senior professionals
H. wouldn't be able to work full-time
I. less qualified full-time employees
J. people would prefer to work full-time
K. part-time female employees
L. they don't have to offer training to part-timers

Example Many employees _____. ***Answer*** H

1. Although there are many more part-time jobs, _____.
2. Often smaller organisations prefer to hire _____.
3. Senior staff might leave the organisation, _____.
4. Men are thought to lack ambition, _____.
5. Nearly one mllion disabled people _____.

6. Although employers are required not to discriminate against parttimers, ______.

Reading Passage 2

Do We Need Cities Any More?

A I don't want to live in a city. Perhaps we divide naturally into two types: those for whom cities are vibrant and exciting, a focus for human activity; and those for whom they are dirty, noisy and dangerous. It may be unfashionable, but I'm in the latter camp. I do not believe that we are a species whose behaviour improves in overcrowded conditions.

B A new study proposes a significant increase in the capacity of towns and cities through a combination of increased housing densities, lower on-plot provision for cars and more on-street parking, and the re-use of marginal open space that is 'devoid of any amenity value'. The benefit of this approach is to reduce the loss of green fields and to help 'move towards more sustainable patterns of development'.

C This study suggests that it would be possible to achieve a 25% increase in density in a typical provincial city without changing the traditional street scene, although it would be necessary to reduce the size of the houses and substitute parking spaces for garages. Therefore, the cost of this approach is to have more people living in smaller homes at higher densities, along streets that are lined with parked cars. Can we really accept the notion that space within dwellings may be reduced even further? In times when, we are told, living standards are rising in real terms, is it realistic to seek to reduce personal space standards?

D The streets of many inner suburbs are already lined with cars on both sides, reducing movement to a single lane. Increasing densities means accepting urban streets that are designed as linear car parks, bounded by even smaller living units and tempered only by occasional trees sprouting from the tarmac. Would the benefits of higher density be worth the disadvantages of increasing on-street parking? Can we achieve a satisfactory visual environment from such raw naterials? Higher urban densities may be communally good for us, but they will fail to meet the aspirations of many prospective home owners.

E Those without economic choice can be directed to live in this way, but if we are to continue to rely on the private sector to produce this urban housing, it will need to appeal to the private developers' customers. Who will choose to live in these high-density developments of small dwellings, with minimal open space and a chance to park on the highway if you are lucky enough to find a space? The main consumers will be single people, couples without children, and perhaps some 'empty nesters' (people whose children have grown up and left home). These are people who can choose to spend much of their time outside their home, making the most of those urban cultural opportunities or getting away an weekends to a country cottage or sporting activities.

F The combination of a young family and a mortgage restricts the mobility and spending power of many couples. Most people with a family will try to avoid bringing up their children in a cramped flat or house. Space for independent activity is important in developing the individual and in maintaining family equilibrium. The garden is the secure place where the children can work off excess energy.

G There is a danger that planners may take a dispassionate, logical view of how we should live, and seek to force society into that mould. A few years ago a European Commission study provided a good example of this. It took the view, quite sensibly, that housing should not be under-occupied because this is a waste of resources. Therefore, it would be much better if the many thousands of old ladies who live alone in large detached houses would move into small urban flats, thus releasing the large houses for families. What the study failed to recognise was that many of those old ladies prefer to continue to live in their family home with their familiar surroundings and, most importantly, with their memories. What is good for us is not necessarily what we want.

H The urban housing option may be technically sustainable, but individually unacceptable. There still seems to be a perception among planners that new housing investment can be forced into those areas that planners want to see developed, without proper consideration of where the prospective purchasers want to live. There is a fatal flaw in this premise. Housing developers run businesses. They are not irrevocably committed to building houses and they are not obliged to invest their resources in housing development. Unless there is a reasonable prospect of a profit on the capital at risk in a housing project, they may simply choose to invest in some other activity.

Questions 1-6

*Choose **ONE** phrase (A-G) from the box to complete each of the following key points. Write the appropriate letters (A-G) in boxes 1-6 on your answer sheet.*

The information in the completed sentences should be an accurate summary of points made by the writer.

NB Yor may use any phrase more that once.

A. people likely to want to live in high-density accommodation
B. living in higher density accommodation
C. if houses are built smaller
D. where old people should live
E. if residential density in cities is increased
F. where people do not want to live
G. attitude towards city livng

Example There will be more green space available _____.

Answer E

1. Residential density in cities will be increased _____.
2. There are two types of _____.
3. There are three types of _____.
4. Developers are unlikely to build houses _____.
5. Planners might try to dictate _____.
6. Many people will not be happy _____.

Reading Passage 3

Graveyard of Green Intentions

A It was a promising moment for enviro-capitalism. Credit card maker NBS Technologies Inc. issued a press release in December touting a new 'Green Earth Card' credit card using a biodegradable plastic made by Monsanto, known in some quarters for its toxic chemicals and pesticides. But behind the scenes, Monsanto was quietly pulling the plug on its biodegradable plastics division, such as it was. 'We came to the conclusion that the jury is out [on biodegradable plastics], and it's not apparent that people are willing to pay a premium,' acknowledged Michael Berezo, the former general manager of Monsanto's Biopol unit. Berezo said that Monsanto could have sold its plant-derived plastic for US $1.35 to US$1.80 a kilogram at best. That's almost ten times as much as what ordinary plastic sells for, and the card world have been that much more expensive—too expensive to make it competitive. Write-off: undisclosed. Sales: virtually nil.

B The evidence is that when environmentalism and economics clash, all the professed good intentions of big corporations to create 'green' products disappear as if in a puff of smoke. Monsanto is by no means alone. Several companies have lost hundreds of millions of dollars on biodegradable plastic schemes since the late 1980s. What wonderfully good intentions they had! But business has to cover its costs. ACX Technologies, the Adolph Coors Co. packaging spin-off, killed a highly-touted biodegradable plastics venture, Chronopol, last fall after deciding that it would take at least an additional US $100 million to build a full-scale plant and sell the stuff commercially. After finding no partners to commercialize the business, ACX took a US $17 million write-off and buried the news of Chronoplo's death in a quarterly financial filing.

C Despite these failures, the biodegradable business continues to attract dreamers and schemers, some of whom manage to convince public investors to go along with them. Planet Polymer Technologies of San Diego has lost US $9.4 million of its shareholders' money since its founding in 1991 and doesn't expect to make a profit 'for the foreseeable future'. Then there's EarthShell Corp., which raised US $250 million in an initial public offering last March with promises from Essam Khashoggi, chairman of the board and 73% shareholder, that it had come up with a limestone based, biodegradable replacement for polystyrene foam formerly used most prominently in McDonald's containers. 'Finally, fast-food packaging that Mother Earth can love!' Khashoggi pronounced in the company's prospectus. Maybe Mother Earth, but not the auditor, who, noting more than US $74 million in operating losses since 1992, questioned the company's viability.

D EarthShell is depending heavily on a tentative deal with McDonald's, according to Vince Truant, an EarthShell vice-president. Truant said that if the deal goes through, the new product's future is assured, but there is 'no binding commitment'. When asked for a delivery date, he explained, 'We have agreed with McDonald's to make every effort to keep a low profile.' Meantime, investors who got in at US $21 last March have seen the price fall to US $14. 'The reality is, as of today, they are basically nothing,' sneered Frederic Scheer, whose privately-held Biocorp Inc. of Redondo Beach, California, is making biodegradable garbage bags and cutlery for a European McDonald's franchise. Scheer claims he's got the only meaningful sales of biodegradable plastics—which he claims are less than $5 million. 'That's peanuts,' he commented. 'Most big companies are sincere in their efforts to develop environmentally-friendly products,' commented John Webber, who teaches sustainable economics at a college in California. 'The t rouble is that pioneering "green" products is costly. The research and development phase is the most expensive part, and investors want quick profits.'

E But the real reason for the dramatic downturn in interest in developing biodegradable plastics may be the fact that efforts to reduce the amounts of solid waste cluttering up the environment are beginning to pay off. A Cargill and Dow Chemical joint venture to produce corn-based biodegradable plastics prefers not to acknowledge that it's developing such products at all. Instead, the companies want to first compete on price with traditional plastics for applications such as clothing fibers and food wrapping. Then they'll promote bildegradability. 'People don't need a biodegradable product,' declared James Stoppert, the president of the joint venture. 'Where in the world are there solid-waste problems? There certainly isn't one in the U.S. today. When you look at the current degradable market, it's probably 14 millon to 18 million kg, growing to maybe 112 million kg, compared with a petroleum-based plastics market of 112 billion kg a year. Do we want to compete for 14 million kg—or 112 billion kg?'

Questions 1-4

Complete each of the following statements (Questions 1-4) with the best ending (A-G) from the box below. Write the appropriate letters A-G in boxes 1-4 on your answer sheet.

A. it abandoned its good intentions
B. ACX failed to find any partners for the venture
C. garbage bags and cutlery
D. only after achieving competitiveness in traditional plastics
E. it would have cost almost ten times as much as an ordinary plastic card
F. the fast food industry
G. when they find a substitute for corn

1. Monsanto scrapped plans to make the 'Green Earth Card' because ____.

2. The death knell sounded for Chronopol when ____.

3. EarthShell Corp. sees the future for its new plastic substitute in ____.

4. Cargill and Dow Chemical will put more effort into biodegradable products ____.

Reading Passage 4

Solar Energy: the Myths? the Facts!

Solar and other renewable energy supply options have the capability to supply a large proportion of our energy requirements. The increased use of renewable energy technologies will reduce pollutants and greenhouse-gas emissions as the energy is derived from the natural source of sun, wind, water and biomass.

Renewable energy technologies already exist in a wide range of forms suitable for satisfying energy demands for many end uses. However, the implementation of these technologies is hampered by myths and misinterpretations.

This information has been produced by the Australian and New Zealand Solar Energy Society to clarify the issues and to dispel some of the more commonly held misconceptions.

MYTH A

REALITY:

Solar (renewable) energy includes the production of electricity and heat directly from solar radiation for many applications. Designing your house to use solar energy passively can provide 60%-100% of your heating and cooking requirements. Photovoltaics (solar cells), wind generators and hydro can supply electricity for any use. Biomass fuels include wood, alcohol, and methane for heating, electricity generation or transportation.

MYTH B

REALITY:

Solar heat can be stored in thermal mass or thermochemical reactions so it is available on demand at any time. In a solar efficient designed house, the building elements themselves store the energy in their thermal mass for nighttime comfort and for cloudy days.

Electricity from photovoltaics can be stored in batteries.

Wind generators run day and night.

Hydropower, derived from the solar evaporation of the oceans can be used at any time, with water storage buffering the effect of river flow variations.

Solid fuel crop, biogas (methane) and alcohol fuels can be stored and used when needed.

MYTH C

REALITY:

Some solar technologies require no additional costs, e.g., houses designed to make use of natural energy flows employ 'design', not devices or additional equipment.

Some solar equipment costs less than conventional alternatives to buy and install and also has lower running costs, e.g., solar pool heaters compared with gas heaters; solar clothes lines compared with electric dryers; and photovoltaic panels for lighting or power supplies in areas too costly to connect to power from the grid. Some solar equipment costs more up front, but is cheaper overall due to lower running and environmental costs, e.g., water heaters for domestic, commercial and industrial purposes; wind turbines for electricity generation and pumping.

Also, many costings are distorted to solar's disadvantage, e.g., solar water heaters would be even more attractive if you could get the same loan terms that the utility gets to build a power station. Remember, consumers don't have to pay for the power station when they buy their electric water heater.

MYTH D

REALITY:

While researchers continue to produce further improvement in a wide range of renewable energy technologies, the big breakthrough needed is equality of financing terms with conventional energy, e.g., Australia leads the way in solar pool heating. There is a wide range of Australian and New Zealand solar water heaters which are amongst the best in the world.

MYTH E

REALITY:

There is 25 times the yearly energy needs of Australia and New Zealand falling on those land areas on an average day.

The southern coastline of Australia and New Zealand is in the 'Roaring Forties', one of the best wind regimes in the world.

Biomass resources (fuel crops) could supply all of Australia and New Zealand's liquid fuels from crops covering 2% of the land area.

MYTH F

REALITY:

There is sufficient roof space on homes alone to produce the total electricity requirements of Australia and New Zealand using existing photovoltaic technology.

Wind generators occupy only a small space for the tower with the rest of the land area being available for agricultural uses.

Solar supply allows decentralisation and the use of small modules which can be accurately matched to the load and which minimise electricity distribution.

MYTH G

REALITY:

Energy statistics tend to be biased, e.g., they include energy used in drying food by oil fired driers, but ignore energy used in drying food in the sun. Even ignoring the bias in the statistics, solar (renewable) energy supplies 28% of the world's energy now, made up of 14.4% biomass and 7.5% hydro. In comparison nuclear supplies 4.4%.

Solar supplies all the energy used to grow plants, to evaporate water for rain and to maintain the temperature of the planet, all necessary for human life.

Hydro and geothermal power stations already supply 30% of Australia and New Zealand's electricity requirements.

MYTH H

REALITY:

A solar water heater will repay its energy 'debt' in only 6 to 18 months, depending on the location, and will last well in excess of fifteen years.

A photovoltaic module will collect over its operating life four times the energy used in its production.

A wind generator will produce the energy used in its manufacture in 1 to 4 years, depending on the wind regime.

Questions 1-3

Complere the sentences below with words taken from the reading passage use ***NO MORE THAN THREE WORDS*** *for each answer. Write your answer in boxes 1-3 on your answer sheet.*

1. Using renewable energy can help reduce ____.
2. To reduce costs and conserve energy, houses should be designed to make use of ____.
3. The article suggests energy statistics are ____.

Reading Passage 5

The Future of the Grizzly Bear

A Grizzly bears (Ursrs Arctos) are distributed around the Northern Hemisphere, but their major habitat is North America. There are only about 58,000 left, more that half in Alaska. There were more than twice that number living in the rest of the continent two centuries ago, but by 1975 these had been reduced to fewer than 1,000, and listed as a threatened species. However, numbers in some areas appear to have stabilized and may be rebounding slighty, bringing the total to about 1,100.

B Apart from not being killed, the bears' main requirments are lots of room and lots of food. Their diet is very varied and they devour almost any source of nutrition, as they have to live on stored-up body fat for nearly half a year while hibernating in a den. So they are not fussy eaters. Salmon, which they catch with great skill in roaring rivers, is a favorite, but grizzlies also eat elk and other deer, hornet larva, roots and bulbs, gophers, horses and horse fodder, and even clams dug up on beaches.

C Over the winter, a large grizzly can lose 150 pounds , which needs to be replaced. Size and body fat affect how many cubs a female produces. For males, getting big means competing more successfully for mates. Observers have calculated that a grizzly can eat 2,500 moths an hour, and 40,000 a day. A month of such steady feasting could fulfill nearly half a bear's energy requirements for a year.

D Although hunting decimated the grizzly population in the past, sharp curbs have been put on both commercial and sport huting in North America's wilderness areas. A bigger problem for the grizzlies is the restriction of their habitats by road building, both highways and logging roads in forests. A female grizzly will roam in an area 50 to 300 square miles, while a male grizzly can forage in territory of up to 1,000 square miles. The bears will seldom cross a highway, no matter how unfrequented, and so local governments have erected special 'wildlife ovepasses' to encourage them to continue their normal wanderings.

E Grizzlies perform a useful service for the well-being of the ecological environment, according to scientists. As they dig in the ground, their claws turn over the soil, releasing scarce nitrogen and allowing wild seeds to lodge. Vegetation such as glacier lilies grow better and produces more seeds in swaths dug by bears. The bears, too, can eat and spread seeds from as many as 70,000 berries a day. In the coastal forests of the west coats of the U.S. and Canada, where the rivers are rich in salmon, it is grizzlies which make possible the growth of what ecologists call 'salmon trees'. As the fish fight their way upstream, transporting tons of nutrients harvest from the oceans, grizzlies carry that bounty across the forest floor in the form of urine, feces and left-over fish carcasses. These nutrients, together with the nitrogen that the grizzlies scratch up from the soil, enable the 'salmon trees' to grow 60 percent faster. Over the centuries, grizzles have thus helped to produce the temperate rain forests with giant conifers, able to produce more bio-mass per acre than tropical rain forests.

F To solve the problem of shrinking grizzly populations, wildlife managers are beginning to look beyond the traditional borders of the national parks. The Yellowstone to Yukon (Y2Y) Conservation Initiative is a joint effort by more than 200 U.S. and Canadian organizations. It aims to connect all the wild areas along the Rocky Mountains chain. Indeed, some scientists think that the long-term survival of isolated grizzly populations may well depend on the creation of such linkage zones, narrow strips of bear-friendly habitats that would restore connections between these endangered animals in North America.

Questions 1-4

Complete the following statements using words or phraese from the box below.

NB there are more words and phraese than statements, so you will not use them all.

fewer than 1,000	cubs	grizzlies	giant conifers
continent	traditional borderd	a threatened species	national parks
Rocky Mountains	salmon trees		

1. By 1975, the guizzly had become _____.

2. Size and body fat can determine the number of ___.

3. Trees fertilized by fish remains are called _____.

4. Y2Y will follow the _____.

Chapter Seven
Cracking Multiple Choice Questions
多项选择题题型突破

内容提示

- IELTS 考试的——Multiple Choice 题解题技巧点拨
- Multiple Choice 题实例讲解

特别提醒

- Multiple Choice 题或许是 IELTS 阅读考试中你最熟悉的题型，但是这绝不意味着你可以忽视本章的学习。相反，你应该用心去体会 IELTS 考试中的 Multiple Choice 题与其他英语测试中的 Multiple Choice 题的异同
- 尽管 Multiple Choice 题在 IELTS 考试中出现频率较低，但它却是你在 IELTS 考试中最有可能全部解答正确的题型，因此请你重视本章的学习

Part 1
Guide to Answering Multiple Choice Questions
多项选择题解题方法透析

一、题型介绍

在 IELTS 阅读考试的众多题型当中，选择题毫无疑问是考生最熟悉的一种题型，因为在雅思以外的其他英语考试中，选择题几乎统领全部江山。

特别提醒……

从开始宣传雅思考试的那天起，British Council 就立志要使 IELTS 考试成为全球最具特点的英语水平考试。正是因为这个原因，在 IELTS 考试中，你很少看到在别的英语考试中大量出现的选择题！

和其他考试中的选择题一样，IELTS 考试中的选择题也要求从备选项中挑选出正确的答案。一般情况下，正确答案为备选项中的某一项。在 IELTS 考试中，如果要求从备选项中挑选出多项作为正确答案，那么题目一般会用大写字母提醒需要挑选出几项。例如：

Which ***THREE*** *of the following factors contribute to the water crisis in poorer countries?*

二、题型要求

Multiple Choice 题强调的是对细节信息的辨认能力，题目给出的几个备选项均经过命题专家的精心设计，正确选项往往是阅读文章中具体细节的描述。

需要提醒的是，IELTS 考试中，如果 Multiple Choice 题本身没有特别指明需要挑选出多个答案，则只需要挑选出一项即可。

三、题型地位

IELTS 考试的出题机构尽力避免 IELTS 考试在风格上与 TOEFL（托福）等其他英语水平测试有雷同现象。因此，在 IELTS 考试中选择题不仅出题频率较低，而且所占比例较小。Multiple Choice 题属于 IELTS 阅读考试的非主流题型。

特别提醒……

不仅阅读考试中选择题比例较小，而且听力考试中选择题的比例也不高。大量非选择题的题型，构成了 IELTS 考试最明显区别于其他英语测试的风格！

四、破题原则

（1）排除原则

①排除错误选项

阅读各个选择项，把错误的选择项挑出来，排除掉。如果恰好只剩下一项没被排除，那么这项就是正确答案了。

②排除同义选择项

如果在 A、B、C 和 D 四个选择项中，A、B 两个选择项意思相同，那么就排除 A 和 B 两个项，因为它们不可能成为正确答案。如果它们当中的任何一项成为题目的正确答案，寻么另外一项必定也可以成为题目的正确答案，而题目规定只有一个正确选项，因此惟一的可能就是两个选项都为错误选项。

（2）选择项定位原则

在 IELTS 考试中，有一部分 Multiple Choice 题无法直接从题干中寻找到合适的单词用作定位正确答案，这时就需要把目光投向选择项，从各个选择项下手，结合排除法确定正确答案。例如：

According to the reading passage，which of the following is right?

像这样的题目，显然无法从题干中搜索出可作关键词使用的单词，因此只能寄希望于选择项中，从各个选项中挑选出关键词，逐一定位。

五、解题步骤

第一步　选择关键词

仔细阅读 Multiple Choice 题的题干，从题干中挑选出关键词。如果题干中没有适合的关键词，请千万不要气馁。把目光投向选择项，一定可以发现很多能够充当关键词的单词。逐一定位这些关键词，就等于逐一定位各个选项。

例 1：

题目　Vegetarianism is growing in popularity because ________.

A. it is economical　　B. red meat is bad for you

C. it is healthier　　D. more and more people live in the countryside

分析　这道题目问的是 Vegetarianism is growing in popularity because（素食主义越来越流行的原因是）。题干中出现的名词 Vegetarianism 就可以直接作为定位词。回阅读文章中定位 Vegetarianism 就一定能够确定正确选项。

例 2：

题目　Which of the following is true according to the reading passage?

A. The lawyer demands 500，000 pounds for the Guildford Four.

B. The lawyer demands 500，000 pounds for each of the Guildford Four.

C. The lawyer demands 500，000 pounds for each family of the Guildford Four.

D. The lawyer demands 500，000 pounds for wives of the Guildford Four.

分析　显然直接从这道题的题干中挑选关键词是不现实的，因此需要将目光投向各个选择项。选择项中出现的数字 500,000 可以作为关键词，在阅读文章中搜索出 500,000，就能确定这道题的正确选择项。

第二步　定位挑选出的关键词

由于关键词特点鲜明，一般很容易在阅读文章中搜索到这些词语，进而确定题目正确答案在阅读文章中的大致位置。

第三步　比较定位得到的语句与选择项之间的差别

仔细比较定位得到的阅读文章中的语句与 Multiple Choice 题的选择项之间的差别，挑选意思与原文吻合的选择项作为答案。

特别提醒……

通过定位关键词，你可以很快地找到题目的正确答案。如果发现阅读文章中的文字刚好与题目中某一选项完全吻合，这时你要千万小心，因为很有可能在这段文字后面出现单词 but / however 之类的词语，进而使得这个选择项成为错误选择项。你要记住，在 IELTS 考试中，与阅读原文文字完全吻合的选择项往往都不是正确答案！

Part 2
Analysis of Multiple Choice Questions
多项选择题实例透析

Reading Passage 1

UNICEF, Malnutrition and Micronutrients

A UNICEF has continued to be at the forefront of advocacy and support for the implementation of programs to combat child malnutrition. A condition for designing effective programs to fight malnutrition is understanding the causes of the problem and recognising how complex they are.

B Micronutrients

IODINE: Some of the most rapid and important progress in UNICEF programs is in the area of salt iodisation. The strategy of universal salt iodisation (USI) has been widely accepted in all regions, and the goal of USI by end-1995 has been met in virtually all of Latin America and in many countries in other regions. During the year, a number of countries with a high prevalence of iodine deficiency in which salt iodisation was previously thought to be virtually impossible, such as Pakistan and Indonesia, started to iodise at least half of all salt reaching consumers. To achieve this, UNICEF offices supported a range of innovative and flexible approaches, for example the establishment of an 'Iodised Salt Support Facility' in Pakistan, to provide training, supplies and quality control to the 800 or so small salt crushers in the country.

C Enormous Progress was seen not only in getting iodine into salt but also in the promulgation of laws to give teeth to monitoring and quality control efforts. UNICEF, WHO and the International Council for the Control of Iodine Deficiency Disorders (ICCIDD) sponsored a forum in 1995 to consider the iodisation and monitoring challenges faced by countries in which salt is brought to market by many small producers rather than larger enterprises.

D A technical monograph on practical ways of monitoring salt iodisation programs was developed jointly with WHO, ICCIDD and PAMM and widely distributed. Many UNICEF country programs are monitoring household availability of iodised salt, utilising a simple test kit, as part of the Multi-Indicator Cluster Surveys being undertaken to assess progress in meeting the goals of the World Summit.

E VITAMIN A: WHO-UNICEF estimates now indicate that over 250 million children still suffer from vitamin A deficiency (VAD) with many millions more at risk. The known effects of VAD on the immune system and thus on child mortality make this a high-priority challenge for UNICEF. In 1995, UNICEF supported surveys of vitamin A status that resulted in widespread deficiency being recognised for the first time in Egypt, South Africa. Kenya and Botswana.

F With support from the Micronutrient Initiative in Canada, UNICEF launched projects in 14 countries that will enable innovation in systems of distribution of vitamin A supplements and improvements in monitoring the mortality and morbidity impact of supplementation. A number of countries are building on the successful experience of Guatemala in fortification of sugar with vitamin A. Bolivia and Brazil both launched sugar fortification with vitamin A on a pilot basis in 1995. In Namibia and South Africa, the feasibility of fortifying maize meal with vitamin A is being considered.

G UNICEF supports dietary diversification and the consumption of appropriate fruits and vegetables as one of the most potentially sustainable ways for communities to overcome micronutrient malnutrition. Research completed in 1995 with UNICEF assistance pointed to the need to pay further attention to the types of vegetables grown and the type of cooking in order to maximise the impact of home gardening on the vitamin A status of children. In Bangladesh, UNICEF is collaborating with Helen Keller International to assess the impact of a large home gardening project on the vitamin A status of mothers and young children. This information should help to ensure that future programs of this type are designed in the most cost effective way.

H IRON: The statement on strategies for reducing iron deficiency anaemia, developed and adopted by WHO and UNICEF in 1995, calls for general supplementation with iron in any population of pregnant women or young children where the prevalence of anaemia exceeds 30%. The results of research trials investigating the impact on anaemia of weekly iron supplements have started to become available. Weekly iron or iron and vitamin A supplements now appear to be a feasible intervention to combat iron deficiency anaemia on a population basis in some vulnerable groups.

I UNICEF supported a meeting, jointly with the Thrasher Research Fund and Cornell University, to explore ways of increasing the micronutrient content of foods commonly consumed in countries where micronutrient malnutrition is common. Plant breeders, soil scientists and human nutritionists met to consider the problem and agreed that the micronutrient content of foods had been neglected in the breeding of high yielding (green revolution) varieties of cereals such as rice. With the realisation of the tremendous importance of the micronutrient content of staple food crops to human development, plant breeders agreed that future breeding work should take micronutrient goals into account. The participants also called for research in other priority areas to exploit the potential food-based systems, including the development of programs and policies that influence the choices of consumers and producers to increase the supply and consumption of micronutrient-rich foods.

Questions 1-4

Choose the appropriate letter A-D to answer Questions 1-4.

1. In which country or area was an 'Iodised Salt Support Facility' established?
   A. Indonesia.
   B. Latin America.
   C. Botswana.
   D. Pakistan.
2. What common food has vitamin A been added to?
   A. Salt.
   B. Maize meal.

C. Sugar.

D. Rice flour.

3. Why does UNICEF support fruit and vegetable consumption and a more varied diet?

A. It's cheaper.

B. It's sustainable.

C. It's more easily obtainable.

D. It's more cost effective.

4. In what aspect of the green revolution was micronutrient content not taken fully into account?

A. Development of high-yielding varieties of cereals.

B. Excessive use of pesticides.

C. Programs designed to influence consumer choice.

D. Application of chemical fertilisers.

答案透析

Question 1

答案 D

分析 第1题的题干中出现了加有引号的名词短语"Iodised Salt Support Facility"，选定"Iodised Salt Support Facility"作为关键词，在阅读文章中搜索"Iodised Salt Support Facility"，可以发现"Iodised Salt Support Facility"位于文章B段的末尾句中：...for example the establishment of an 'Iodised Salt Support Facility' in Pakistan...（……比如说在巴基斯坦建立的"Iodised Salt Support Facility"……），所以正确答案为D。

Question 2

答案 C

分析 第2题的题干中出现了带有大写字母的名词短语vitamin A，选定vitamin A作为关键词，在阅读文章中搜索vitamin A可以发现正确答案位于阅读文章F段第2句话中：A number of countries are building on the successful experience of Guatemala in fortification of sugar with vitamin A.（很多国家都把希望寄托于Guatemala成功的经验，那就是加大食糖中vitamin A的含量。）由此可以得出正确答案为C。

Question 3

答案 B

分析 第3题的题干中出现了名词短语 fruit and vegetable，选定 fruit and vegetable 作为关键词，在阅读文章中搜索 fruit and vegetable，可以发现正确答案位于阅读文章G段第1句话中：UNICEF supports dietary diversification and the consumption of appropriate fruits and vegetables as one of the most potentially sustainable ways for communities to overcome micronutrient malnutrition.（UNICEF 支持把饮食多样化和适当进食水果、蔬菜，作为社区对抗微量营养素缺乏症的最有可能持续的方法之一。）因此正确答案为B。

Question 4

答案 A

分析 第4题的题干中出现了名词短语 green revolution，选定 green revolution 作为关键词，在阅读文章中搜索 green revolution，可以发现 green revolution 位于阅读文章I段第2句话中：... that the micronutrient content of foods had been neglected in the breeding of high yielding (green revolution) varieties of cereals such as rice.（在高产谷物品种例如稻米的生产中，食物的微量营养素往往被忽视。）因此正确答案为A。

Reading Passage 2

Global Water Crisis

A According to a report released by the World Water Organization (WWO), two-thirds of the world's population will be facing water shortages by 2025. The report states that the world's water supply is not keeping pace with demands being made upon it—consumption rose six-fold between 1900 and 1995, more than twice the rate of population growth. The report also says that while most wealthy countries will cope with falling water supplies due to efficient water management, poorer countries will suffer on a huge scale, making it even harder for them to escape poverty.

B The WWO says the scale of the crisis is such that the world will increasingly witness a new phenomenon, 'water refugees' —millions of people being forced to leave their homes in search of clean water. Chronic water shortages are already being experienced around the world. Lake Chad in Africa, which provides water to 20 million people in six countries, has shrunk by 95% in the past 38 years. Two-thirds of China's cities are facing severe water shortages and Delhi in India is predicted to run out of groundwater by 2015 at current usage rates.

C The world's water supplies are stretched to the limilt due to escalating populations, rising agricultural use, poor management and the effects of global warming. Consequently the WWO is urging governments and institutions to take urgent action by:

1. Giving the water crisis high priority at the World Summit on Sustainable Development in 2002.

2. Increasing investment in water supply sanitation and water resources to ensure that the basic needs of poorer communities are met before the luxury needs of the wealthy.

3. Increasing efforts to meet commitments to reduce greenhouse gas emissions by 5% by 2012.

4. Reintroducing traditional methods of water conservation in poorer countries. For example, water harvesting could significantly help to meet India's water needs if land was set apart for rainfall collection.

D Water is our most essential and basic requirement. Although water has been successfully harnessed for energy, irrigation and industry we are increasingly paying a high cost for it as people in poorer countries die from lack of a fresh, regular supply. Worldwide water shortages will begin to threaten food production in many countries too. By 2025 the amount of water needed for food production around the world will rise by 50%, due to population growth and higher standards of living. Poorer countries will face having to choose between using water for crop irrgation or domestic and industrial use. Consequently many may be forced to risk the vagaries of international markets by importing food. For the 1.3 billion people who live on $1 a day or less, high grain prices could quickly become life threatening.

E The primary reasons for the water supply crisis are:

1. Lack of water regulation, management and investment by governments in poorer countries.

2. Global warming which causes deserts to expand, rivers to dry up, droughts to intensify and melting of the polar ice caps which may lead to the intrusion of salt water into freshwater supplies.

3. Unsustainable use of groundwater which occurs in every continent except Antarctica.

F According to the WWO, even though water shortages and hosepipe bans exist in the UK, each person still has an average of 150 litres of water a day at their disposal—enough to wash 15 cars. In some of the poorest countries, however, people are surviving on a daily ration of less than a bucket of water.

Questions 1-5

Choose the appropriate letters A-D and write them in boxes 1-5 on your answer sheet.

1. Between 1900 and 1995 world water consumption increased _____.
   A. sixty times
   B. six-fold
   C. at the same rate as the population
   D. at six times the population rate

2. The world's water supplies are running out because _____.
   A. there are too many people
   B. of poor water management
   C. the earth is getting hotter
   D. all of the above

3. By 2025 many poorer countries may be forced to _____.
   A. buy water
   B. revert to traditional methods of water conservation
   C. import food
   D. stop farming

4. More than a billion people live _____.
   A. on ten dollars a week
   B. on a dollar a day or less
   C. near Lake Chad
   D. in Africa

5. Global warming causes ______.
A. drought
B. flooding
C. decreased evaporation rates
D. lower sea levels

答案透析

Question 1

答案　B

分析　第1题的题干中出现了数词1900和1995，选定1900和1995作为关键词，在阅读文章中搜索1900和1995，可以发现1900和1995出现于阅读文章的A段中。正确答案位于A段的第2句：The report states that the world's water supply is not keeping pace with demands being made upon it—consumption rose six-fold between 1900 and 1995，...（报道指出，世界供水没有跟上需求的步伐——从1900年到1995年，世界水消耗量增加了6翻，……），不难得出正确答案为B。

Question 2

答案　D

分析　第2题问的是世界范围内水资源缺乏的原因是什么。阅读文章的E段专门叙述The primary reasons for the water supply crisis（世界范围内供水危机的主要原因），阅读E段的第1点：Lack of water regulation，management...（缺乏对水的规范和管理……），以及第2点：Global warming...（全球变暖……），可以得知B、C两项均为正确答案，因此正确答案为D：all of the above（以上各项均正确）。

Question 3

答案　C

分析　第3题的题干中出现了数词2025，选定2025作为关键词，在阅读文章中搜索2025，可以发现2025出现于阅读文章的D段中。正确答案位于D段的倒数第2句：Consequently many may be forced to risk the vagaries of international market by importing food.（因此很多国家将被迫冒由进口食物带来的国际市场变化无常的风险。）显然正确答案为C。

Question 4

答案　B

分析　第 4 题的题干中出现了数词 a billion，选定 billion 作为关键词，在阅读文章中搜索 billion，可以发现 billion 出现于阅读文章 D 段的末句：For the 1.3 billion people who live on $1 a day or less，...（对于 13 亿每天仅仅依靠 1 美元甚至更少的钱来生活的人而言，……），显然正确答案为 B。

Question 5

答案　A

分析　第 5 题的题干中出现了名词 global warming，选定 global warming 作为关键词，在阅读文章中搜索 global warming，可以发现 global warming 位于阅读文章的 E 段中：Global warming which causes deserts to expand，rivers to dry up，droughts to intensify...（全球变暖导致沙漠扩张、河流干涸、干旱加剧……），显然正确答案为 A。

Part 3
Exercises of Multiple Choice Questions
多项选择题实战练习

Reading Passage 1

Search-and-Rescue Robots

A A competition held in Seattle, USA, explored an intriguing new field—the use of robots in search and rescue operations for the victims of earthquakes and other disasters.

B Some of the robots were small, motorized machines resembling remote-cotrolled cars. They were equipped with heat sensors enabling them to locate an injured person. Others, equipped with cameras which can send pictures of the inside of a damaged building, were able to climb unsteady stairs. Still others, could detect cries for help. They were tested on an obstacle course meant to simulate an earthquake disaster as part of the annual RoboCup competition, in conjunction with the International Joint Conference on Artificial Intelligence.

C As they rambled and rolled through the carefully constructed obstacle course, the robots encountered rubble, stairs, slippery paper, venetian blinds and other tricky debris likely to be encountered after an earthquake, fire or bombing. Their mission was to find dummies lying under desks, caught under fallen beams, trapped in small spaces or crushed under fallen beams.

D The utility of the research was more than theoretical to Lieutenant Colonel John Blitch, director of robotics technology for the National Institute for Search and Rescue. Blitch, one of the judges of the competition, took part in the rescue operation following the Oklahoma City bombing. He is familiar with the type of robots used to defuse or explode bombs, but these robots are the size of desks, weigh as much as 450 kg and cannot get into places a human can because of their size. 'So in the past we had to send human rescuers into dangerous situations. Robots need to be made smaller, lighter and more maneuverable for this type of work.'

E For a long time, autonomy was the main goal in creating search-and-rescue robots. But it is most important for the robots to work with the rescue teams and supplement what rescue workers can't do. One function is for a robot to go into a collapsed building and map the rubble and structural conditions, a job that can be highly dangerous and slow for a human rescue worker.

F 'Everyone has tried to make the robot like a person,' said Robin Murphy, an associate professor of computer science at the University of South Florida in Tampa, 'but what we really need is something more with the intelligence of a dog that you can tell where to go. Add to that the advantage of a robot that can work everywhere, take lots of camera pictures and send them back to the rescue headquarters. These are things that neither people nor dogs can do. They can't carry all that sensor equipment. People are too big, and dogs don't know how to look in corners or how to look for structural details.'

G Other advantages of robots for search-and-rescue work are that they cannot be overcome by smoke, electrocuted or drowned. Also, they are expendable; if one gets crushed by falling masonry, a replica can be brought in to do exactly the same job. 'Humans, of course, are not expendable,' said Ms. Murphy, 'and neither are dogs. It takes time to train a dog, and there is a tendency not to put them in risky situations if it can be helped.'

H But it could be a long time before robots are employed in real-life emergencies. At the competition, four teams—from Swarthmore College, Sharif University of Technology in Tehran, Iran, the University of Edinburgh and Utah State University—let loose the robots they had designed in a specially constructed full-size mock-up of a building interior. There was no winner, however, as none of the teams met the minimum requirement of finding four victims in 25 minutes in an easy section of the obstacle course.

Questions 1-4

Choose the appropriate letters A-D, and write them in boxes 1-4 on your answer sheet.

1. In the RoboCup Competition, the robots were set the task of locating ____.
   A. injured people
   B. unexploded bombs
   C. dummies
   D. obstacles
2. Which of the following disasters is NOT mentioned in the passage?
   A. Plane crash.
   B. Earthquake disaster.
   C. Bomb explosion.
   D. Fire.
3. Robots are expendable because _____.
   A. they are cheap to make
   B. they can reproduce themselves
   C. they have no human or animal feelings
   D. they can be easily replaced
4. What do you think a 'mock-up' is?
   A. An amusing design.
   B. A replica.
   C. An insult.
   D. A damaged building.

Reading Passage 2

Family Planning

A Based on the 1990 census, the Philippines has a population of 60.7 million people and of this number, 49 per cent reside in urban areas. The Philippines Demographic and Health Survey of 1993 reports a total fertility rate (TFR) of

4.09 among women in the reproductive age group. Among currently married women, contraceptive prevalence is 40 per cent, with 25 per cent using modern methods. Among the 15 per cent using traditional methods, natural family planning accounts for 7.3 per cent of use (PDHS, 1994).

B National family planning efforts began in the Philippines in 1968 with the establishment of the Office of Maternal and Child Health in the Department of Health. By 1970, the Population Commission was established as a coordinating body to promote government and private sector efforts to reduce fertility as a means of fostering national welfare. Currently, about 60 per cent of modern contraceptive users receive services from the public sector. Government services are offered through various outlets such as Rural Health Units, Barangay (village) Health Stations, hospitals, social hygiene clinics, city health centres and mobile outreach services.

C Non-Governmental Organizations have always played significant roles in family planning service delivery. Prior to government involvement, non-profit organizations were early advocates of family planning. Private volunteer family planning organizations pioneered the use of voluntary surgical contraception, initiated adolescent fertility management projects that focused on sex education (USAID, 1992) and led the way in the rapid expansion of clinical services, operating more than 14 per cent of family planning clinics (United Nations, 1991).

D The Government of the Philippines continues to rely on the help of non-profit organiztations in meeting the demand for family planning services. The Government and select industries have contracts with private volunteer organizations to deliver services. The Philippines Demographic and Health Survery (1994) shows that non-profit organizations are significant sources of supply for the IUD, providing 28 per cent of the total. Volunteer organizations also meet about 14 per cent of the demand for pills and about 14.5 per cent of the need for condoms. Further, non-profit organizations performed 7.5 per cent of the female sterilizations in the country (PDHS, 1994: 50).

E Metropolitan Cebu is located in the Province of Cebu which has 48 municipalities and five cities. Three of the cities and six of the municipalities comprise 'Metro Cebu'. Based on the 1990 Census of Population and Housing, Metro Cebu has a population of 1,252,339 (NSO, 1990). Cebu is experiencing high levels of urban growth as a result of new employment opportunities in the city's emerging industries. Both men and women are taking advantage of employment opportunities in the city. About 71.3 per cent of the men and 48 per cent of the women are in the labour force.

F Cebu is located in the Central Visayas region of the country. Within this region, about 46.1 per cent of currently married women are current users of family planning, with 28.8 per cent using modern methods and 17.3 per cent relying on traditional methods (PDHS, 1994). Of the 17.3 per cent using traditional methods, 8.8 per cent use natural family planning.

G As in most other areas of the country, the Government is the primary provider of modern family planning services and supplies in Metro Cebu. Family planning users can obtain public services and supplies from more than 170 government health centres and stations in the metropolitan area. Within the private sector, family planning services and supplies can be received from 253 pharmacies, 55 employer-based companies, 50 obstetric / gynaecological and family physicians and 33 non-profit organizations including religious organizations.

H Volunteer organizations complement government services and the commercial sector by providing low-cost services and supplies for poor families and individuals in acceptable, familiar settings. Religious organizations provide a range of natural family planning methods for couples concerned about the religious implications of artificial birth control. Development organizations engaged in income-generating activities provide information, services and supplies to the hard-core urban poor. Health and family planning agencies integrate their services with those of the Government and industries to fill gaps in service delivery.

I This study is based on a census of private volunteer organizations in Cebu that provide clinical and non-clinical family planning services and supplies. Interviews were conducted with 33 non-profit organizations in 1994. Agencies were identified through a number of different sources. Initial lists of organizations were obtained from the regional office of the Population Commission in Cebu, a government organization that is responsible for coordinating population activities within the province. Additional lists were obtained from other government organizations and from private associations including the Department of Health—Integrated Provincial Health Office, the Department of Labor and Employment Population Program Office, Cebu Medical Society and USAID (United States Agency for

International Development / Manila) . Staff of the Office of Population Studies, University of San Carlos, visited each institution and selected organization to ensure that they provide family planning services.

Questions 1-6

Choose the appropriate letters A-D and write them in boxes 1-5 on your answer sheet.

1. Among the traditional contraceptive users, natural family planning users account for ____.
   A. 25%
   B. 15%
   C. 7.3%
   D. almost 50%
2. The main function of the Population Commission is ____.
   A. to make government and private sector work more effectively in family planning
   B. to provide enough modern family planning services and supplies
   C. to reduce the fertility rate among the married women
   D. to conduct the Demographic and Health survey
3. The body which first promotes the family planning is ____.
   A. government
   B. non-profit organizations
   C. Office of Maternal and Child Health
   D. commercial sector
4. Metropolitan Cebu includes ____.
   A. 5 municipalities and 48 cities
   B. 48 municipalities and 5 cities
   C. 6 municipalities and 3 cities
   D. 3 cities and 48 municipalities
5. Among the currently married women in Cebu, ____ use modern contraceptive methods.
   A. 46.1%
   B. 40%
   C. 28.8%
   D. 8.8%

6. In Metropolitan Cebu, the modern family planning services and supplies are mainly provided by ____.
A. government
B. private sector
C. commercial sector
D. the Department of Health

Reading Passage 3

Turning Farms into Factories

A Until about 20 years ago, there were four intimate aspects of our personal lives that we assumed to be produced by individual skilled activity. They were medicine, entertainment, sports, and vegetables. Some penetration of capital into those spheres had, of course, occurred, but they were invisible to us. Since then, our family physician has become a corporate health care practitioner; television, popular music, books and films are owned by a few major conglomerates; baseball players are paid millions by owners, who are paid millions by television networks, who, in turn, are paid millions by advertisers.

B One consequence of this has been a false nostalgia for an idyllic life never experienced: the independent family farmer, tilling the soil, in touch with nature, making decisions about what and when to plant and harvest from his craft knowledge, sitting down to a dinner of home-grown victuals prepared by his wife. This is a life we want to preserve. Unfortunately, we are 100 years too late.

C The history of European and American agriculture over the last 100 years has been a history of the increasing dominance of industrial capital over farming. In 1900, when over 50% of the US population worked on the land, the inputs into farming were predominantly self-produced. The farmer saved seeds from the previous year's crop to plant; the plow and tillage machinery were pulled by mules fed by forage grown on the farm; 40% of planted acreage was in feed crops; and livestock produced manure to go back on the fields. In those days, the farmer was largely self-sufficient. But nowadays, the seed is purchased from Pioneer Hi-bred, the mules are John Deere tractors, the feed is supplied by Exxon and the manure is bought from the Terra company.

D The rise in purchased industrially produced inputs has had two effects. A major increase in yields per acre has driven down the price paid to farmers for their products. Simultaneously, the farmers' costs of production have risen. There has been no escape from this dilemma for the individual farmer. Because the price paid for farm products is determined by the aggregate production from all farms, no individual farmer can push prices up by holding down production. Thus, he must increase production when other farmers do, but the result of all these individually economically rational acts is mass suicide. Smaller and smaller margins between farm income and expenses have led to increasing farm debt and bankruptcies.

E The consequence of the growing dominance of industrial capital in agriculture for the class 'family farm' has been the progressive conversion of the independent farmer into an industrial employee. The 'pure' farm population nowadays in the US is about 7% of the total. More and more farm operators and their spouses are only part-time farmers, trying to support their farming from outside income. According to 1997 statistics some 60% of farm operators are also employed off the farm, and 40% work at alternative employment for more than 200 days a year. They work as truck drivers, salespeople, secretaries and factory hands. Car companies now put their assembly plants in the rural counties of the farm belt to take advantage of this work force.

F The creation and adoption of genetically modified organisms are the latest steps in this long historical development of capital-intensive industrial agriculture. Round-up Ready, herbicide-resistant soybeans have been created by the Monsanto Company so that farmers will be able to use Monsanto powerful herbicide, called Roundup, while at the same time buying Monsanto seeds. The farmers accept the cost of the new variety of genetically modified soybeans and its chemical partner because the use of such a powerful general weed killer will reduce the number of herbicide treatments or mechanical tillage passages through the fields, freeing them for the hours in the automobile assembly plant or other employment that they need to work in order to keep their farms. For the farmer, there is no escape from engineering, whether it be mechanical, chemical, electrical or genetic.

Questions 1-5

Choose the appropriate letters A-D, and write them in boxes 1-5 on your answer sheet.

1. The farmer's life used to be idyllic because ____.
   A. he tilled the soil
   B. his wife prepared his meals
   C. he was independent
   D. he grew green crops
2. The encroachment of industrial capital has resulted in ____.
   A. 60% of farmers holding part-time jobs
   B. 40% of farmers holding part-time jobs
   C. 40% of planted acreage raising feed crops
   D. 50% of farmers leaving the land
3. The most recent development of capitalized agriculture is ____.
   A. automobile assembly plants in rural areas
   B. diminishing margins between farm income and expenses
   C. false nostalgia for an idyllic life
   D. genetically modified crops
4. Industrial capital began to take control of agriculture ____.
   A. about 20 years ago
   B. about 100 years ago
   C. in 1997
   D. when farmers started using Pioneer Hi-bred seeds
5. The John Deere company supplies ____.
   A. mules
   B. manure
   C. tractors
   D. fodder

Chapter Eight
Cracking Matching Questions
匹配题题型突破

内容提示

- IELTS 特色题型——Matching 题解题技巧点拨
- Matching 题实例讲解

特别提醒

- *从 2000 年闪亮登场到今天，Matching 题一直是 IELTS 阅读考试的"明星"。在你即将参加的 IELTS 考试中，不仅很有可能遇到 Matching 题，而且很有可能遇到为数不少的 Matching 题*
- *Matching 题是最让 IELTS 出题机构自豪的题型，因为它是你在其他任何英语考试中都不曾见过的题型，或许它也是 IELTS 考试中最让你茫然不知所措的题型，因此请重视本章的学习*

Part 1
Guide to Answering Matching Questions
匹配题解题方法透析

一、题型介绍

Matching（匹配）题，是 IELTS 考试在不断发展的过程中，为了适应全球英语学习者学习和测试状况的改变而新加入的题型，是 IELTS 阅读考试中历史最短的题型。在 IELTS 考试中，往往会提供两个集合，要求考生根据阅读文章的具体内容，将两个集合中的元素，按照一定的关系匹配起来。比如第一个集合为歌手，第二个集合为唱片名，则题目要求把各位歌手和与其相对应的唱片名进行匹配。例如：

Use the information in the text to match the people (listed A-E) with opinions or deeds (listed 1-7) below. Write the appropriate letter (A-E) in boxes 1-4 on your answer sheet. Some people may match more than one discovery.

特别提醒……

Matching 题中，两个集合内元素的数目往往并不相等，因此在匹配的过程中，某些元素可能被多次使用，而某些元素却一次都未被使用。

二、题型要求

Matching 题强调的是题目中各个元素之间的正确匹配，例如唱片名和歌手之间的正确匹配关系。从阅读难度的角度出发，Matching 题要求的是一种比较低级的阅读能力，因为在阅读文章中，相互对应或可以匹配的两个元素（例如某歌手和某唱片），往往出现在同一位置，比较容易辨认。

特别提醒……

Matching 题的这一特点，决定了在 IELTS 考试中，即使你根本无法读懂阅读文章，也有希望正确解答全部的 Matching 题，所以你必须高度重视 Matching 题，确保在考试中拿到高分！

三、题型地位

从 2000 年 IELTS 考试正式引入 Matching 题以来，Matching 题一直是 IELTS 阅读考试中出现频率最高的题型，无论是在 A 类考试中，还是在 G 类考试中，Matching 题所占据的比例一直保持在一个较高的水平上，可以毫不夸张地说，Matching 题已经成为雅思阅读考试最核心的题型之一。

2002 年在中国大陆区的一场 A 类 IELTS 考试中，曾经出现多达 21 道 Matching 题的情况，Matching 题在 IELTS 阅读考试中的重要性，由此可见一斑。

四、破题原则

Matching 题的破题原则是充分定位原则。

IELTS 考试中的 Matching 题，考查的是阅读文章中两个具体信息之间简单的匹配关系，并不涉及复杂的阅读理解。在解答 Matching 题时，不需要对阅读文章进行全局把握，也不需要深刻了解文章中语句的含义，只要简单确认两个信息之间的匹配关系就可以了。因此，如果能够在阅读文章中充分定位 Matching 题的每一个元素，就一定可以顺利解答全部的 Matching 题。

特别提醒……

定位答案的主要方式为先确认关键词。Matching 题中的关键词相对比较容易确认，因为 Matching 题所给出的很多元素（例如人名、地名等）本身就可以直接充当关键词用来定位。

五、解题步骤

第一步 仔细阅读解题说明，明确两个集合及其相互之间的匹配关系类型

IELTS 考试中所有的 Matching 题都必定在解题说明中指明需要匹配的两组集合的类型，以及两组集合之间的关系。例如：

Use the information in the text to match the people (listed A-E) with opinions or deeds (listed 1-7) below. Write the appropriate letter (A-E) in boxes 1-4 on your answer sheet. Some people may match more than one discovery.

阅读完这道 Matching 题的解题说明以后，你可以了解到题目给出的两个集合，分别是被标号为 A-E（listed A-E）的集合，这组集合表示的是 people（人），以及标号为 1-7（listed 1-7）的集合，这个集合表示的是 opinions or deeds（看法或功绩）。题目要求的是“人”和“人的看法或功绩”之间的匹配关系。

第二步 回阅读文章中充分定位某一集合的元素

和解答其他题型的定位方法一样，解答 Matching 题时定位答案的主要方式为先确认关键词，然后在阅读文章中搜索关键词，通过定位关键词来定位题目的正确答案。

第三步 通过定位另外一个集合来匹配第二步中尚未匹配出去的元素

如果第二步中还有一些元素没有被匹配出去，可以考虑以这些元素本身作为定位词，回阅读文章中搜索这些元素，从而定位题目的正确答案。

Part 2
Analysis of Matching Questions
匹配题实例透析

Reading Passage 1

Saving the Unique Wildlife of the Galapagos Island

A When Charles Darwin, whose visit to the Galapagos Islands in 1835 inspired his monumental work on evolution, *The Origin of Species*, arrived at the islands, there were fewer than 300 human inhabitants, and they had only been there for six years. Today, the permanent population has swelled to 16,109. This influx of people, combined with the approximately 65,000 eco-tourists who visit the islands annually, is placing a heavy strain on the natural balance of life in the Galapagos.

B The Galapagos Islands are home to many unique species of animals, birds and plants, and have become known as a 'natural laboratory of evolution'. Darwin himself wrote, 'In that little world within itself, we seem to be brought somewhat near to that great fact—that mystery of mysteries—the first appearance of new beings on this earth.' The best known of these creatures is the giant tortoise, which has evolved into 14 distinct forms on different islands. This process is known to scientists as 'adaptive radiation'. Other classic examples of this phenomenon are several species of plants, especially those of the daisy family, which have spread to different islands and adapted to the distinct conditions there. In addition, the 13 species of 'Darwin's finches', small brown finches which eat different foods, are important to scientists trying to understand how evolution occurs.

C The islands are volcanic in origin, and lie in the Pacific Ocean, about 1,000 km from South America and straddling the Equator. There are 13 large islands, six smaller ones and 107 islets and rocks. They were officially 'discovered' in 1535 by Tomas de Berlanga, bishop of Panama, when his ship was blown off course. There were no aboriginal human inhabitants, and no permanent population at all until Ecuador annexed the Galapagos in 1832, and used them as a penal colony.

D One of the biggest threats to the wildlife and ecosystem as a whole on the Galapagos is the exploding population of domestic animals and plants which were brought in by early settlers and allowed to become feral 'wild': Goats compete for grazing with native herbivores 'vegetarian animals' such as tortoises and iguanas, and on some islands, have devastated natural vegetation. Feral dogs and cats prey on iguauas and sea bird chicks. Some introduced plants are seriously threatening the survival of native species.

E In 1959, Ecuador designated 97% of the land area of the Galapagos as a national park. In 1986, the Galapagos Marine Resources Reserve was established to protect the waters around the archipelago group of islands. The islands have also been recognized internationally as a Man and Biosphere reserve and as a World Heritage Site by Unesco. Ecuador manages the islands through the Galapagos National Park Service. In addition, the Charles Darwin Research Station (CDRS), which is operated by the international Charles Darwin Foundation, carries out scientific research and assists the Park Service in what the latter's director Juan Sanchez calls, 'a successful example of cooperation between national and international agencies.'

F To ensure that the human population does not spiral out of control, Ecuador enacted the Special Law for the Galapagos in 1998. Under the law, the government recognizes as permanent residents of the islands only those who were born there to at least one resident parent; those who, on the date the law took effect, had lived in the Galapagos for five continuous years; and those married to a permanent resident. Meanwhile, the government is preparing a database of all permanent residents, who will be issued identification cards.

G In order to boost the awareness of the fragile nature of the ecology on these unique islands, environmental impact assessments are regularly made by a team headed by Sanchez, and both locals and tourists are educated in the importance of conservation.

H At the same time, eradication programs aimed at eliminating alien species are being put into effect, as well as strict quarantine inspections—even bacteria brought to the islands on the soles of tourists' shoes carry potential harm. An imaginative program encourages tour operators to purchase food and supplies locally. According to a spokesman for the CDRS, this will have the advantages of both aiding the local economy and avoiding possible transport of invasive species from the mainland.

I The spokesman commented, 'Though far more pristine than other archipelagos, the Galapagos are being degraded at an accelerating rate.' All the experts agree that the principal threat to the bio-diversity of the Galapagos is the presence of alien plants, diseases, insects and other organisms that people bring inadvertently to the islands.

Questions 1-7

Use the information in the text to match the people (listed A-E) with opinions or deeds (listed 1-7) below. Write the appropriate letter (A-E) in boxes 1-7 on your answer sheet. Some people may match more than one discovery.

A. Charles Darwin
B. Juan Sanchez
C. Tomas de Berlanga
D. The spokesman for the CDRS
E. Unesco

Example The Galapagos are less spoiled than other groups of islands.

Answer D

1. The discovery of the Galapagos.
2. The Galapagos Islands are a self-contained world.
3. National and international agencies cooperate successfully in the Galapagos.

4. Local purchasing will have a dual benefit for the islands. D

5. Recognition of the islands as a World Heritage Site. E

6. The theory of evolution. A

7. Environmental impact assessments. B

答案透析

Question 1

答案 C

分析 在阅读文章中搜索第一个集合中出现的全部人名，可以发现第 1 题的正确答案位于阅读文章 C 段第 3 句话：They were officially 'discovered' in 1535 by Tomas de Berlanga, ...（它们是在 1535 年由 Tomas de Berlanga 正式发现的，……），显然正确答案为 C。

Question 2

答案 A

分析 在阅读文章中搜索第一个集合中出现的全部人名，可以发现第 2 题的正确答案位于阅读文章 B 段第 2 句话：Darwin himself wrote, 'In that little world within itself, ...'（Darwin 自己写到，在那个完全自成一体的小世界里，……），显然正确答案为 A。

Question 3

答案 B

分析 在阅读文章中搜索第一个集合中出现的全部人名，可以发现第 3 题的正确答案位于阅读文章 E 段的末尾句：... Juan Sanchez calls, 'a successful example of cooperation between national and international agencies.'（……Juan Sanchez 称之为"本土机构与国际机构合作的成功范例"），显然正确答案为 B。

Question 4

答案　D

分析　在阅读文章中搜索第一个集合中出现的全部人名，可以发现第4题的正确答案位于阅读文章H段第3句话：According to a spokesman for the CDRS, this will have the advantages of both aiding the local economy and avoiding possible transport of invasive species from the mainland.（据CDRS的一位发言人称，这将带来两个好处，一是促进地方经济，二是避免从大陆运输而来的入侵性物种。）显然正确答案为D。

Question 5

答案　E

分析　在阅读文章中搜索第一个集合中出现的全部人名，可以发现第5题的正确答案位于阅读文章E段第3句话：The islands have also been recognized internationally as a Man and Biosphere reserve and as a World Heritage Site by Unesco（这些岛屿同样被国际上认定为人类生态保护区，并被Unesc认定为世界文化遗址。）显然正确答案为E。

Question 6

答案　A

分析　在阅读文章中搜索第一个集合中出现的全部人名，可以发现第6题的正确答案位于阅读文章A段第1句话：Charles Darwin，whose visit to the Galapagos Islands in 1835 inspired his monumental work on evolution，*The Origin of Species*,...（达尔文1835年对Galapagos岛屿的访问，激发了他在进化方面的不朽著作《物种起源》的创作,……）显然正确答案为A。

Question 7

答案　B

分析　在阅读文章中搜索第一个集合中出现的全部人名，可以发现第7题的正确答案位于阅读文章G段第1句话：...，environmental impact assessments are regularly made by a team headed by Sanchez，...（……，一支由Sanchez带领的队伍定期进行环境影响评估，……），显然正确答案为B。

Part 3
Exercises of Matching Questions
匹配题实战练习

Reading Passage 1

Wolves, Dogs and Humans

A There is no doubt that dogs are the oldest of all species tamed by humans and their domestication was based on a mutually beneficial relationship with man. The conventional view is that the domestication of wolves began between 10,000 and 20,000 years ago. However, a recent ground-breaking paper by a group of international geneticists has pushed this date back by a factor of 10. Led by Dr. Robert Wayne, at the University of California, Los Angeles, the team showed that all dog breeds had only one ancestor, the wolf. They did this by analysing the genetic history through the DNA of 162 wolves from around the world and 140 domestic dogs representing 67 breeds. The research also confirms, for the first time, that dogs are descended only from wolves and do not share DNA with coyotes or jackals. The fact that our companionship with dogs now appears to go back at least 100,000 years means that this partnership may have played an important part in the development of human hunting techniques that developed 70,000 to 90,000 years ago. It also may even have affected the brain development in both species.

B The Australian veterinarian David Paxton suggests that in that period of first contact, people did not so much domesticate wolves as wolves domesticated people. Wolves may have started living at the edge of human settlements as scavengers, eating scraps of food and waste. Some learned to live with human beings in a mutually helpful way and gradually evolved into dogs. At the very least, they would have protected human settlements, and given warnings by barking at anything approaching. The wolves that evolved into dogs have been enormously successful in evolutionary terms. They are found everywhere in the inhabited world, hundreds of millions of them. The descendants of the wolves that remained wolves are now sparsely distributed, often in endangered populations.

C In return for companionship and food, the early ancestor of the dog assisted humans in tracking, hunting, guarding and a variety of other activities. Eventually humans began to selectively breed these animals for specific traits. Physical characteristics changed and individual breeds began to take shape. As humans wandered across Asia and Europe, they took their dogs along, using them for additional tasks and further breeding them for selected qualities that would better enable them to perform specific duties.

D According to Dr. Colin Groves, of the Department of Archaeology and Anthropology at Australian National University, early humans came to rely on dogs' keen ability to hear, smell and see—allowing certain areas of the human brain to shrink in size relative to other areas. 'Dogs acted as humans' alarm systems, trackers and hunting aids, garbage disposal facilities, hot-water bottles and children's guardians and playmats. Humans provided dogs with food and security. This symbiotic relationship was stable for over 100,000 years and intensified into mutual domestication,' said Dr. Groves. In his opinion, humans domesticated dogs and dogs domesticated humans.

E Dr. Groves repeated an assertion made as early as 1914—that humans have some of the same physical characteristics as domesticated animals, the most notable being decreased brain size. The horse experienced a 16 per cent reduction in brain size after domestication while pigs' brains shrank by as much as 34 per cent. The estimated brain-size reduction in domesticated dogs varies from 30 per cent to 10 per cent. Only in the last decade have archaeologists uncovered enough fossil evidence to establish that brain capacity in humans declined in Europe and Africa by at least 10 per cent beginning about 10,000 years ago. Dr. Groves believes this reduction may have taken place as the relationship between humans and dogs intensified. The close interaction between the two species allowed for the diminishing of certain human brain functions like smell and hearing.

Questions 1-5

Match one of the researchers (A-C) to each of the findings (1-5) below.

A. Dr. Wayne
B. Dr. Paxton
C. Dr. Groves

Example Found the common ancestor of the dog.

Answer A

1. Studied the brain size of domesticated animals.
2. Claims that wolves chose to interact with humans.
3. Established a new time frame for domestication of wolves.
4. Believes that dogs and humans domesticated each other.
5. Studied the DNA of wolves and dogs.

Reading Passage 2

Computer Hacking Becoming Easier

A Computer vandals toting nothing more than a Sega game device, handheld computer, or even a compact disc can slip into offices and launch 'phone home' attacks via remote computers under their control, speakers at a U.S. hackers convention said. Lonely office printers aren't any safer, and can be hacked into through an Internet connection via a corporate network, one speaker said as the annual Defcon conference of computer security enthusiasts and mischievous network tinkerers.

B More than 5,000 pelple are expected for the three-day meeting, which started on Friday and is held in an out-of-the-way Las Vegas hotel at the edge of the Nevada desert. The decade-old event has become the biggest annual gathering of the computer counterculture.

C Basically, any device that sits on a network 'can run malicious code, can be made to do attacks and can do anything you want them to do,' said Chris Davis, a security consultant at RedSiren, a computer security firm in Reston, Virginia. 'The idea is any computer can pose a potential threat,' he said.

D 'More and more things are embedded in computers. We could put the same code on a TiVo (news-web sites) if we wanted to,' Aaron Higbee, a security consultant at Foundstone of Mission Viejo, California. TiVo allows people to record TV programs while away or while watching other programs at the same time. Firewalls—the computer security barriers that organizations depend on to defend against outside intrusions—are worthless against such attacks, Higbee said. While they are configured to block suspicious traffic from getting into the network, they also permit any type of traffic to get out, he said.

E To create a tunnel to a remote computer, an attacker must first get physical access to devices or network connections in the building. Sometimes they can rely on unsuspecting souls inside the company to do their dirty work for them by sending them an innocent-looking compact disc that contains tunneling software. A disc containing a special program to activate itself can find the network and reach the Internet on its own, creating the opening for a hacker to wreak havoc inside the company's network, Davis said. Another method of unlocking the network door and opening the tunnel is for the hacker to gain physical access to an office building and plug simple devices onto the network. 'Five minutes on the inside is all you need,' said Davis, who does penetration testing for companies to see how easy it is to compromise their systems.

F The speakers demonstrated for the crowd how an attacker can slip a tunneling CD into a CD-ROM drive, a Sega Dreamcast (newsweb sites) gaming console, or a Compaq iPaq, and connect to the network. Once a connection is established, devices such as the Sega game player can analyze the network for routes data, can travel to the Internet and establish a secret tunnel to an outside computer controlled by the hacker.

G With printers, attackers don't even have to enter the building, said Dennis Mattison, a computer scientist at Science Applications International Corp., a top military contractor in the communications research arena based in San Diego. Printers are increasingly becoming more complex, with more sophisticated software and funcitons, making them easy and unsuspecting targets, he said. Still, there is little evidence such attacks have become widespread, the experts said. But with more and more devices every day being connected to computer networks, the exposure to such threats makes such attacks inevitable one day. 'These are theoretical attacks,' he said. 'There are not many known attacks out there.'

H Striking back against a computer that is attacking you may be illegal under U.S. law, but a security researcher says people should be allowed to neutralize one that is unwittingly spreading destructive Internet worms like Nimda. 'Arguably the biggest threat the Internet faces today is the propagation of a big worm,' Timothy Mullen, chief information officer of AnchorIS Inc., based in Charleston, South Carolina. Worms are a form of self-propagating virus that once set in motion can wreak havoc by taking control of other machines and then use these to launch attacks on the wider Internet.

I Mullen said his hack back idea is different because it is designed to improve the security of cyberspace and would not harm any computer systems. To counter this, Mullen has come up with a way for machines that have been attacked but not infected to trace the worm back to the attacking machine and prevent it from spreading the worm to other computers. Using his technique, the computer that launches an attack is paralyzed and requires an administrator to restart it, but it stays online and is not otherwise harmed, said Mullen. 'What we're doing, according to the letter of the law, is illegal,' he acknowledged. 'I would like to see the law changed... We've illustrated not just a reasonable recourse, but a minimal responsibility.'

Questions 1-6

In the Reading Passage, four speakers are cited as saying the following ideas. Decide which idea (1-6) corresponds to each speaker by putting short forms of their names before the sentences below. Write your answers in boxes 1-6 on your answer sheet.

You may write

ChD *for Chris Davis*

AH *for Aaron Higbee*

DM *for Dennis Mattison*
TM *for Timothy Mullen*

Example Any computer can be a potential threat.

Answer ChD

List of ideas

1. Firewalls are not very much helpful in blocking off malicious codes.
2. Neutralizing a computer that launches attacks should be protected by law.
3. One way to attack a system is to plug simple devices onto the network.
4. Printers are targets of attack from outside.
5. It is a minimal responsibility to hack back the Internet hackers.
6. Some attacks are just theoretical ones.

Reading Passage 3

Mystery of the Mummies

A In 1992, a German scientist made a discovery which was to upset whole areas of scientific study from history and archeology to chemistry and botany. Dr. Svetlana Balabanova, a forensic specialist, was performing tissue tests on an Egyptian mummy, part of a German museum collection. The mummified remains were of a woman named Henut-Taui who had died over 3,000 years ago. Amazingly, the tests revealed that her body contained large quantities of cocaine and nicotine. Dr. Balabanova had regularly used the same testing methods to convict people of drug consumption but she had not expected to find nicotine and coca in an Ancient Egyptian mummy. It is generally accepted that these two plants, native to the Americas did not exist on other continents prior to European exploration.

B Dr. Balabanova repeated the tests then sent out fresh samples to three other labs. When the results came back positive she published a paper with two other scientists. If Balabanova was shocked by the results of her tests she was even more shocked at the hostile response to her publication. She received many insulting letters, accusing her of fraud.

C There were two explanations that came immediately to mind. One was that something in the tests could have given a false result. The second was that the mumies tested were not truly Ancient Egyptian. Perhaps they were relatively modern bodies, containing traces of cocaine. Dr. Balabanova then examined tissue from 134 naturally preserved bodies over a thousand years old discovered in an excavated cemetery in the Sudan. About a third of them tested positive for nicotine or cocaine.

D But something had happened even earlier which should have initiated serious discussion. In 1976 the mummified remains of Ramses Ⅱ arrived in Paris for repair work. Dr. Michelle Lescot of the Natural History Museum (Paris) was looking at sections of bandages and within the fibres found a plant fragment. When she checked it under a microscope she was amazed to discover that the plant was tobacco. Fearing that she had made some mistake she repeated her tests again and again with the same result every time: a New World plant had been found on an Old World mummy. The results caused a sensation in Europe. Was it possible that a piece of tobacco had been dropped by chance from the pipe of some forgotten archaeologist? Dr. Lescot responded to this charge of contamination by carefully extracting new samples from the abdomen, with the entire process recorded on film. These samples, which could not be 'droppings', were then tested. Once again they were shown to be tobacco. The discovery of tobacco fragments in the mummified body of Ramses Ⅱ should have had a profound influence upon our whole understanding of the relationship between Ancient Egypt and America but this piece of evidence was simply ignored. It raised too many questions and was too far outside of commonly accepted scientific views.

E So now the question had returned. Could Ancient Egyptian trade have stretched all the way across the Atlantic Ocean? This was an idea so unbelievable it could only be considered after all the other possibilities had been eliminated. Could Egyptians have obtained imports from a place thousands of miles away, from a continent supposedly not discovered until thousands of years later? Was it possible that coca—a plant from South America had found its way to Egypt 3,000 years ago? If the cocaine found in mummies could not be explained by contamination, or fake mummies or by Egyptian plants containing it, there appeared to be another interesting possibility: a trade route with links all the way to the Americas.

F The Egyptians did make great efforts to obtain incense and other valuable plants used in religious ceremonies and herbal medicines, but to the majority of archeologists, the idea is hardly worth talking about. Professor John Baines, an Egyptologist from Oxford University states: 'I don't think it is at all likely that there was an ancient trade network that included America. The essential problem with any such idea is that there are no artefacts... found either in Europe or in America.' But other experts aren't so sure. Professor Martin Bernal, an historian, from Cornell University says, 'We're getting more and more evidence of world trade at an earlier stage. You have the Chinese silk definitely arriving in Egypt by 1000 BC.' In his opinion, it is arrogance on the part of modern people to believe that a transoceanic trading network could only have been set up in recent times.

G The discoveries in the mummies from Egypt and Sudan have challenged conventional beliefs. It is no longer possible to exclude the hypothesis of transoceanic trade in ancient times. The tale of Henut Taui and the story of Ramses II show that, in science, facts can be rejected if they don't fit with our beliefs, while what is believed to be proven, may actually be uncertain. It is understandable then, how a story of a scientist, a few mummies and some routine tests, could upset whole areas of knowledge we thought we could take for granted.

Questions 1-5

Match ***ONE*** *of the researchers (A-D) to each of the statements (1-5) below. There may be more than one correct answer.*

A. Dr. Svetlana Balabanova
B. Dr. Michelle Lescot
C. Professor John Baines
D. Professor Martin Bernal

1. First to find a substance from the Americas in a mummy.

2. Argues against transoceanic trade because of lack of evidence.

3. Had to defend against attacks on research methodology.

4. Gives evidence of extensive Egyptian trade in ancient times.

5. Publication of research results was controversial.

Chapter Nine
Cracking Table Questions
图表题题型突破

内容提示

- IELTS 特色题型——Table 题解题技巧点拨
- Table 题实例讲解

特别提醒

- Table 题是 IELTS 阅读最容易的题型之一，学习本章，你惟一的目标应该是——正确解答 IELTS 中的每一道 Table 题
- Table 题是 G 类 IELTS 考试中最重要的题型之一，如果你打算移民海外或赴海外参加短期培训，请特别重视本章的学习

Part 1
Guide to Answering Table Questions
图表题解题方法透析

一、题型介绍

IELTS 考试中，图表题（Table Questions）和流程图题（Flow Chart Questions）属于同一大类型的考题。由于两种题型中都出现文字以外的图表或表格，因此它们被统称为图片类考题。

与 IELTS 考试中的其他题型不一样，图表题的问题既不是以空格的形式出现在某一段文字中，也不是以问句的形式出现，而是以表格中的空白这样一种比较特殊的形式出现。题目给出一个有若干空白处的表格，要求根据阅读文章的内容，往表格中的空白处填写对应的单词。例如：

Use the information from the reading passage to complete the table below. Use **NO MORE THAN TWO WORDS OR A NUMBER***. Write your answers in boxes 1-4 on your answer sheet.*

DATE	EVENT
393AD	1 came to an end
2	First Women's events
Example 1901	First Nordic Games
1908	First 3 included in Olympics
4	First Winter Olympic Games

二、题型要求

图表题考察考生能否充分把握阅读文章中某个具体的信息点，因此题目涉及到的均是文章中比较零散的细节性内容。

除了对细节内容的考查之外，和 IELTS 阅读考试中的大多数题型一样，Table

题本身还专门针对答案设计了一些限制性要求，常见的这类要求有：

- Use No More Than Three Words
- Use a number only
- Use words or phrases taken from the reading passage

三、题型地位

虽然在 IELTS 考试中偶有出现，但整体上讲，图表题在 IELTS 阅读中出现的频率较之其他题型要低很多，因而并不属于 IELTS 阅读考试的核心题型。

IELTS 考试中虽然不会经常出现 Table Questions，但是一旦考到，一组 Table Questions 题往往出现至少 4 道题，因此在出现 Table Questions 题的 IELTS 考试中，图表题往往占据较大的比例。

四、破题原则

（1）定位简便原则

IELTS 考试中的表格题需要填写的答案，往往集中于人名、地名、公司名等专有名词，或是事件发生的年代、商品的价格等数字型答案这两大类型。无论是专有名词还是数字，在文章中都相对显眼，因而定位正确答案相对比较容易。

在实际 IELTS 考试中，阅读完解题说明和 Table 后，如果确认题目要求的答案为专有名词或是数字，就可以直接回阅读文章中搜索专有名词或数字，而不再需要从题目中挑选关键词定位正确答案。

特别提醒……

图表题的题目本身就是图表，文字内容较少，因此你几乎不能从题目中挑选出关键词，你所能够做的，是认真推测答案可能的形式，然后直接回阅读文章中搜索同类型的单词。

（2）表格平行原则

在 IELTS 考试中，可能在找到 Table 题的正确答案以后，依然感觉困难重重，因为不知道应该将正确答案以怎样的形式填入表格中。

其实，如果解题说明中没有特殊要求，就可以考虑表格的平行性：同一个表格中，平行的各格之间的内容在形式上相同，例如：如果第 3 列第 3 行的单词为某动词的现在分词，那么第 3 列第 2 行的空格中需要填写的单词，也必须采用动词的现在分词形式。

五、解题步骤

第一步 仔细阅读解题说明，明确题目要求和表格的大致内容

在 IELTS 考试中，很有必要仔细阅读 Table 题的解题说明。如果为了节约时间而忽视这一步，就很有可能因为无法理解表格的内容而耽误更多的答题时间。

第二步 阅读表格中和空格平行的内容，预测空格中内容的大致形式

预测空格中内容的大致形式是一项非常重要的任务，因为如果发现题目的答案为数字或是专有名词，则定位正确答案的难度将大大降低。

第三步 回阅读文章中搜索正确答案

确定空格中内容的大致形式以后，可以直接回到阅读文章中搜索符合这种形式的内容。例如，如果确认空格中的内容为数字，那么只要直接回到阅读文章中搜索数字，就一定能够顺利找到题目的正确答案。

特别提醒……

在某些情况下，你或许无法直接推测题目答案的形式，这时可以考虑你已经非常熟悉的关键词定位正确答案的方法。Table 题中的关键词，往往来自于表格中空格以外的其他内容。

Part 2
Analysis of Table Questions
图表题实例透析

Reading Passage 1

Foster Families in Rwanda

A Sperantia Nyirantibenda vividly recalls the night she was unceremoniously turned into a foster parent by soldiers who brought her five children and two sacks of maize. They came knocking at her door in the town of Gitarama as the civil war in Rwanda was winding down. Nyirantibenda, a 34-year-old school teacher, nervously opened the door and immediately recognised the smiling faces before her. 'I have brought you children,' one of the soldiers told Nyirantibenda this time. 'I will see you later.'

B The maize the soldiers left behind did not last very long, and they never came back. Nyirantibenda is still caring for the children. She says she will gladly keep them so long as she receives some assistance.

C Food for the Hungry International (FHI), a US-based voluntary organisation supported by the UN High Commissioner for Refugees, has come in to help the school teacher. In Rwanda and Zaire, FHI supports families which have taken in orphans and lost children, as well as unaccompanied minors who have formed into groups to live together. Over 7,000 people receive blankets, shelter materials and a regular supply of corn, beans and oil.

D FHI originally began the program to help children separated from their families at Mugunga camp, near Goma in eastern Zaire, one month after more than a million Rwandan refugees flooded into Goma in July 1994, fleeing victorious troops of the Rwandan Patriotic Front.

E An estimated 95,000 children were separated from their families during the war. Nearly half of them were inside Rwanda and the rest were in refugee camps in Zaire, Tanzania, Burundi and Uganda, which together hold more than 2.1 million refugees.

F At the outset of the refugee influx into Goma, conditions in the camps were appalling. Thousands of refugees were dying every day of cholera, dysentery and other diseases. Youngsters were being picked up beside bodies lying along the roads. Starving parents were abandoning their children or sending them to centres for unaccompanied minors in the camps.

G Rachel Poulton, an FHI spokes-person in Gitarama, said that during a visit to a tent for separated children, a 5-year-old girl followed her and asked for help. She said her parents were dead. The girl kept glancing over her shoulder at a woman who Poulton subsequently discovered was her mother. The woman later told Poulton she could no longer feed her daughter.

H Poulton said that, over a four-day period, 184 childern arrived at the tent and 16 others were brought by elders. 'There were also a lot of people fostering—mostly grandmothers and aunts. And there were sibling groups,' she said. She said that a system was developed whereby FHI supported groups of unaccompanied children.

I 'The challenge was to support these children in the community rather than in institutions. This shows another way of caring,' Poulton said. She said that it was preferable for children to grow up in a family setting rather than in orphanages.

J Myra Adamson, a 63-year-old nurse, born in South Africa to American missionary parents, works with care givers and foster parents living in bombed-out houses in Kigali. 'These separated children in the communities need food. They need someone to give them stability. They need someone they can turn to,' she said. 'The family would be destroyed if the children were brought to orphanages.'

K While a large proportion of children—about 60 per cent—are with foster families or ad hoc groups, a large number of unaccompanied minors also turn up in orphanages, such as the redbrick compound of Saint Andrew's church at Kabgayi. Run by Abundant Life International—an organisation of former Rwandan exiles from Uganda—this orphanage was started 3 months ago and it now houses 536 children. The youngsters were either brought to the institution or fetched by workers who had been informed of their location.

L 'Soldiers would come to us to tell us where we could find children and we would go and pick them up,' said an official. He said he himself had packed in his car 30 children he had picked up from nearby Kibuye prefecture where camps for displaced people had been colsed. 'We get groups of 60, 70 children,' he said.

M Throughout Rwanda and Zaire, United Nations International Children's Fund (UNICEF) and several other relief organisations are not only supporting various programs for unaccompanied minors, but are also pooling resources to help track missing relatives. As of March, over 7,000 children had been reunited with their families.

Questions 1-5

Complete the table below by writing **NO MORE THAN THREE WORDS** *in boxes 1-5 on your answer sheet.*

Location	Person or organisation	Activity
Gitarama	***Example*** Nyirantibenda	looking after five children
1	FHI	started helping lost children
2	Rachel Poulton	working for FHI
Rwanda and Zaire	3	finding relatives and reuniting families
Kigali	4	nursing
Kabgayi	Abundant Life International	5

1.

2.

3.

4.

5.

答案透析

Question 1

答案 Mugunga Camp

分析 选定 FHI 作为定位的关键词，可以发现第 1 题的正确答案位于阅读文章 D 段第 1 句话：FHI originally began the program to help children separated from their families at Mugunga camp, ...（FHI 最初是在 Mugunga camp 开始启动帮助与家人失散的儿童的项目，……）显然正确答案为 Mugunga Camp。

Question 2

答案 Gitarama

分析 选定 FHI 作为定位的关键词，可以发现第 2 题的正确答案位于阅读文章 G 段第 1 句话：Rachel Poulton, an FHI spokes-person in Gitarama, ...（Rachel Poulton 是 FHI 在 Gitarama 地区的发言人，……）显然正确答案为 Gitarama。

Question 3

答案 UNICEF

分析 如果选定 Rwanda and Zaire 作为定位的关键词，就会发现阅读文章中反复出现 Rwanda and Zaire，因此改选名词 relative 作为关键词，可以发现第 3 题的正确答案位于阅读文章 M 段第 1 句话：Throughout Rwanda and Zaire, United Nations International Children's Fund （UNICEF） and several other relief organizations are not only supporting various programs for unaccompanied minors, but are also pooling resources to help track missing relatives.（在整个卢旺达和扎伊尔地区，联合国儿童基金会以及其他的救援组织，不仅支持各项帮助无依靠未成年人的项目，而且集中力量帮助他们寻找失散的亲人。）显然正确答案为 UNICEF。

Question 4

答案 Myra Adamson

分析 选定 Kigali 作为定位的关键词，可以发现第 4 题的正确答案位于阅读文章 J 段第 1 句话：Myra Adamson, a 63-year-old nurse, born in South Africa to American missionary parents, ...（63 岁的护士 Myra Adamson 出生在南非，父母是美国的传教士，……）显然正确答案为 Myra Adamson。

Question 5

答案 running an orphange

分析 选定 Kabagayi 作为定位的关键词，可以发现第 5 题的正确答案位于阅读文章 K 段第 2 句话：Run by Abundant Life International—an organization of former Rwandan exiles from Uganda—this orphanage was started 3 months ago... [由 Abundant Life International（由从乌干达流亡的前卢旺达人组织）运作的这间孤儿院，是在 3 个月前开设的……] 显然正确答案为 running an orphange。

Part 3
Exercises of Table Questions
图表题实战练习

Reading Passage 1

The Hemp Revival

A The hemp plant, one of the world's oldest industrial resources, is back. The rediscovery of this renewable resource is making it the fibre of choice for future textiles, personal care products, building materials, paper and fuel.

B Hemp has been grown for paper, textiles, food and medicine throughout human history. The earliest known woven fabric, made of hemp, dates back to the eighth millennium (8,000-7,000 BC). The majority of all sails, clothes, tents, rugs, towels, paper, rope, twine, art canvas, paints, varnishes and lighting oil were made from hemp. Hemp seeds were regularly used as a source of food and protein for centuries.

C Hemp's drastic decline in use and importance within a matter of fifty years is widely considered to have been brought about by the timber and petrochemical industries in America. By the mid-1930s, changes in technology were beginning to impact on the hemp industry. Mechanical stripping equipment and machines to conserve hemp's hige-cellulose pulp became available and affordable. Timber and paper holding companies stood to lose billions of dollars if hemp were to be grown on a large scale. A resurgence of the hemp industry also threatened the emerging petro-chemical companies which had patented the chemicals for pulp processing.

Newspaper articles began to appear, linking hemp with violent crime. The term used, however, was 'marijuana' to distance it from hemp used for industrial purposes. Because few people realised that marijuana and hemp came from the same plant species, virtually nobody suspected that the Marijuana Prohibition of 1938 would destroy the hemp industry.

D Supporting the theory that marijuana was banned to destroy the hemp industry, were two articles written just before the Marijuana Prohibition, claiming that hemp was on the verge of becoming a super crop. These articles, which appeared in well-respected magazines, praised the usefulness and potential of hemp. 'Hemp can be used to produce more than 25,000 products', and 'hemp will prove, for both farmer and public, the most profitable and desirable crop that can be grown.' This was the first time that 'billion dollar' was used to describe the value of a crop. Less than one year after these articles were written the Marijuana Prohibition took effect. To what extent a conspiracy was involved is still being debated, but the important thing is that for thousands of years, hemp was used extensively. Then over a short period, it became illegal in many parts of the world.

E Now, however, the focus is on the development of hemp as an industrial resource. Initially, a distinction needs to be made between the two types of hemp. 'Cannabis has evolved into two basic species. Plants grown for fibre and seed are universally called hemp. Cannabis grown for its drug content is commonly called marijuana or drug cannabis. Drug-type cannabis varies widely in THC content from approximately 1%-2% in unselected strains to 10% in the best modern varieties.' (as cited from Watson 1994). Hemp contains virtually none of the active ingredients of drug-type cannabis (THC). It is not feasible to 'get high' on hemp, and most marijuana produces very low-quality fibre. Hemp should never be confused with marijuana, as their roles can not be reversed.

F It is evident that hemp is an extraordinary fibre. Both stems and seeds can be utilised. Most significantly, hemp can be grown without pesticides and herbicides. The plant also has the ability to suppress weeds and soil-borne diseases. Based on the hemp industries which have been established overseas, there is a large demand for hemp products and hemp is proving to be a highly profitable industry. On an annual basis, one acre of hemp will produce as much fibre as 2 to 3 acres of cotton. The fibre is stronger and softer than cotton, lasts twice as long and will not mildew. Cotton grows only in warm climates and requires more water and more fertiliser than hemp as well as large quantities of pesticide and herbicide.

G Hemp can also be used to produce fibreboard that is stronger and lighter than wood, and is fire retardant. Unlike paper from wood pulp, hemp paper contains no dioxin, or other toxic residue, and a single acre of hemp can produce the same amount of paper as four acres of trees. The trees take 20 years to harvest and hemp takes a single season. In warm climates hemp can be harvested two or even three times a year. On an annual basis, one acre of hemp will produce as much paper as 2 to 4 acres of trees. From tissue paper to cardboard, all types of paper products can be produced from hemp. The quality of hemp paper is superior to tree-based paper. Hemp paper will last hundreds of years without degrading and it can be recycled many more times than tree-based paper.

H Today, industrialised nations around the world are waking up to the enormous potential of hemp. While some countries, like China and India, have never had laws against hemp cultivation, others are legalising industrial hemp after many years of lumping it together with marijuana. The products and fabrics that are emerging from the international hemp industry are finding strong demand in an eco-aware global community. Hemp is indeed an agricultural crop for the twenty-first century.

Questions 1-2

Complete the following table using **NO MORE THAN THREE WORDS** *from the passage.*

	Hemp	Marijuana
Fibre	strong and durable	___1___
Drug Content	___2___	up to 10% THC

1. ______

2. ______

Reading Passage 2

Fossil Birds Force an Evolutionary Re-think

A Archaeopteryx, the first known bird, may have flown, according to a new analysis. Some palaeontologists had doubted this, saying that the bird's flight muscles were too light to power it. They claimed that instead the crow-sized bird used its feathers for gliding or cooling itself, and was unable to launch itself into flight from the ground.

B John Rubin of Oregon State University, believes Archaeopteryx had the muscles of a cold-blooded reptile. These are more than twice as powerful per unit weight as those of warm-blooded animals, and may have allowed Archaeopteryx to fly short distances, he says.

C Rubin's theory is only one jigsaw piece in a new picture which is emerging of how birds evolved. Another piece has come from the discovery of a fossil bird in China, the size of a sparrow. The bird, which is only slightly younger than Archaeopteryx, lived in trees and was capable of true flight. Birds evolved from dinosaurs, but palaeontologists do not know precisely how. Archaeopteryx, which lived 150 million years ago, is an enigma, because it is part bird and part dinosaur. The creature's wings and feathers are those of a bird, but its skeleton is very much like that of a dinosaur. It has no breastbone to anchor flight muscles. Also, it has a long dinosaur-like tail, hollow one, which enables modern birds to fly.

D These features have led some researchers to conclude that Archaeopteryx could not fly by flapping its wings, but must have glided instead. Other scientists have objected to this, saying that a flightless Archaeopteryx did not make evolutionary sense, and could not have survived on the ground. Rubin believes the puzzle can be solved if Archaeopteryx had the same type of muscles as a modern reptile. It would still have lacked the endurance of a modern bird, says Rubin, but it would have been able to fly between 1.5 and 2 kilometres without stopping. According to Rubin, such a short-distance flyer makes more ecological sense than a warm-blooded Archaeopteryx which was unable to take off from the ground.

E Now, with the discovery of a fossil bird in northeastern China, palaeontologists have a further piece that may enable them to complete the puzzle of avian evolution. The bird, found by a 10-year-old boy and as yet without a name, is the first evidence that fairly modern tree-perching birds had evolved by 135 million years ago, 15 million years after Archaeopteryx. Archaeopteryx had flat claws, which mark it as a ground dweller. But the sparrow-sized Chinese bird had an opposable first digit and slender, curved claws. According to Paul Sereno of the University of Chicago, these would have allowed it to firmly grasp a tree branch. The small bird also sported a breast-bone, which could have anchored strong flight muscles. Sereno believes that the bird would have looked much like a modern bird.

F Sereno and Cheng Gangrao of the Beijing Natural History Museum, China, have studied the bird closely and found other modern features. For instance, the creature had a pygostyle—a fused cluster of tail vertebrae to which long tail feathers are attached. This gave the Chinese bird a centre of gravity in the wings, which is desirable for flight, says Sereno. The long feathered tail of Archaeopteryx, on the other hand, put its centre of gravity above its feet, which is a better position for a creature that runs on the ground.

G The Chinese bird retained some primitive traits, however. Its wings reveal small remnants of claws and fingers, and the bird may have had teeth. It also has stomach ribs. According to Kevin Padian of the University of California at Berkeley, these are present in Archaeopteryx and carnivorous dinosaurs, but not in modern birds.

H Rubin believes that the Chinese bird was warm-blooded, because its skeleton would have supported heavier muscles. He says that the advantages of greater endurance may have driven the gradual evolution of a warm-blooded physiology. Sereno thinks that birds evolved tree-dwelling features fairly rapidly, because that ecological niche was open and attractive. Although pterosaurs could fly and climb trees, they never evolved the claws needed to dwell there for long periods. Only insects had both flown and lived in trees before the advent of birds.

I The Chinese fossil also highlights how the patchy fossil record makes bird evolution difficult to interpret. It is one of very few terrestrial fossils from lake sediments. Archaeopteryx and most other bird fossils come from shallow marine sediments. Fossils of perching birds 125 million years old have been found in Spain and Mongolia, but the next oldest bird fossils are about 50 million years younger.

Questions 1-6

Complete the table by contrasting Archaeopteryx with the fossil bird discovered in China. Choose ***NO MORE THAN THREE WORDS*** *from the passage for each answer. Write your answers in boxes 1-6 on your answer sheet.*

Bird	Dwelling place	Claws	Size	Centre of gravity	Fossil
Archaeopteryx	***Example*** Ground	2	4	Above its feet	6
Chinese bird	1	3	Sparrow	5	Lake sediments

1.
2.
3.
4.
5.
6.

Reading Passage 3

Industrialisation Brought about by Tea and Beer

A Alan Macfarlane thinks he could rewrite history. The professor of anthropological science at King's College, Cambridge has, like other historians, spent decades trying to understand the enigma of the Industrial Revolution. Why did this particular important event—the world-changing birth of industry—happen in Britain? And why did it happen at the end of the 18th century?

B Macfarlane compares the question to a puzzle. He claims that there were about 20 different factors and all of them needed to be present before the revolution could happen. The chief conditions are to be found in history textbooks. For industry to 'take off', there needed to be the technology and power to drive factories, large urban populations to provide cheap labour, easy transport to move goods around, an affluent middle-class willing to buy mass-produced objects, a market-driven economy, and a political system that allowed this to happen. While this was the case for England, other nations, such as Japan, Holland and France also met some of these criteria. All these factors must have been necessary but not sufficient to cause the revolution. Holland had everything except coal, while China also had many of these factors. Most historians. however, are convinced that one or two missing factors are needed to solve the puzzle.

C The missing factors, he proposes, are to be found in every kitchen cupboard. Tea and beer, two of the nation's favourite drinks, drove the revolution. Tannin, the active ingredient in tea, and hops, used in making beer, both contain antiseptic properties. This, plus the fact that both are made with boiled water, helped prevent epidemics of waterborne diseases, such as dysentery, in densely populated urban areas.

D Historians had noticed one interesting factor around the mid-18th century that required explanation. Between about 1650 and 1740, the population was static. But then there was a burst in population. The infant mortality rate havled in the space of 20 years, and this happened in both rural areas and cities, and across all classes. Four possible causes have been suggested. There could have been a sudden change in the viruses and bacteria present at that time, but this is unlikely. Was there a revolution in medical science? But this was a century before Lister introduced antiseptic surgery. Was there a change in environmental conditions? There were improvements in agriculture that wiped out malaria, but these were small gains. Sanitation did not become widespread until the 19th century. The only option left was food. But the height and weight statistics show a decline. So the food got worse. Efforts to explain this sudden reduction in child deaths appeared to draw a blank.

E This population burst seemed to happen at just the right time to provide labour for the Industrial Ravolution. But why? When the Industrial Revolution started, it was economically efficient to have people crowded together forming towns and cities. But with crowded living conditions comes disease, particularly from human waste. Some research in the historical records revealed that there was a change in the incidence of waterborne disease at that time, especially dysentery. Macfarlane deduced that whatever the British were drinking must have been important in controlling disease. They drank beer and ale. For a long time, the English were protected by the strong antibacterial gent in hops, which were added to make beer last. But in the late 17th century a tax was introduced on malt. The poor turned to water and gin, and in the 1720s the mortality rate began to rise again. Then it suddenly dropped again. What was the cause?

F Macfarlane looked to Japan, which was also developing large cities about the same time, and also had no sanitation. Waterborne diseases in the Japanese population were far fewer than those in Britain. Could it be the prevalence of tea in their culture? That was when Macfarlane thought about the role of tea in Britain. The history of tea in Britain provided an extraordinary coincidence of dates. Tea was relatively expensive until Britain started direct trade with China in the early 18th century. By the 1740s, about the time that infant mortality was falling, the drink was common. Macfarlane guesses that the fact that water had to be boiled, together with the stomach-purifying properties of tea so eloquently described in Buddhist texts, meant that the breast milk provided by mothers was healthier than it had ever been. No other European nation drank tea so often as the British, which, by Macfarlane's logic, pushed the other nations out of the race for the Industrial Revolution.

G But, if tea is a factor in the puzzle, why didn't this cause an industrial revolution in Japan? Macfarlane notes that in the 17th century, Japan had large cities, high literacy rates and even a futures market. However, Japan decided against a workbased revolution, by giving up labour-saving devices, even animals, to avoid putting people out of work. Astonishingly, the nation that we now think of as one of the most technologically advanced, entered the 19th century having almost abandoned the wheel. While Britain was undergoing the Industrial Revolution, Macfarlane notes wryly, Japan was undergoing an industrious one.

H The Cambridge academic considers the mystery solved. He adds that he thinks the UN should encourage aid agencies to take tea to the world's troublespots, along with rehydration sachets and food rations.

Questions 1-4

Complete the table using **NO MORE THAN THREE WORDS** *from the passage.*

CENTURY	SOCIAL CHANGE IN BRITAIN	REASON	EFFECT ON POPULATION
mid 17th century	***Example*** main drinks were still beer and ale	hops helped to make beer last longer	no significant change
late 17th century	gin becomes more popular, especially with poor people	beer becomes expensive because of ___3___	mortality rate goes up
early 18th century	___1___ drinking starts to become widespread	Britain starts trade with China	mortality rate goes down
mid 18th century	decline in urban deaths caused by ___2___	___4___ water used for tea and beer; antibacterial qualities of tannin	infant mortality rate goes down by half

1. ______
2. ______
3. ______
4. ______

Chapter Ten
Cracking Short Answer Questions
简答题题型突破

内容提示

- 雅思的 Short Answer 题与同类英语考试的 Short Answer 题的异同
- Short Answer 题解题技巧点拨
- Short Answer 题实例讲解

特别提醒

- 如果你是 A 类考生，那么只需要对本章作简单了解，因为 A 类考试中一般不会出现 Short Answer 题
- 如果你是 G 类考生，则请高度重视本章的学习，因为在 G 类考试中，Short Answer 题占据相当大的比例
- Short Answer 题，或许是雅思考试中你最熟悉的题型，但是你千万不要因为熟悉它而忽视了对它的研究，因为 IELTS 考试的 Short Answer 题与普通英语考试的 Short Answer 题有着很大的差异

Part 1
Guide to Answering Short Answer Questions
简答题解题方法透析

一、题型介绍

在雅思考试的9种题型之中，Short Answer（简答题）可能是你最熟悉的题型。但是千万不要因为熟悉 Short Answer 题的形式，而忽视了对它的复习。在G类 IELTS 考试中，Short Answer 题比重相当大，可谓占据了大半壁江山。

与一般的英语测试中常见的简答题一样，IELTS 中的简答题要求考生根据对阅读文章的理解，就题目给出的若干个问题，作出简单的回答。如：

Read Reading Passage One and answer the following questions using ***NO MORE THAN THREE WORDS.***

1. Where can you find the batch number on the jars?
2. What information do they ask you to provide about the jar of Chicken Curry you ate?

在这道例题中，题目要求在阅读完指定的阅读文章以后，回答这些问题，并且特别注明要使用"NO MORE THAN THREE WORDS"（不超过3个单词）。IELTS 中的简答题与一般英语考试中的简答题最大的区别在于，IELTS 中的简答题往往对答案有字数方面的限制，常见的字数限制有如下几种表述方式：

NO MORE THAN THREE WORDS
ONE OR TWO WORDS
USE A MAXIMUM OF THREE WORDS

特别提醒……

Short Answer 题是 IELTS 考试中最能够体现英国人做事一丝不苟的风格的题型。由于题目本身设定了答案的字数限制，在解答 Short Answer 题时，你一定要小心谨慎，认真确认最终的答案应该是哪几个单词。请记住，你的答案一定要精确到每一个单词！

二、题型要求

Short Answer 题不仅要求充分理解阅读文章，而且要求答案必须精确。雅思对考生的要求之高，在 Short Answer 题里得到了淋漓尽致的体现。

解答 Short Answer 题时，请思考如下问题：

- **题目问的是什么？我的答案是否答非所问？**
- **题目要求答案的形式是什么？我的答案是否在格式上和题目要求有所出入？**

三、题型地位

(1) 在 A 类考试中的地位

在 A 类 IELTS 考试中，Short Answer 题曾是必考题型，几乎每次考试中都会出现。但是最近几年，在 A 类 IELTS 考试中都没出现 Short Answer 题。

(2) 在 G 类考试中的地位

在 G 类 IELTS 考试中，Short Answer 题一直都是主流题型。不仅每次考试都会出现，而且每次考试中 Short Answer 题的题量也较大。

特别提醒……

在 G 类 IELTS 考试中，曾经出现在一场阅读考试全部 40 道题目中，Short Answer 题占了 23 道，超过了半数。如果你打算参加 G 类 IELTS 考试，请特别留意 Short Answer 题的解题方法和常见技巧！

四、破题原则

（1）直接定位答案原则

由于 Short Answer 题的特殊性，或许很难从题目中找到任何特殊的字符用来寻找答案，但是如果将思路转向答案本身，或许会立即感到“柳暗花明又一村”。例如：

题目 What is the average number of people you would expect to find in automobiles during commuting hours?

分析 从这道 Short Answer 题的题目中，很难发现任何可以用来定位的单词或词组。请从答案开始思考，题目问的是“What is the average number”，说明正确答案必定是 number（数字）。抛开所有的阅读文字，你现在需要做的，就是去文章中直接寻找数字，解题难度自然也就大大降低了。

（2）答案精确原则

IELTS 考试中的 Short Answer 题，十分强调答案的精确性。正所谓“失之毫厘，谬以千里”，解答 Short Answer 题时，稍不小心，就有可能全盘皆输。例如：

原文 Scientist explained that the surface crust of Mars is not formed of a network of plates，like the Earth's.

题目 Answer the questions below USING NO MORE THAN THREE WORDS.
What distinguishes the Earth's crust from that of Mars?

答案 （a） network of plates

分析 阅读原文，可以知道地球地壳和火星地壳的区别在于，火星地壳不是由 a network of plates（板块网）组成的，问题的答案自然应该是：a network of plates。不幸的是，如果你把答案写成 a network of plates，就不能满足题目本身对答案格式作出的要求。题目的要求是“NO MORE THAN THREE WORDS”（不超过 3 个单词），而 a network of plates 这个词组是由 4 个单词组成的。对这个词组稍微进行调整，省略冠词“a”，改写为 network of plates，就符合题目的要求了。

特别提醒……

一个并不起眼的单词“a”，却有可能彻底改变 IELTS 考试中你的答案的正误。Short Answer 题对答案精确度的要求，由此可见一斑。实际考试时，千万记住仔细阅读题目的要求，确保你所填写的答案的精确性。

五、Short Answer 题正确答案的形式

(1) 数字后面必须加单位

在 IELTS 考试中，稍微疏忽，就会忘记在数字后面还应该加单位。常见的单位：

时间	a.m. / p.m. / o'clock
货币	\$ (dollar) / £ (pound)
距离	km (kilometers)
面积	km^2 (square kilometers)
质量	kg (kilogram)

特别提醒……

在 IELTS 考试中，你或许还会犯一个非常低级的错误，那就是在阅读文章中找到答案为数字“7 million”后，就兴奋地在答题卡上填写数字“7”，却忽视了“7”后面应该有一个非常关键的单词——million！

(2) 答案不需要使用大写字母，但专有名词除外

(3) 答案切记要满足题目的字数限制

字数限制，是 IELTS 考试中的 Short Answer 题与一般英语考试中的 Short Answer 题最大的区别所在。在 IELTS 考试中，如果发现你的答案已经超过了题目的字数限制，那么就要省略一些修饰成分，留下答案的核心词。

特别提醒……

在 IELTS 考试中你很有可能遇到这样的情况，题目要求答案不能超过 3 个单词，而你找到的答案却恰恰多出一个单词。请你注意，这样的情况下，如果你找出来的答案中有冠词，就可以果断地把冠词去掉，或是加上括号。例如，你的答案是 a set of machine，而题目却要求答案 NO MORE THAN THREE WORDS，那么你可以直接把答案改写为 set of machine，或是（a）set of machine。请记住，英语中只有三个冠词：a、an 以及 the。

（4）答案都来自阅读原文，很少需要考生自己写答案

在 IELTS 考试中，一定要看清楚题目本身的要求。如果题目要求使用阅读文章中出现的单词来回答，就必须使用阅读文章中出现的单词，即使使用该单词的同义词，也将被视为错误答案。

题目 Answer the following questions with NO MORE THAN THREE WORDS taken from the reading passage.

How many people were evacuated from the mountain before Mount St. Helens erupted?

原文 Urgent steps were taken by the local government to evacuate the local population around the mount. Five hundred people were evacuated from the mountain before it erupted suddenly in the morning.

答案 Five hundred

分析 这道 Short Answer 题的答案为：Five hundred。题目的说明中指出，必须使用“NO MORE THAN THREE WORDS taken from the reading passage”，即答案首先不可以超过 3 个单词，其次必须是阅读文章中的单词，不能是同义词。因此，如果把答案写成阿拉伯数字“500”，就是错误答案，因为阿拉伯数字“500”并不存在于阅读文章中。

六、解题步骤

第一步 仔细阅读解题说明，了解题目本身对答案的要求

在 IELTS 考试中，仔细阅读 Short Answer 题的解题说明，可以了解题目本身对答案是否有如下限制：

- 字数方面的限制 **NO MORE THAN THREE WORDS**
- 单词来源方面的限制 **With words taken from the reading passage**

第二步 仔细阅读问句，猜测可能的答案形式，或找出定位使用的关键词

在IELTS考试中，绝大多数Short Answer题，只需要阅读完问句，就可以推测出答案可能的形式，然后直接回阅读文章中搜索形式相同的信息。例如：

题目 What was the cost of the revised budget for the Sydney bid?

分析 这道Short Answer题问的是cost（费用），不难推测出正确答案不仅必定为数字，而且必定为带有货币单位符号的数字。直接回到阅读文章中搜索带有货币单位符号的数字，就一定可以找到正确答案。

特别提醒……

IELTS考试中的Short Answer题，如果你已经确定答案为数字，那么寻找正确答案的道路将因此而变得平坦了很多。不过请注意，Short Answer题中，如果正确答案为数字，一般在解题过程中会涉及到简单的四则运算。例如，文章中告诉你学校里女生比例为30%，题目却问你学校里男生的比例为多少。类似这样的简单四则运算，自然难不倒聪明的你，不过你千万不可以掉以轻心，因为大意而未能正确地回答。

在IELTS考试中，有小部分Short Answer题不能直接从问句中推测出正确答案的格式，这时就要从问句中寻找关键词，通过定位关键词来定位正确答案。例如：

题目 How will the electronic sniffer contribute to stopping terrorist contaminating the water supply?

分析 从这道Short Answer题的问句中，恐怕很难推测出正确答案的格式。因此，需要选定“electronic sniffer”这个表示名称的词组作为关键词，通过定位“electronic sniffer”来定位正确答案。

第三步 定位正确答案

根据第二步采取的策略的不同，需要定位的可能是：

- 阅读文章中符合正确答案格式的文字（如果已经从问句中推测出了正确答案的格式）
- 第二步中确定的关键词（如果无法直接从问句中推测出正确答案的格式）

第四步 正确书写所找的答案

特别提醒……

毫无疑问，如果你已经找到了题目的正确答案，却不幸将答案书写错误，那将是一件非常吃亏的事情！在将答案填到答题卡上的相应位置之前，请确认你的答案满足了题目中的各项限制！

Part 2
Analysis of Short Answer Questions
简答题实例透析

Reading Passage 1

Vital Role in World Airline Industry

A Telecommunications play a vital part in the world airline industry where there is a need for speedy contact over long distances, and where the sheer size of the number of people and freight being carried today would overwhelm systems lacking the most modem technology.

B Most of the world's airlines have highly advanced systems, although some of them have tended to be outpaced by the explosive growth enjoyed by the industry over the past decade, particularly in areas such as the Middle East, parts of Africa, and the Far East. Estimates made at the beginning of the 1970s of the number of messages which would be passed by 1980 proved in most cases to be far too low, with the result that there was a scramble during the late 1970s for new equipment.

C But while the equipment is available, the highly skilled manpower needed to operate it and to service it remains scarce for the airlines which have to compete with the many other users of advanced telecommunications. Most of the bigger airlines now have their own training schools, while the smaller ones send their trainees to schools such as that operated by International Aeradio at Bath. There is still a residual glamour about working for an airline for some recruits, and the prospect of cheap staff travel also attracts people.

D Airline communications break down into four main sections: radio, teletype, telephone and data processing. Radio is used for passing messages between ground and the airliners, although in remote parts of the world it may also be used for messages between various bases. Each operator will have a selective call band over which it can pass company messages to its crews in flight wherever they are.

E Routine low-speed internal company messages generally come over the company teletype system, but in most airlines they have reached such large numbers that they are distributed by computer.

F SITA, the internationai airlines communications consortium, and a similar organization in the United States, play a major part in this vast message-passing operation. Saudia, the national airline of Saudi Arabia, a medium-sized operator, passes, for instance, 30,000 routine low-speed messages every 24 hours, rising to 40,000 in 24 hours at the peak travel season.

G It is in the area of data communications that telecommunications have had, and will continue to have, the greatest impact on the airline industry, however. To take the case of Saudia again, the airline is to install its own in-house computer in 1982, but in the meantime 'piggybacks' on the British Airways computer at West London air terminal 3,000 miles away for its reservations, and on the Alitalia computer in Rome for its engineering inventory.

H The link with the BA computer BABS in London is achieved by way of land lines in both Saudi Arabia and Britain and in between by satellite, one over the Indian Ocean, the other over the Atlantic. Reservations clerks in Jiddah can interrogate BABS by way of their keyboards and have the answer back on their video screens in the amazingly short time of two seconds.

I When Saudia installs its own computer it will cope not only with reservations and the engineering inventory at present carried in Rome, but such extra tasks as payroll, finance, flight-crew scheduling, and flight operations rosters.

J Modern telecommunications help Saudia to answer up to 7,000 calls a day at its Jiddah office alone, 90 per cent of them being replied to within 20 seconds against an airline industry average of 80 per cent.

K Computer and telecommunications sharing is common in the airline industry.

British Airways' BABS, in fact, holds the schedules for, 70 airlines, in addition to its own, and also provides the airline with facilities for payroll calculations, pensions; accounting, statistics, cost control, component control, flight planning and in-flight data analysis.

L The system uses a vast network of communications links around the world consisting of more than 50 computers linked to 3,500 visual displays units and 1,000 teleprinters in 650 cities. The network extends from Oslo and Helsinki in the north to Cape Town and Christchurch in the south, and east to west from Tokyo and Auckland to Los Angeles. BA has worked out that BABS represented 800 man-years to establish.

M The system is equipped with four million characters of highspeed memory and more than 4,200 million characters of backing storage. BABS holds details of every flight for a year ahead and full booking details for some 15 million passengers a year.

N The airline's offices, and those of many others, have access to the BABS system through a worldwide communications network of satellite, cable and microwave links operating at speeds of up to 9,600 bits per second.

O Offices in such faraway places as Australia and South Africa receive replies to booking requests in two or three seconds. The computers in London handle such inquiries at the rate of 60 per second at peak times, and in total the system handles more than 1,250,000 messages every day. BA offices around the world can also make hotel reservations for passengers through BABS and can ask it for package-tour bookings and fares quotations. Later this year each office with a computer terminal will be able to use the computer in London for the construction of fares, in the past a laborious and time-consuming task with enormous possibilities for error and therefore loss of revenue for the airlines.

P Modern telecommunications are expensive to develop and install, but once in and operating they have great potential for saving money as well as time. British Airways has estimated that its BABS system has reduced the costs per passenger for reservations from 12p in 1973 to 9.4p today. When the effect of inflation is considered, the latter figure drops still further to 5.9p.

Questions 1-6

Answer the following questions using ***NO MORE THAN THREE WORDS*** *from the passage.*

What are the four main sections of airline communications?

1. ______
2. ______
3. ______
4. ______
5. What is radio used for? ______
6. What is teletype used for? ______

答案透析

Questions 1-4

答案 1. radio 2. teletype 3. telephone 4. data processing

分析 直接从这道 Short Answer 题的问句中推测出正确答案的形式是比较困难的，因此需要考虑寻找关键词定位正确答案。

选定题目中出现的 airline communications 作为定位的关键词，在阅读文章 D 段首句中可以找到这个词组：Airline communications break down into four main sections：radio，teletype，telephone and data processing.（航班通讯可以分为四个部分：无线电、电传、电话和数据处理。）显而易见，题目的答案为：radio、teletype、telephone 和 data processing。

Question 5

答案 passing messages

分析 要从这道 Short Answer 题的问句中推测出答案的形式似乎非常困难，因此需要考虑寻找关键词。选定问句中的单词 radio 作为关键词，很快可以找到 radio 位于阅读文章 D 段的第 2 句话：Radio is used for passing messages between ground and the airliners，…（无线电被用在地面和飞机之间传输信息，……）显然正确答案为：Passing messages。

Question 6

答案 come over messages

分析 从这道 Short Answer 题的问句中，很难推测出答案的形式，因此需要考虑寻找关键词。选定问句中的单词 teletype 作为关键词，很快可以找到 teletype 位于阅读文章 E 段的第 1 句话：Routine low-speed internal company messages generally come over the company teletype system，…（公司内部的信号通常使用公司的电子信号系统来传递，……）显然正确答案为：come over messages。

特别提醒……

这篇阅读文章的阅读量巨大，如果你逐字阅读，很有可能耗费大量时间，导致无法完成其他考题。在 IETLS 考试中，如果你能够采用分析中所使用的定位关键词的方法来解答 Short Answer 题，不仅可以节约大量宝贵的阅读时间，而且还巧妙地躲避了阅读文章中一些难度较大的语句，自然会如虎添翼，事半功倍！

Reading Passage 2

Model Atmosphere Show Signs of Life

A Life could exist on planets that are much farther from their stars than the Earth is from the Sun. Planetary scientists at NASA's Ames Research Center in California have developed models for climates on other planets that make the existence of life in other solar systems much more likely.

B The scientists, James Kasting, O. Brian Toon and James Pollack, have increased by more than 75 million kilometers the distance an Earth-sized planet may be from a star and yet support life. The atmosphere on such a planet could be unlikely to support human life, but it could support some forms of life, according to the researchers. 'We're saying that these planets may be habitable, but not necessarily inhabited,' Kasting, an atmospheric physicist, told *New Scientist.*

C The models suggest that the concentrations of carbon dioxide in the atmosphere would be enough to warm planets and prevent water from freezing as far away as the orbit of Mars from the Sun an average distance of 228 million kilometres. The average distance of Earth from the Sun is 150 million kilometres.

D In the past, scientists doubted that 'civilizations' could exist in other solar systems because the chance of an Earth-like planet evolving is slim. Michael Hart of NASA's Goddard Space Flight Center in Maryland has calculated that if the Earth were 5 per cent closer to the Sun, its oceans would evaporate, or if it were 1 per cent farther away, glaciation would take over. Hart's work suggests that only a narrow range of orbits—within a few million kilometers either side of the Earth's orbit of the Sun—would provide a habitable environment in another solar system.

E But the scientists at Ames have pushed the range of orbits for Earth-like planets by more than 50 per cent. Habitable planets could be found from 0.95 to 1.5 astronomical units, they say. One astronomical unit (AU) is the distance from the Earth to the Sun. 1.5 AU is about the distance from the Sun to Mars.

F The work at Ames might also help to explain what planetary scientists call the 'Goldilocks paradox'. Earth and its two neighbouring planets, Mars and Venus, were formed at the same time, about 4.6 billion years ago, from the same ingredients, including water, carbon dioxide and nitrogen. But only Earth developed life. Mars is too cold. Venus is too hot, but Earth is just right, like Goldilock's porridge.

G The scientists say that earlier models, including Hart's, failed to include the stabilizing effect of the exchange of carbon dioxide between the atmosphere and the silicate rocks in the Earth's crust. This exchange helps to regulate atmospheric and surface temperatures. Exchange of CO_2 also regulated temperatures in the early history of Venus and Mars before Venus became too hot and Mars became too cold.

H In its first few hundred million years, Venus may have had a thin atmosphere and hot oceans, like the Earth, that were capable of supporting life. The scientists have developed a new model called 'wet greenhouse' to explain how Venus evolved into its current hell-like state where clouds of sulphuric acid fill the sky and surface temperatures reach 460℃. The model challenges the generally accepted 'runaway greenhouse' model that Fred Hoyle first suggested in the 1950s.

I According to the 'runaway greenhouse', Venus has always had a heavy atmosphere which traps the Sun's heat. In primordial times, the atmosphere was a mix of water vapour and CO_2. The water vapour would have risen to the upper atmosphere, well above the level at which water condenses. Ultraviolet radiation from the magnetically active young Sun would have split the water molecules into hydrogen and oxygen and the hydrogen would have escaped into space. The result would be a dry planet, with no oceans and high concentrations of CO_2 in the atmosphere.

J But, Say Kasting and his colleagues, there are two problems with this model. Where is the oxygen stored and why is there no surplus water? Escape of hydrogen from the stratosphere would have ceased when the level of water vapour in the lower atmosphere reached about 20 per cent of saturation. The stratosphere would have become dry but water should have remained in the Venusian atmosphere.

K By adding a mechanism to recycle CO_2 on early Venus as happens today on Earth—the two objections can be met. The water carried by the lumps of rock from which Venus formed could well have condensed out to form oceans with at least one-tenth of the volume of those currently on Earth. The oceans were hot, about 100 ℃, but the pressure of the atmosphere would have prevented excessive evaporation.

L An exchange of CO_2 occurred for several hundred million years between the atmosphere and carbonate rocks on the surface of the planet. The process, known as 'weathering', reduced the density of the Venusian atmosphere to about that of the Earth. The thinner atmosphere allowed most of the hydrogen to escape. The remainder escaped more slowly over the next few billion years, so that Venus now has about 100,000 times less water than Earth. According to Kasting and his colleagues the early interaction between the atmosphere and the surface rocks may also have locked up most of the planet's oxygen.

M After the water was gone, exchange of CO_2 would have ceased and the level of CO_2 in the atmosphere would have risen causing a severe 'greenhouse' effect.

Clouds of sulphuric acid would also have evolved. On Mars, according to the model, carbonates were recycled for about a billion years but eventually the exchange broke down because the planet was too small to retain its internal heat. The CO_2 has become trapped in carbonate rocks. The thin atmosphere caused the planet's surface to freeze.

Questions 1-5

Answer the following questions using **NO MORE THAN THREE WORDS** *from the passage.*

List the three elements that were formed on the Earth 4.6 billion years ago.

1.

2.

3.

4. What helps regulate atmospheric exchange and surface temperature?

5. What was the effect of "weathering" on venus?

答案透析

Questions 1-3

答案 1. water 2. carbon dioxide 3. nitrogen

分析 从这道 Short Answer 题的问句中，不容易推测出答案的格式。但是，你肯定会发现题目中出现了"4.6 billion"这个数词，选定"4.6 billion"作为关键词，通过定位"4.6 billion"来定位正确答案。

"4.6 billion"位于阅读文章 F 段的第 2 句话：Earth and its two neighbouring planets, Mars and Venus, were formed at the same time, about 4.6 billion years ago, from the same ingredients, including water, carbon dioxide and nitrogen.（地球和与它邻近的两颗行星——火星和金星，都是在 46 亿年前同时形成的，而且它们是由同样的成分构成的，这些成分包括水、二氧化碳以及氮。）显然，正确答案为：water、carbon dioxide 和 nitrogen。

Question 4

答案 exchange (of) carbon dioxide

分析　从这道 Short Answer 题的问句中，很难推测出答案的格式。选定 atmospheric exchange 或 surface temperature 作为定位使用的关键词，很快可以在阅读文章的 G 段找到这关键词。

仔细阅读关键词所在的语句：This exchange helps to regulate atmospheric and surface temperature.（这种交换有利于大气和地表温度的调节。）从上一句话中可以得知，此处的 this exchange，意指 exchange of carbon dioxide，因此答案为：exchange （of） carbon dioxide。

Question 5

答案　reduced density

分析　这道 Short Answer 题的问句中出现了带有引号的单词 “weathering”。选定 “weathering” 作为定位词，可以先在文章中搜索带有引号的单词。很容易发现，“weathering” 出现于阅读文章 L 段的第 2 句话：The process，known as ‘weathering’，reduced the density of the Venusian atmosphere to about that of the Earth.（这个被称为 ‘weathering’ 的过程，把金星大气层的密度降低到了地球的水平。）显然，题目的答案为：reduced the density。

Reading Passage 3

Survivor from the Sky

A In a remarkable documentary，*Wings of Hope*，German director Werner Herzog recounts the true story of an eighteen year old girl，the sole survivor of a plane crash in the Amazon jungle in 1971. Twenty-nine years later，Herzog returns to the jungle with Juliane Koepke，now a 47 year old biologist，and she tells her amazing story on film.

B Juliane had just graduated from high school in Lima，Peru and，with her mother，was flying out to spend Christmas at her father's research station in the jungle. A half hour into the flight they encountered a horrific storm. In the midst of wild turbulence, the plane was struck by lightning and fell into a nosedive. Passengers screamed as baggage flew around the compartmen. Then the plane broke into pieces and suddenly Juliane found herself outside free-falling 30,000 feet. 'I was suspended in mid-air, still in my seat. It wasn't so much that I had left the plane but that the plane had left me. It simply wasn't there any more. I was all alone with my row of seats', says Julianel, 'I sailed on through the air, then I tumbled into a fall, The seatbelt squeezed my stomach and I couldn't breathe any more.' Before she lost consciousness, Juliane saw the dense jungle below, 'a deep green, like broccoli', with no clearings for hundreds of miles.

C Somehow, miraculously, Juliane survived that fall from the sky. In the film, she speculates on a number of factors which may have combined to save her. First, the storm had produced a strong updraft from the thunder clouds. Secondly, being strapped into a row of seats, she was aware of falling in a spiralling movement, like a maple seed pod. Then, hitting the canopy of trees, she tumbled through a maze of vines which slowed her landing in deep mud.

D But surviving the fall, though miraculous in itself, was just the beginning. When Juliane awoke hours later, wet and covered with mud, she was still strapped to her seat. Staggering to her feet, she assessed her injuries: a fractured bone in the neck. concussion and deep cuts in her leg and back. She was also in shock, lost and totally alone in the Amazon jungle.

E No doubt it was her familiarity with the wilderness that enabled her to cope. Her parents were biologists and Juliane had grown up in the jungle. She realised her only hope was to follow a little stream of water nearby, trusting that it would eventually lead to a larger river and rescue. With noe provisions, dressed in the miniskirt she had worn on the plane and wearing just one shoe, she set off through the jungle. She passed broken fragments from the plane—a wheel, an engine. 'Initially, I saw planes circling above me, but after a few days I realised the search had been called off,' she said.

F Surprisingly she felt no hunger but as the days passed, her health was deteriorating rapidly. The gash in her shoulder, where flies had laid their eggs was now crawling with maggots. 'I knew I'd perish in the jungle so I stayed in the water.' Walking in the stream however presented one risk more serious than any others. Before each step, she had to poke ahead in the sand with a stick, to avoid treading on poisonous sting rays, lying hidden on the bottom.

G As the stream grew into a river, swimming was the only option. However, here in deeper water, there were new threats. Crocodiles basking on the shores slipped silently into the water as she passed. Juliane trusted that they feared humans and were entering the water to hide. She swam on. On the tenth day. starving and barely coscious, she spotted a hut and a canoe. They belonged to three woodcutters working nearby. Rescue was at hand.

H For this 46 year old woman, re-living such a traumatic experience on film must have been a great challenge. But she shows little emotion. Flying back into the jumgle she sits in the same seat (19F) as on that fateful day. She is dispassionate, unemotional in descriging the flight. On the ground, when they finally locate the crash site, in dense jungle, Juliane is scientific in her detachment, looking through the debris, now buried under dense vegetation. She examines a girl's purse, the skeleton of a suitcase. Walking along the stream, she spots the engine which she remembers passing on the third day. Her arms and legs are covered with mosquitoes, but she seems to ignore all discomfort. Then, back in the town, standing in front of a monument erected in memory of the victims of the crash, entitled *Alas de Esperanza* (*Wings of Hope*), Juliane comments simply, 'I emerged, as the sole embodiment of hope from this disaster.'

Questions 1-3

Answer the following questions using **NO MORE THAN THREE WORDS** *from the passage.*

1. How old was Juliane at the time of the crash? ______
2. What is her occupation now? ______
3. What was the cause of the plane crash? ______

答案透析

Question 1

答案　18 years old

分析　阅读题目的问句，可以发现题目问的是"How old"（年龄多大）的问题，毫无疑问正确答案应该为数字。在文章中直接搜索表示年龄的数字，很快可以发现正确答案位于阅读文章的A段之中。

通过阅读 A 段中含有数字的句子，一定可以发现 crash（飞机失事）是在 1971 年，而在 29 年后 Juliane 是 47 岁（Twenty-nine years later，...now a 47 year old...），通过简单的四则运算可以得出，飞机失事时，Juliane 应该是 17 岁，所以答案为：18 years old。

特别提醒……

这就是一道非常典型的答案为数字的 Short Answer 题。在 IELTS 考试中，这样的 Short Answer 题往往就会涉及到比较简单的四则运算，所以要千万小心才是！

Question 2

答案 biologist

分析 这道 Short Answer 题的答案碰巧和上一道题目的答案在同一句话里，从这句话可以看到，Juliane 的职业应该是 biologist（生物学家）。

Question 3

答案 lightning

分析 从这道 Short Answer 题的问句里无法判断答案的形式，因此需要从问句中挑选出关键词。选定名词 "plane crash" 作为定位关键词在文章中搜索，发现 "plane crash" 在阅读文章 B 段第 3 句话中：...，the plane was struck by lightning and fell into a nose dive.（……，飞机被闪电击中后开始俯冲。）所以正确答案为：lightning。

Part 3
Exercise of Short Answer Questions
简答题实战练习

Reading Passage 1

UNICEF, Malnutrition and Micronutrients

A UNICEF has continued to be at the forefront of advocacy and support for the implementation of programs to combat child malnutrition. A condition for designing effective programs to fight malnutrition is understanding the causes of the problem and recognising how complex they are.

Micronutrients

B IODINE: Some of the most rapid and important progress in UNICEF programs is in the area of salt iodisation. The strategy of universal salt iodisation (USI) has been widely accepted in all regions, and the goal of USI by end-1995 has been met in virtually all of Latin America and in many countries in other regions. During the year, a number of countries with a high prevalence of iodine deficiency in which salt iodisation was previously thought to be virtually impossible, such as Pakistan and Indonesia, started to iodise at least half of all salt reaching consumers. To achieve this, UNICEF offices supported a range of innovative and flexible approaches, for example the establishment of an "Iodised Salt Support Facility" in Pakistan, to provide training, supplies and quality control to the 800 or so small salt crushers in the country.

C Enormous progress was seen not only in getting iodine into salt but also in the promulgation of laws to give teeth to monitoring and quality control efforts.

UNICEE, WHO and the International Council for the Control of Iodine Deficiency Disorders (ICCIDD) sponsored a forum in 1995 to consider the iodisation and monitoring challenges faced by countries in which salt is brought to market by many small producers rather than larger enterprises.

D A technical monograph on practical ways of monitoring salt iodisation programs was developed jointly with WHO, ICCIDD and PAMM and widely distributed. Many UNICEF country programs are monitoring household availability of iodised salt, utilising a simple test kit, as part of the Multi-Indicator Cluster Surveys being undertaken to assess progress in meeting the goals of the World Summit.

E VITAMIN A: WHO-UNICEF estimates now indicate that over 250 million children still suffer from vitamin A deficiency (VAD) with many millions more at risk. The known effects of VAD on the immune system and thus on child mortality make this a high-priority challenge for UNICEF. In 1995, UNICEF supported surveys of vitamin A status that resulted in widespread deficiency being recognised for the first time in Egypt, Sorm Africa, Kenya and Botswana.

F With support from the Micronutrient Initiative in Canada, UNICEF launhed proiects in 14 countries that will enable innovation in systems of distribution of vitamin A supplements and improvements in monitoring the mortality and morbidity impact of supplementation. A number of countries are building on the successful experience of Guatemala in fortification of sugar with vitamin A. Bolivia and Brazil both launched sugar fortification with vitamin A on a pilot basis in 1995. In Namibia and South Africa, the feasibility of fortifying maize meal with vitamin A is being considered.

G UNICEF supports dietary diversification and the consumption of appropriate fruits and vegetables as one of the most potentially sustainable ways for coinmunities to overcome micronutrient malnutrition. Research completed in 1995 with UNICEF assistance pointed to the need to pay further attention to the types of vegetables grown and the type of cooking in order to maximise the impact of home gardening on the vitamin A status of children. In Bangladesh, UNICEF is collaborating with Helen Keller International to assess the impact of a large home gardening project on the vitamin A status of mothers and young children. This information should help to ensure that future programs of this type are designed in the most cost effective way.

H IRON: The statement on strategies for reducing iron deficiency anaemia, developed and adopted by WHO and UNICEF in 1995, calls for general supplementation with iron in any population of pregnant women or young children where the prevalence of anaomia exceeds 30%. The results of research trials investigating the impacton anaemia of weekly iron supplements have started to become available. Weekly iron or iron and vitamin A supplements now appear to be a feasible intervention to combat iron deficiency anaemia on apopulation basis in some vulnerable groups.

I UNICEF supported a meeting, jointly with the Thrasher Research Fund and Cornell University, to explore ways of increasing the micronutrient content of foods commonly consumed in countries where micronutrient malnutrition is common. Plant breeders, soil scientists and human nutritionists met to consider the problem and agreed that the micronutrient content of foods had been neglected in the breeding of high yielding (green revolution) varieties of cereals such as rice. With the realisation of the tremendous importance of the micronutrient content of staple food crops to human development, plant breeders agreed that future breeding work should take micronutrient goals into account. The participants also called for research in other priority areas to exploit the potential food-based systems, including the development of programs and policies that influence the choices of consumers and producers to increase the supply and consumption of micronutrient-rich foods.

Questions 1-4

Answer the following questions using ***NO MORE THAN THREE WORDS*** *and according to the information in the reading passage.*

1. What strategy for overcoming iodine deficiency did UNICEF plan to have in place by the end of 1995? ____________
2. In which two countries was iodised salt thought unlikely to succeed? ____________
3. What did WHO, PAMM and ICCIDD collaborate to produce? ____________
4. What kind of common food has vitamin A been added to? ____________

Reading Passage 2

The Future of the Grizzly Bear

A Grizzly bears (Ursus Arctos) are distributed around the Northern Hemisphere, but their major habitat is North America. There are only about 58,000 left, more than half in Alaska. There were more than twice that number living in the rest of the continent two centuries ago, but by 1975 these had been reduced to fewer than 1,000, and listed as a threatened species. However, numbers in some areas appear to have stabilized and may be rebounding slightly, bringing the total to about 1,100.

B Apart from not being killed, the bears' main requirements are lots of room and lots of food. Their diet is very varied and they devour almost any source of nutrition, as they have to live on stored-up body fat for nearly half a year while hibernating in a den. So they are not fussy eaters. Salmon, which they catch with great skill in roaring rivers, is a favorite, but grizzlies also eat elk and other deer, hornet larva, roots and bulbs, gophers, horses and horse fodder, and even clams dug up on beaches.

C Over the winter, a large grizzly can lose 150 pounds, which needs to be replaced. Size and body fat affect how many cubs a female produces. For males, getting big means competing more successfully for mates. Observers have calculated that a grizzly can eat 2, 500 moths an hour, and 40, 000 a day. A month of such steady feasting could fulfill nearly half a bear's energy requirements for a year.

D Although hunting decimated the grizzly population in the past, sharp curbs have been put on both commercial and sport hunting in North America's wilderness areas. A bigger problem for the grizzlies is the restriction of their habitats by road building, both highways and logging roads in forests. A female grizzly will roam in an area 50 to 300 square miles, while a male grizzly can forage in territory of up to 1,000 square miles. The bears will seldom cross a highway, no matter how unfrequented, and so local governments have erected special 'wildlife overpasses' to encourage them to continue their normal wanderings.

E Grizzlies perform a useful service for the well-being of the ecological environment, according to scientists. As they dig in the ground, their claws turn over the soil, releasing scarce nitrogen and allowing wild seeds to lodge. Vegetation such as glacier lilies grow better and produces more seeds in swaths dug by bears. The bears, too, call eat and spread seeds from as many as 70,000 berries a day. In the coastal forests of the west coasts of the U.S. and Canada, where the rivers are rich in salmon, it is grizzlies which make possible the growth of what ecologists call 'salmon trees'. As the fish fight their way upstream, transporting tons of nutrients harvest from the oceans, grizzlies carry that bounty across the forest floor in the form of urine, feces and left-over fish carcasses. These nutrients, together with the nitrogen that the grizzlies scratch up from the soil, enable the 'salmon trees' to grow 60 percent faster. Over the centuries, grizzlies have thus helped to produce the temperate rain forests with giant conifers, able to produce more bio-mass per acre than tropical rain forests.

F To solve the problem of shrinking grizzly populations, wildlife managers are beginning to look beyond the traditional borders of the national parks. The Yellowstone to Yukon (Y2Y) Conservation Initiative is a joint effort by more than 200 U.S. and Canadian organizations. It aims to connect all the wild areas along the Rocky Mountains chain. Indeed, some scientists think that the long-term survival of isolated grizzly populations may well depend on the creation of such linkage zones, narrow strips of bear-friendly habitats that would restore connections between these endangered animals in North America.

Questions 1-3

Answer the following questions using **NO MORE THAN THREE WORDS** *and according to the information in the reading passage.*

1. How did Grizzlies assist the growth of vegetation? ______
2. What is the function of the linkage zones? ______
3. What is the aim of the Yellowstone to Yukon (Y2K) Conservation Initiative? ______

Chapter Eleven
Cracking Flow Chart Questions
流程图题题型突破

内容提示

- IELTS 特色题型 Flow Chart 题解题技巧点拨
- Flow Chart 题实例讲解

特别提醒

- IELTS 考试中，你可能会因为错误理解 Flow Chart 题的要求而导致整个解题过程的失败，因此请你重视本章的学习
- 从 2003 年 9 月开始，A 类 IELTS 考试作文部分 Task One（第 1 题）正式引入 Flow Chart 写作。本章的学习，不仅可以帮助你彻底攻克 IELTS 阅读考试中的 Flow Chart 题，而且可以助你作文考试一臂之力

Part 1
Guide to Answering Flow Chart Questions
流程图题解题方法透析

一、题型介绍

Flow Chart（流程图）题是 IELTS 考试一开始就采纳的题型，也是 IELTS 考试中最具特色的题型之一，用于考查考生对阅读文章中细节内容的把握。在海外英语语言测试中，IELTS 是惟一以流程图的形式考查学生对细节内容把握的考试。

如果阅读文章考到 Flow Chart 题，那么在阅读文章后一定附有一张标有箭头的 Flow Chart。整个 Flow Chart 所介绍的，往往是阅读文章中涉及到的某个特定的工艺流程，或是某个分成若干步骤的过程。在题目中，用文字来描述整个流程具体的每一步，文字描述中有一些空格，要求考生根据阅读文章中提供的信息，往这些空格中填写正确的单词或词组。例如：

Read the reading passage and use the information in the passage, complete the chart below. Write your answers in boxes 1-5 on your answer sheet. Use **ONE OR TWO WORDS** *for each answer.*

Waste paper collected from:
Factories
Retail stores
(1) ________
Paper converters and printers
Households

→

The paper is then
(2) ________

↓

and
(3) ________
by adding water

↓

Chemicals are
added in order to
(4) ________

←

The fibres are then
(5) ________

二、题型要求

Flow Chart 题考查的是考生能否清晰地了解阅读文章中介绍的工艺流程的每一个步骤。题目往往涉及一些非常具体的细节，因此阅读要比较仔细。

由于 Flow Chart 题涉及的往往是复杂的工艺，所以通常只需要对阅读文章中介绍的工艺有简单的字面认识即可，不需要对文字的意义有太深的理解。从这种意义上来说，Flow Chart 题对阅读要求高，但是对理解要求却很低。因为在缺乏背景知识的情况下，考生根本不可能完全理解阅读文章中所介绍的工艺流程。

三、题型地位

从整体上讲，Flow Chart 题在 IELTS 阅读中出现的频率较低，不属于 IELTS 阅读考试的主流题型。

IELTS 考试中虽然不会经常出现 Flow Chart 题，但是一旦考到，一组 Flow Chart 题往往至少有 5 道小题。因而在涉及到 Flow Chart 题的 IELTS 考试中，Flow Chart 题的比重相对较大。

四、破题原则

（1）与阅读文章顺序一致原则

Flow Chart 题以 Flow Chart 的形式介绍某种工艺的各个步骤，而 Flow Chart 采用的顺序，往往与阅读文章中的行文顺序一致，因此一组 Flow Chart 题的正确答案，往往在阅读文章中按照题目顺序依次出现。

Flow Chart 题的这种特点，将极大方便解题。在 IELTS 考试中，如果感觉解答某道 Flow Chart 题难度较大，可以先跳过这个题目，直接解答下一道 Flow Chart 题，然后再回过头来往前阅读，就一定可以找到这道题的正确答案。

特别提醒……

在实际 IELTS 考试中，阅读部分 40 道题目的答案在文章中出现的位置，并不全部和阅读文章的行文顺序一致。请你记住，只有 Flow Chart 题和 Summary 题，题目答案出现的顺序才会和阅读文章的行文顺序完全一致。

（2）答案集中原则

作者通常会用一个段落或相邻的几个段落来介绍一个工艺流程的各个步骤，而一组 Flow Chart 题通常是考查一个工艺流程，因此 Flow Chart 题的答案往往集中在阅读文章的同一个段落中，或是集中在相邻的几个段落中。

特别提醒……

答案集中原则意味着如果你找到一组 Flow Chart 题中任意一道小题的答案，你就已经找到了整组题目的答案。但是在极个别情况下，也会出现答案不集中的情况，例如整篇阅读文章就是在介绍某种工艺流程，而 Flow Chart 题的答案散布于阅读文章的各个段落之中。

五、解题步骤

第一步　仔细阅读解题说明，弄清 Flow Chart 的介绍对象

在 IELTS 考试中，很有可能因为没有理解 Flow Chart 题的具体要求，而错误地解答 Flow Chart 题。更为严重的是，有时候甚至会完全无法从 Flow Chart 本身推测出其描述的对象究竟是何物。正因为这样，在解答 Flow Chart 时，请首先仔细阅读解题说明，弄清楚整个 Flow Chart 介绍的是什么样的一个过程或流程。

第二步　从整个 Flow Chart 中挑选出一个关键词，定位关键词

解答 Flow Chart 题时，并不需要从每一道小题中寻找关键词。相反，只需从某一个步骤中挑选出一个关键词就可以了。因为 Flow Chart 题的答案分布顺序和题目顺序往往是一致的，而且答案往往比较集中，因此通过定位这一个关键词，就能准确定位整组 Flow Chart 题的答案了。

第三步　在阅读文章中出现关键词的语句前后按照题目顺序寻找正确答案

定位到关键词以后，根据题目顺序往关键词的前面或后面寻找其他题目的答案。例如：整个 Flow Chart 题涉及到第 11 至 16 题，如果已经定位出第 13 题的关键词，那么在阅读文章中，第 11、12 题的答案，一定出现于第 13 题答案的前面，第 14 至 16 题的答案必定出现于第 13 题答案的后面。

Part 2
Analysis of Flow Chart Questions
流程图题实例透析

Reading Passage 1

Doctors Divided over Heart Pills

A A group of drugs now being marketed in the United States under a variety of brand names have been proved to reduce deaths among heart-attack survivors by more than 40% over five years. The drugs are collectively known as statins, and are currently being taken by over 10 million Americans. Doctors are currently wondering if statins will be just as effective in preventing heart attacks in people who do not necessarily fit the profile of a 'high-risk' patient.

B The people the doctors are targeting for possible prescription of statins are those whose LDL, or 'bad' cholesterol, is somewhat high, or their HDL, or "good" cholesterol is a little low. Again, maybe they have diabetes, which commonly leads to cardiovascular disease, but do not yet show symptoms of the latter. A study report in the British Medical Journal concluded that statins could reduce by 30% the risk of dying from a heart attack, even among people with normal cholesterol levels and no signs of cardiovascular disease.

C Leading pharmaceutical companies have gone so far as to petition the US Food and Drug Administration (FDA) to allow consumers to buy some low-dose statins without having to first obtain a physician's prescription, or 'over the counter'.

D Statins work by partly blocking an enzyme, known as HMG, found in the liver that turns some of the food that you eat into cholesterol. The body, in fact, needs some cholesterol to produce hormones and Vitamin D. Excess cholesterol builds up in the arteries, reducing the blood flow and increase the danger of heart disease. By slowing down the function of the HMG enzyme, statins reduce the amount of cholesterol entering the blood stream, and force the body to draw on the cholesterol already in the arteries to make up the shortfall in its needs. Thus, there is a regular clearing out of cholesterol from the arteries. Doctors emphasize that statins work best when a person adopts a low-fat diet.

E There are, however, certain drawbacks to statins. Apart from the fact that they are expensive—about $3 per pill, and you would presumably have to take them for the rest of your life—they can cause liver damage or a breakdown of muscle tissue. Anyone taking statins needs to undergo periodic blood tests to check for signs of liver trouble. Most people on the pills report no complaints; those who do commonly list fatigue as the major side-effect.

F Companies manufacturing dietary supplements became interested in statins when it was discovered that Chinese red yeast fermented on rice contains small amount of the same active ingredient found in statins. They then made a dietary supplement containing this ingredient and publicized it as a wonder drug for preventing heart attacks. The FDA banned its sale over the counter, and the sides are still locked in a lengthy court case.

G In the meantime, another intriguing possibility has convinced doctors that making statins more freely available may be a good thing. Research has shown that taking an aspirin a day can reduce a heart patient's risk of suffering a heart attack. Would combining aspirin with a statin have a powerful effect in preventing heart disease? Similarly, many cardiologists are impressed by the ability of a group of drugs called ACE inhibitors to normalize high blood pressure and reduce the strain on the heart. Do they work better alone, or would a combination of ACE inhibitors and statins enhance their efficacy?

Questions 1-7

The flow chart below outlines how statins work, as described in the Reading Passage. Complete the flow chart. Choose your answers from the box below and write your answers in boxes 1-7 on your answer sheet.

List of words

FDA	hormones	"high-risk"	cardiovascular
LDL	diet	dying	Vitamin D
arteries	fatigue	heart	HMG
pills	draws on	doctors	physicians
shortfall	HDL		

How Statins Work

Example An enzyme in the liver turns some of the food you eat into ______.
Answer cholesterol

The body uses cholesterol to produce __1__ and __2__.

Excess cholesterol builds up in the __3__, posing a risk of __4__ disease.

Statins slow the action of __5__.

The body __6__ cholesterol from the blood to make up for the __7__.

1. ______
2. ______
3. ______
4. ______
5. ______
6. ______

答案透析

特别提醒……

你需要了解，流程图未必一定要标有箭头，例如这道题中出现的 Flow Chart 就没有标箭头，但是你依然应该从题目的解题说明里明确这就是一组 Flow

Chart。

事实上，这是一组非常典型的 Flow Chart 题，选定例子项中出现的名词 liver 作为关键词，根据前面介绍的 Flow Chart 题答案集中性原则可以知道，只要定位出作为关键词的 liver 在阅读文章中的位置，就可以在这个位置附近顺利找到整组 Flow Chart 题（共计 7 小题）的正确答案了。

在这道 Flow Chart 题中，你还需要特别留意，整个流程图的第一步，不是第一题，例子项才是这个 Flow Chart 真正的第一步。

在阅读文章中定位关键词的 liver，很快可以发现 liver 出现在阅读文章 D 段的第 1 句话中：Statins work by partly blocking an enzyme, known as HMG, found in the liver that turns some of the food that you eat into cholesterol.

Question 1

答案　hormones

Question 2

答案　Vitamin D

分析　确定关键词 liver 在阅读文章中出现的位置以后，只需要往后再阅读一句话，就可以发现第 1 题和第 2 题的答案了。第 1 题和第 2 题的答案都位于阅读文章 D 段的第 2 句话中：The body, in fact, needs some cholesterol to produce hormones and Vitamin D.（实际上，身体需要一些胆固醇来制造激素和维生素 D。）正确答案分别为 hormones 和 Vitamin D。

Question 3

答案　arteries

Question 4

答案　heart

分析　由于 Flow Chart 题的答案出现顺序和阅读文章的行文顺序一致，因此只要从第 1 题和第 2 题答案出现的位置向后阅读，就肯定可以找到第 3 题和第 4 题的答案。第 3 题和第 4 题的答案出现于阅读文章的 D 段第 3 句话中：Excess cholesterol builds up in the arteries, reducing the blood flow and increase the danger of heart disease.（多余的胆固醇在动脉中堆积起来，阻碍了血液流动，而且增加了心脏病发病的危险。）正确答案分别为 arteries 和 heart。

Question 5

答案 HMG

分析 同样由于 Flow Chart 题的答案出现顺序和阅读文章的行文顺序一致，只要从第 3 题和第 4 题答案出现的位置向后阅读，就肯定可以找到第 5 题的答案。第 5 题的答案出现于阅读文章 D 段的第 4 句话中：By slowing down the function of the HMG enzyme, . . .（通过减慢 HMG 酶的功效，……）正确答案为 HMG。

Question 6

答案 draws on

Question 7

答案 shortfall

分析 你只要从第 5 题答案出现的位置向后阅读，就可以找到第 6 题和第 7 题的答案。第 6 题和第 7 题的答案出现于阅读文章 D 段的第 4 句话的后半部分中：..., statins reduce the amount of cholesterol entering the blood stream, and force the body to draw on the cholesterol already in the arteries to make up the shortfall in its needs.（statin 减少了进入到血流的胆固醇的含量，从而迫使身体吸收已经在动脉中的胆固醇以弥补所需胆固醇的不足。）正确答案分别为 draws on 和 shortfall。

Part 3
Exercises of Flow Chart Questions
流程图题实战练习

Reading Passage 1

Paper Recycling

A Paper is different from other waste product because it comes from a sustainable resource: trees. Unlike the minerals and oil used to make plastics and metals, trees are replaceable. Paper is also biodegradable, so it does not pose as much threat to the environment when it is discarded. While 45 out of every 100 tonnes of wood fibre used to make paper in Australia comes from waste paper, the rest comes directly from virgin fibre from forests and plantations. By world standards this is a good performance since the world-wide average is 33 per cent C waste paper. Governments have encouraged waste paper collection and sorting schemes and at the same time, the paper industry has responded by developing new recycling technologies that have paved the way for even greater utilisation of used fibre. As a result, industry's use of recycled fibres is expected to increase at twice the rate of virgin fibre over the coming years.

B Already waste paper constitutes 70% of paper used for packaging and advances in the technology required to remove ink from the paper have allowed a higher recycled content in newsprint and writing paper. To achieve the benefits of recycling, the community must also contribute. We need to accept a change in the quality of paper products: for example stationery, may be less white and of a rougher texture. There also needs to be support from the community for waste paper collection programs. Not only do we need to make the paper available to collectors but it also needs to be separated into different types and sorted from contaminants such as staples paperclips, string and other miscellaneous items.

C There are technical limitations to the amount of paper which can be recycled and some paper products cannot be collected for re-use. These include paper in the form of books and permanent records, photographic paper and paper which is badly contaminated. The four most common sources of paper for recycling are factories and retail stores which gather large amounts of packaging material in which goods are delivered, also offices which have unwanted business documents and computer output paper converters and printers and lastly households which discard newspapers and packaging material. The paper manufacturer pays a price for the paper and may also incur the collection cost.

D Once collected, the paper has to be sorted by hand by people trained to recognise various types of paper. This is necessary because some types of paper can only be made from particular kinds of recycled fibre. The sorted paper then has to be repulped or mixed with water and broken down into its individual fibres. This mixture is called stock and may contain a wide variety of contaminating materials particularly if it is made from mixed waste paper which has had little sorting. Various machinery is used to remove other materials from the stock. After passing through the repulsing process the fibres from printed waste paper are grey in colour because the printing ink has soaked into the individual fibres. This recycled material can only be used in products where the grey colour does not matter such as cardboard boxes but if the grey colour is not acceptable, the fibres must be de-inked. This involves adding chemicals such as caustic soda or other alkalis, soaps and detergents, water-hardening agents such as calcium chloride, frothing agents and bleaching agents. Before the recycled fibres can be made into paper they must be refined or treated in such a way that they bond together.

E Most paper products must contain some virgin fibre as well as recycled fibres and unlike glass, paper cannot be recycled indefinitely. Most paper is down-cycled which means that a product made from recycled paper is of an inferior quality to the original paper. Recycling paper is beneficial in that it saves some of the energy, labour and capital that goes into producing virgin pulp. However, recycling requires the use of fossil fuel, a non-renewable energy source, to collect the waste paper from the community and to process it to produce new paper. And the recycling process still creates emissions which require treatment before they can be disposed of safely. Nevertheless, paper recycling is an important economical and environmental practice but one which must be carried out in a rational and viable manner for it to be useful to both industry, and the community.

Questions1-5

Look at paragraphs C, D, and E and using the information in the passage, complete the flow chart below. Write your answers in boxes 1-5 on your answer sheet. Use ***ONE OR TWO WORDS*** *for each answer.*

Waste paper collected from:
Factories
Retail stores
_____1_____
Paper converters and printers
Households

→

The paper is then
_____2_____

↓

and
_____3_____
by adding water

↓

Chemicals are
added in order to
_____4_____

←

The fibres are then
_____5_____

1. ________
2. ________
3. ________
4. ________
5. ________

Reading Passage 2

Development of Time

A We sense the passage of time in our personal experience and observe it in the world around us. We feel, think, and act in the flow of time.

B Einstein saik, 'Space and time are modes by which we think, not conditions under which we live.' Time—the time that we know through clocks and calendars—was invented.

C The measurement of time is an ancient science, though many of its discoveries are relatively recent. The Cro-Magnons recorded the phases of the Moon some 30,000 years ago—but the first minutes were counted auccrately only 400 years ago, and the atomic clocks that allow us to track the approach of the millennium by the billionth of a second are less than 50 years old.

D Timekeeping has been both a lens through which humanity has observed the heavens and a mirror reflecting the progress of science and civilization. Our millennia-long struggle to define and calibrate time through calendars and clocks has meant trying to bring the register of human affairs in line with natural cycles—of the Earth, Sun, Moon, and stars, of the physics of matter—but always, cycles. What vary are the cultural values and goals that dictate which cycles are significant.

E With a religious culture dominated by gods of the Sun and sky, and a civilization dependent on the annual cycle of a river, the ancient Egyptians were expert astronomers who studied the Sun's recurrent movements and their effects on the Earth very closely. By plotting the beginning of the Nile' s flood each year, a reliable harbinger of seasonal change, they measured a cycle 365 days long—a reasonable approximation of the duration of the tropical solar year. This measurement was later improved upon through astronomical observations of the star Sirius, which the Egyptians knew rose in a direct line with the Sun on one day each year. Astronomers found that each year, on the appointed day, Sirius appeared about six hours later than the previous year. This quarter-day difference led them to adjust the solar year to 365.25 days.

F Almost 2,200 years ago, the extraordinary Greek astronomer Hipparchus further refined the year. His adjustments centered on the equinoxes—the two points on the Earth's year-long orbit at which the Sun's apparent path crosses the equator, marking the winter-to-spring and summer-to-autumn transitions. Using nakedeye observations, he found that both points were shifting gradually to the west, at the barely perceptible rate of 2 degrees in 150 years.

G The discovery marked a watershed in the history of time measurement, for Hipparchus realized that the shift in the equinoxes meant that the solar year was slightly shorter than the accepted 365.25 days. By his calculation, the year was 365.242 days long: remarkably close to the present calculation of 365.242,199 days. Hipparchus also more accurately calculated the length of the synodic month (a complete cycle of the phases of the Moon). Again, his value of 29.530,58 is very close to the present-day value of 29.530,59 days.

H Unfortunately for civic and religious leaders of the next 1,600 years, Htipparchus's discoveries were virtually ignored by calendar makers. Julius Caesar's calendrical reforms in 46 BC failed to go far enough, leaving the calendar year at 365.25 days—more than 11 minutes too long. The calendar's inaccuracy went largely unchallenged in Europe until the 1500s, by which time the Julian calendar was 10 days behind the solar year. The shortfall alarmed Christian religious leaders because it meant that holy days, including Easter, were being observed at the wrong times. Finally, in 1582, Pope Gregory XIII officially revised the accepted length of the year to 365.242,2 days, adjusted the leap-year rule, and lopped offthe 10 extra days, creating in the process the calendar in most widespread use today.

Questions1-5

Use the information in the Reading Passage to complete the flow chart below. Write your answers in boxes 1-5. Use **NO MORE THAN THREE** *words for each answer.*

Procession of Time Measurements

___1___ recorded the phases of moon. →	Ancient Egyptians figured out the length of ___2___ year. →	___3___ further improved the figure to 365.25 days. ↓
	Now the accurate length of a year is perfected to ___5___ days. ←	Hipparchus refined ___4___ 2,200 years ago.

1. ________
2. ________
3. ________
4. ________
5. ________

Reading Passage 3

The Hemp Revival

A The hemp plant, one of the world's oldest industrial resources, is back. The rediscovery of this renewable resource is making it the fibre of choice for future textiles, personal care products, building materials, paper and fuel.

B Hemp has been grown for paper, textiles, food and medicine throughout human history. The earliest known woven fabric, made of hemp, dates back to the eighth millennium (8000-7000 BC). The majority of all sails, clothes, tents, rugs, towels, paper, rope, twine, art canvas, paints, varnishes and lighting oil were made from hemp. Hemp seeds were regularly used as a source of food and protein for centuries.

C Hemp's drastic decline in use and importance within a matter of fifty years is widely considered to have been brought about by the timber and petrochemical industries in America. By the mid-1930s. changes in technology were beginning to impact on the hemp industry. Mechanical stripping equipment and machines to conserve hemp's high-cellulose pulp became available and affordable. Timber and paper holding companies stood to lose billions of dollars if hemp were to be grown on a large scale. A resurgence of the hemp industry also threatened the emerging petro-chemical companies which had patented the chemicals for pulp processing. Newspaper articles began to appear, linking hemp with violent crime. The term used, however, was 'marijuana' to distance it from hemp used for industrial purposes. Because few people realised that marijuana and hemp came from the same plant species, virtually nobody suspected that the Marijuana Prohibition of 1938 would destroy the hemp industry.

D Supporting the theory that marijuana was banned to destroy the hemp industry, were two articles written just before the Marijuana Prohibition, claiming that hemp was on the verge of becoming a super crop. These articles, which appeared in well-respected magazines, praised the usefulness and potential of hemp. 'Hemp can be used to produce more than 25,000 products', and 'hemp will prove, for both farmer and public, the most profitable and desirable crop that can be grown.' This was the first time that 'billion dollar' was used to describe the value of a crop. Less than one year after these articles were written the Marijuana Prohibition took effect. To what extent a conspiracy was involved is still being debated, but the important thing is that for thousands of years, hemp was used extensively. Then over a short period, it became illegal in many parts of the world.

E Now, however, the focus is on the development of hemp as an industrial resource. Initially, a distinction needs to be made between the two types of hemp. 'Cannabis has evolved into two basic species. Plants grown for fibre and seed are universally called hemp. Cannabis grown for its drug content is commonly called marijuana or drug cannabis. Drugtype cannabis varies widely in THC content from approximately 1%-2% in unselected strains to 10% in the best modern varieties.' (as cited from Watson 1994) . Hemp contains virtually none of the active ingredients of drug-type cannabis (THC) . It is not feasible to 'get high' on hemp, and most marijuana produces very low-quality fibre. Hemp should never be confused with marijuana, as their roles can not be reversed.

F It is evident that hemp is an extraordinary fibre. Both stems and seeds can be utilised. Most significantly, hemp can be grown without pesticides and herbicides. The plant also has the ability to suppress weeds and soil-borne diseases. Based on the hemp industries which have been established overseas, there is a large demand for hemp products and hemp is proving to be a highly profitable industry. On an annual basis, one acre of hemp will produce as much fibre as 2 to 3 acres of cotton. The fibre is stronger and softer than cotton, lasts twice as long and will not mildew. Cotton grows only in warm climates and requires more water and more fertiliser than hemp as well as large quantities of pesticide and herbicide.

G Hemp can also be used to produce fibreboard that is stronger and lighter than wood, and is fire retardant. Unlike paper from wood pulp, hemp paper contains no dioxin, or other toxic residue, and a single acre of hemp can produce the same amount of paper as four acres of trees. The trees take 20 years to harvest and hemp takes a single season. In warm climates hemp can be harvested two or even three times a year. On an annual basis, one acre of hemp will produce as much paper as 2 to 4 acres of trees. From tissue paper to cardboard, all types of paper products can be produced from hemp. The quality of hemp paper is superior to tree-based paper. Hemp paper will last hundreds of years without degrading and it can be recycled many more times than tree-based paper.

H Today, industrialised nations around the world are waking up to the enormous potential of hemp. While some countries, like China and India, have never had laws against hemp cultivation, others are legalising industrial hemp after many years of lumping it together with marijuana. The products and fabrics that are emerging from the international hemp industry are finding strong demand in an eco-aware global community. Hemp is indeed an agricultural crop for the twenty-first century.

Questions 1-5

Choose a letter (A-F) from the list to complete the flow chart that shows the sepuence of events according to the passage.

A. Timber and petro-chemical industries threatened
B. Articles praise hemp as a potential billion dollar crop
C. Widespread cultivation of hemp Example
D. prohibition of marijuana
E. Newspaper articles link hemp to violent crime
F. Development of stripping machines

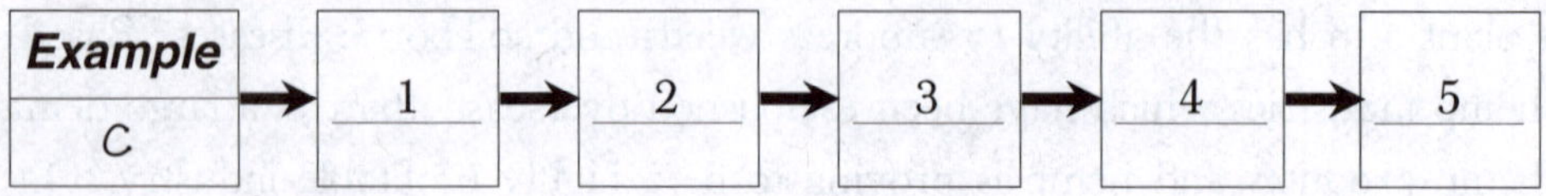

1. ______
2. ______
3. ______
4. ______
5. ______

Chapter Twelve
IELTS Mock Reading Tests
雅思阅读全真模拟试题

内容提示

- 2 套完整的 A 类 IELTS 阅读模拟试题
- 1 套完整的 G 类 IELTS 阅读模拟试题

特别提醒

- 如果你打算赴海外攻读学位，则需要参加 A 类雅思考试；如果你打算移民海外或赴海外参加短期培训，则需要参加 G 类雅思考试
- 模拟考试是 IELTS 复习的重要环节，是你考前热身的最好办法，请认真使用本章的 3 套全真模拟试题
- 解答本章的 3 套全真模拟试题的同时，请你留心记录你的解题速度，为真正的 IELTS 考试留下最权威的解题速度参考
- 模拟考试结束后，除了统计得分以外，请你务必仔细分析错误考题的失分原因；认真总结，你就一定能够获取真正 IELTS 考试的成功

Part 1
Mock Reading Test 1
模拟试题 1

INTERNATIONAL ENGLISH LANGUAGE TESTING SYSTEM

ACADEMIC READING

TIME ALLOWED: 1 hour

NUMBER OF QUESTIONS: 40

Instructions

ALL ANSWERS MUST BE WRITTEN ON THE ANSWER SHEET

The test is divided as follows:

Reading Passage 1	Questions 1–13
Reading Passage 2	Questions 14–27
Reading Passage 3	Questions 28–40

Start at the beginning of the test and work through it. You should answer all the questions. If you cannot do a particular question, leave it and go on to the next. You can return to it later.

READING PASSAGE 1

You should spend about 20 minutes on Questions 1 to 13, which are based on Reading Passage 1.

Questions 1-7

Reading Passage 1 has 8 sections A-H.

From the list of headings below choose the most suitable heading for sections A-F.

Write the appropriate numbers (i-x) in boxes 1 to 7 on your answer sheet.

NB There are more headings than sections so you will not use all of them. You may use any of the headings more than once.

List of headings

i	The feeding habits of feral cats
ii	A pointless campaign
iii	Cats: a dangerous pet
iv	A more realistic campaign
v	An increase in the garden bird population
vi	A false belief
vii	Ways of controlling feral cats
viii	Garden birds: a threatened species
ix	Natural predators of birds
x	The impossibility of controlling feral cats

Example	*Answer*
Section **D**	(viii)

1. Section A
2. Section B
3. Section C
4. Section E
5. Section F
6. Section G
7. Section H

Cats-scoundrels or Scapegoats?

A The campaign against cats has become so exaggerated it has lost its focus. Much energy that could be put to good use is being wasted on futile campaigns that do little more than aggravate cat owners.

B It is widely believed that because cats prey on native birds they could bring about their extermination. But predation seldom leads to extinction in such a simplistic way. If it did there would be no animals left in Africa, as those big cats called Lions would have eaten them all up.

C Enormous numbers of birds are killed by pet cats in gardens, it is true. But while this may sound alarming, ecologically there is nothing wrong with it—predation is a fact of life. Birds are killed in forests too, by a whole gamut of predators including snakes, goannas, falcons, butcherbirds, quolls, dingoes and even spiders. Pet cats are the urban counterparts to a range of native predators.

D Hunting by pet cats would only be a problem if the rate of predation, combined with other deaths, exceeded the breeding rate of the birds. This does not seem to be the case. Several studies show that urban environments actually support a higher density of birds than native forests, despite all the cats. This is partly because of all the garden plants with berries and nectar rich flowers.

E The native garden birds killed by cats are nearly all widespread adaptable species that are thriving in response to urbanisation. Some of them are probably more abundant now than they were before European settlement. This definitely seems to be the case for the common garden skinks that cats often kill.

F Feral cats are a much greater threat to wildlife than pet cats, and in some situ ations they are a major hazard. But not usually to birds, which they seldom eat. Studies of their diet confirm what cartoonists have always known: that cats prefer rats, mice and other small mammals. In a major article on cats (*Nature Australia*, Winter 1993) Chris Dickman stated: 'In most Australian studies, rabbits constitute the single most important prey.'

G I would suggest that foxes pose a greater problem, yet there is no passionate public campaign to oust foxes, presumably because it is obvious we can never eliminate the millions of wild foxes in Australia. Yet the same common sense thinking is not applied to cats. It is thought instead that, if everyone would only spay their cats, string bells around their necks and keep them in at night, cats would no longer kill wildlife. But what of the millions of feral cats in our deserts and woodlands? They are the bigger problem, but they are no more controllable than foxes or cane toads.

H To be useful, the anti-cat campaign should focus on specific situations where cats are a proven problem, and where something can actually be done about it. But to make the sweeping claim that 'Cats threaten the future survival of most wildlife', as the Victorian Department of Environment does in a leaflet, is to exaggerate the case so badly that it probably does more harm than good, by pitting cat owners against conservationists, instead of bringing them together as allies.

Questions 8-13

Do the following statements reflect the claims of the writer of Reading Passage 1? In boxes 8 to 13 on your answer sheet write:

YES *if the statement agrees with the writer*
NO *if the statement contradicts the writer*
NOT GIVEN *if there is no information about this in the passage*

8. The activity of predators, such as lions, causes extinction of other animals.
9. Other animals eat more birds than cats.
10. There are more birds per kilometre in towns and cities than in a forest environment.
11. The large number of plants in gardens has helped to increase the bird population.
12. The author believes that all wild foxes should be killed.
13. Cats are a particular problem in Victoria.

READING PASSAGE 2

You should spend about 20 minutes on Questions 14-27, which are based on Reading Passage 2.

Call for Online Essays to Beat Internet Cheats

A Academics are being encouraged to require all students to submit their essays and assignments electronically, to make it easier to beat web cheats at their own game.

B The University of Melbourne's academic board has approved a tough university-wide attack on the contemporary plague of electronic plagiarism. The Melbourne action follows other moves nationally that indicate the extent of university anxiety about online cheating in an era when a 'whatever you can get away with' attitude often prevails.

C The Australian Vice-Chancellors Committee is assessing plagiarism software that can detect whether student work has been downloaded in part or entirely from the net. And an Australian Universities Teaching Committee project is investigating the scale of the problem and issues in the online assessment of student work.

D The Melbourne academics want the university to set up its own anti-plagiarism website with constantly updated information on electronic checking software and an essay bank for cross-checking.

E The academic board's report on plagiarism says Melbourne has not tried to quantify the extent of electronic cheating, but states that it clearly exists and has the potential to undermine confidence in student assessment.

F The board says that despite existing anti-cheating strategies, such as regular rewording of questions and changes to required reading and research, the problem of electronic plagiarism is acute where large numbers of students are doing the same exercise or where students are able to submit essays on questions of their own choice.

G The board's report lists existing plagiarism-detection methods such as the University Of California's commercial website (www.plagiarism.org) where lecturers pay to have student essays checked against each other and a database of student papers and web materials. But Melbourne's academics believe it is possible for students to rephrase and restructure material to beat this type of system.

H 'Moreover, there is an increasing sophistication of electronic translators which paraphrase plagiarised material, hence making its detection more difficult,' the report says.

I 'This solution potentially requires the instructor to check up to five websites for each essay: a not insignificant task where large classes are concerned.'

J The Melbourne academics believe the knowledge that student work will be checked on cheat-detector websites will help to deter cheats. The report says a holistic rather than 'catch and punish' approach works best and it sets out procedures and penalties for students caught cheating, ranging from redoing the assignment to facing academic misconduct charges.

K Melbourne's head of computer science Leon Sterling said yesterday electronic cheating was an issue in computer science departments worldwide.

L ' Sometimes people just don't pose programming assignments because they worry it's too easy to copy. We think that's the wrong way to teach. But we regularly run comparison software to check if students' assignments are similar, ' he said.

M Professor Sterling's department already requires students to submit work electronically. He said it was often small, telltale signs that gave away the plagiarism-abnormal spacing, or changing the names of variables, but then including comment that referred to the old names.

N Professor Sterling said the university was making it clear to students that 'just taking someone's file, editing it and submitting it as your own isn't acceptable to us here' .

Questions 14-18

Several institutions are mentioned in Reading Passage 2. Which institution is doing each of the following? Classify the following as belonging to

UM *University of Melbourne*
VC *Vice Chancellors Committee*
TC *Universities Teaching Committee*
UC *University of California*

Write the appropriate letters in boxes 14-18 on your answer sheet.

Example	*Answer*
Academics want to set up their own plagiarism website.	**UM**

14. Taking a tough stance on plagiarism.
15. Is presently evaluating software for detecting plagiarism.
16. Assessing the extent of the problem of plagiarism.
17. Has produced a list of plagiarism-detection methods.
18. Has produced a commercial plagiarism-detection website.

Questions 19-24

Do the following statements reflect the claims of the writer in Reading Passage 2? In boxes 19-24 on your answer sheet write:

YES *if the statement agrees with the writer*

NO *if the statement contradicts the writer*
NOT GIVEN *if it is impossible to say what the writer thinks about this*

19. All University of Melbourne students now have to submit their assignments electronically.
20. University of Melbourne students will no longer be able to choose their own essay topics.
21. The University of Melbourne already knows exactly how much electronic cheating is going on.
22. Several University of Melbourne students have already been charged with academic misconduct.
23. The University of Melbourne plans a 'catch and punish' approach to students found plagiarising.
24. Most Internet cheats get caught because they make minor changes that alert the assessor.

Questions 25-27

Complete the notes below. Choose **ONE** *or* **TWO WORDS** *from the passage for each answer.*
Write your answers in boxes 25-27 on the answer sheet.

There are at least three problems with the University of California's commercial plagiarism-detection service:
Lecturers must ___25___ to use the website.
Students can alter an essay so the ___26___ cannot detect changes.
___27___ are constantly changing, making detection difficult.

READING PASSAGE 3

You should spend about 20 minutes on questions 28-40, which are based on ReadingPassage 3.

Food Gamble Divides the Globe

A As the millennium draws to a close, the world stands divided on whether the genetically manipulated dietary promises of tomorrow are a scientific triumph or Frankenstein in green. This could be the cue for Australia to leap into the limelight as the world's healthy food provider. But will it?

B The unrest about genetically modified (GM) foods began in the mid-nineties when in group, educated greenies began very quietly signalling warnings against the work of dedicated and serious scientists in the employ of large biochemical companies. The greenies were seen to have less credibility.

C But committed greenies do not give up. The result has been a marketplace revolt against the biochemical giants and their laboratory alteration of the DNA of living organisms to produce high yields as well as resistance to chemicals and disease.

D Recently the greenies gained an overwhelming victory in the United Kingdom when two of the world's biggest food manufacturers backed away from the use of genetically modified ingredients.

E With Australia's eyes turned firmly towards the United States these days, little note has been taken of the rising anxiety in England and Europe.

F A British Consumer Association poll showed that 92 per cent of people wanted GM foods to be labelled and a recent poll by the *Daily Record* found that '9 out of 10 shoppers would switch supermarkets to avoid genetically modified foods', some saying they were willing to travel double the usual shopping distance to do so.

G Yet here in Australia, floodgates have been open for GM foods and only last week with the closing of the date for applications for approval of GM crops, some 15 new ingredients found their way into consideration by the Australian and New Zealand Food Authority (ANZFA) . These include such things as potatoes, soy, canola, corn and sugar beet.

H This brings to 23 the number of engineered crops which could be present as ingredients in assorted manufactured foods available in our supermarkets-urttested, unassessed and unlabelled.

I While the biotechnical corporations which are developing GM products argue the immense benefits that disease resistant high-cropping and insecticide or pesticide-immune crops may offer the overpopulated world of the future, other scientists, along with environmental groups around the world, protest that these foods are being introduced to the market before their long-term effects have been properly assessed.

J The strongest thrust from the environmental lobby is at least for enforced labelling of GM products—since they may be found in all manner of very ordinary mass consumption items from baby foods to cooking oils. Often food manufacturers don't even know if they are using GM ingredients. The US for example, blends its natural and GM soya beans before export to Australia.

K Director of Australia's GeneEthics Network, Bob Phelps, lamented the last-minute flood of applications for approval by ANZFA saying the country had just lost a 'fantastic opportunity' both to keep its foods free of GM ingredients and be one of the countries to which overseas markets could look for all-natural crops.

L Commenting on last week's burst of last minute GM crop applications, mainly from American-based biochemical super companies, he said the Government was revealing 'a woeful lack of understanding of the world marketplace'.

M 'It is the strongest, most sustained and deepest reaction from the marketplace. These big buying consortia are looking to us for no-GM commodities in very large quantities. They are scouring the world for a very large volume and a sustainable supply. If Australia moves in the GM direction, it would be the stupidest thing we could do to our economy. The market is now wide open. It is the greatest opportunity. The global trend is towards healthier foods. It is not only Britain but all of Europe, most recently and, highly vocally Portugal, Italy and Spain as well, expressing the trend towards natural foods. Japan, too. This trend is retail driven. These new consortia have immense retail strength. And yet we don't have the message. This is a pivotal time for Australia. It is no flash in the pan.'

N Of course, ANZFA has extremely strict guidelines and there is no question that Australian authorities do not intend to safeguard the population as best they can in the testing of new products.

O 'Things are tracking at various stages,' Peter McMahon, food regulations adviser assures us. 'Europe approached this in a different way to us. We have to acknowledge that in attempting to regulate a new technology, standards have yet to be determined. Things are quite tentative at the moment. Governments and regulations are catching up with technology.'

P However, World Scientists, a group of 14 geneticists, immunologists, biologists, toxipathologists, virologists and agronomists, has called for a moratorium on GM crops and a ban on genome patents.

Q They have amassed examples of cross-pollination of herbicide-resistant transgenes to wild relative canola and sugar beet plants, 'creating many species of potential super weeds'. Doubts over the safety of transgenic foods follow revelations of animal feeding experiments such as the headliner rats in Scotland whose diet of GM potato caused internal bleeding. The Greens in Europe have lobbied the European Parliament about sustaining a ban on GM hormones injected into cows to boost milk yields. Cows have been observed to suffer increased foot problems, mastitis, injection site swellings and, with an increase in levels of insulin-like Growth Factor (which occurs naturally in milk), a suspected increased risk of prostate and breast cancer in humans.

R As one environmentalist put it: 'Genetic pollution cannot be recalled.'

Questions 28-32

State whether the following groups or individuals are:

F	*in **F**avour of GM foods*
A	***A**gainst GM foods*
N	***N**either for nor against*

Write the appropriate letters in boxes 15-19 on your answer sheet.

Example	*Answer*
Greenies	A

28. 90% of shoppers in the UK
29. Biochemical giants
30. The Australian and New Zealand Food Authority
31. Bob Phelps
32. World Scientists

Questions 33-36

Do the following statements reflect the claims of the writer in Reading Passaee 3? In boxes 33-36 on your answer sheet write:

YES	*if the statement agrees with the writer*
NO	*if the statement contradicts the writer*
NOT GIVEN	*if it is impossible to say what the writer thinks about this*

33. Genetically modified crops are greater in quantity and more resistant to disease and insects.
34. The United States has done the most extensive testing and so is happy to use GM ingredients and foods.
35. Australia has decided to remain GM-free so that they can sell their produce to Europe and the United Kingdom.
36. Milk from cows fed on GM food has been directly linked to cancer in people.

Questions 37-40

Complete the summary of Reading Passage 3 below. Choose your answers from the box below the summary and write them in boxes 37-40 on your answer sheet.

NB There are more words/phrases than you will need to fill the gaps. You may use a word or phrase more than once if you wish.

SUMMARY

Concerns about genetically modified (GM) foods began in the nineties with a small group of environmentalists. Over time increasing numbers of people have become concerned about foods genetically modified to increase __37__ and decrease disease.

Concern has been greatest in __38__ with the US and Australia continuing to widen the number of GM products regardless of the lack of evaluation and labelling. The environmentalists at least want products with GM ingredients to be __39__.

Bob Phelps of GeneEthics believes Australia is giving up a fantastic opportunity to not only have GM-free food for domestic markets but also be able to supply a world market in which demand for __40__ of GM-free food is growing.

While the ANZFA are in the process of testing and regulaing GM foods one group called World Scientists believe there are enough examples of side-effects in animals eating GM food that all GM crops should be immediately banned while extensive testing is carried out.

consumption	increased supply
England and Europe	labelled
growth	yields
GM-free	numbers
Australia and New Zealand	examples

Answer Sheet

Module taken:

Academic○ General Training○

Version number:

Please enter the number in the boxes and shade the number in the grid.

00	10	20	30	40	50	60	70	80	90
0	1	2	3	4	5	6	7	8	9

		√ ✕			√ ✕
1		○ 1 ○	**21**		○ 21 ○
2		○ 2 ○	**22**		○ 22 ○
3		○ 3 ○	**23**		○ 23 ○
4		○ 4 ○	**24**		○ 24 ○
5		○ 5 ○	**25**		○ 25 ○
6		○ 6 ○	**26**		○ 26 ○
7		○ 7 ○	**27**		○ 27 ○
8		○ 8 ○	**28**		○ 28 ○
9		○ 9 ○	**29**		○ 29 ○
10		○ 10 ○	**30**		○ 30 ○
11		○ 11 ○	**31**		○ 31 ○
12		○ 12 ○	**32**		○ 32 ○
13		○ 13 ○	**33**		○ 33 ○
14		○ 14 ○	**34**		○ 34 ○
15		○ 15 ○	**35**		○ 35 ○
16		○ 16 ○	**36**		○ 36 ○
17		○ 17 ○	**37**		○ 37 ○
18		○ 18 ○	**38**		○ 38 ○
19		○ 19 ○	**39**		○ 39 ○
20		○ 20 ○	**40**		○ 40 ○

Band Score		**Reading Total**	

Part 2
Mock Reading Test 2
模拟试题 2

INTERNATIONAL ENGLISH LANGUAGE TESTING SYSTEM

ACADEMIC READING

TIME ALLOWED：1 hour

NUMBER OF QUESTIONS：40

Instructions

ALL ANSWERS MUST BE WRITTEN ON THE ANSWER SHEET

The test is divided as follows：

Reading Passage 1	Questions 1–13
Reading Passage 2	Questions 14–27
Reading Passage 3	Questions 28–40

Start at the beginning of the test and work through it. You should answer all the questions. If you cannot do a particular question，leave it and go on to the next. You can return to it later.

READING PASSAGE 1

You should spend about 20 minutes on questions 1 to 13, which are based on Reading passage 1.

Does an Aging Society Mean an Aging Culture?

A Especially in the United States, the developed world's obsession with newness, progress and the future has always derived its energy from the numerical heft of each new rising generation. As recently as 1970, when a new youth culture redefined the American dream, the US median age was only 28—not much higher than the median (about age 18 to 20) of the typical pre-modern society. Today with the US median age hitting an unprecedented 35, the American public hears a lot less about the ideals of youth than about the worries of the middle-aged and old.

B And this is just the beginning: by the year 2030, the median age will reach at least 40 in the United States and at least the late 40s in much of Europe. Back when America's baby boomers were warning each other, 'Don't trust anyone over 30', Americans over 30 were in the minority. Over the foreseeable future, they are certain to remain in a solid majority By the year 2030, over one-half of all adults will be aged 50 and over—and thus eligible to join AARP (the American association of retired persons) . While this 50 and over crowd will outnumber all younger adults in the United States, in some European countries it will outnumber all younger adults and all children.

C What do these numbers mean for our culture? Clearly, they mean a much greater focus on the interests and activities of the old over those of the young. For decades, the mass media in the United States and around the world—TV, movies, popular music, and radio—have aggressively courted the all important under 50 demographic. How will the business, as well as the substance, of popular culture change as it becomes evident that the elderly represent the fastest growing component of thc total population and youth the fastest shrinking one?

D We should not be surprised to see pension issues eclipsing college issues on the front pages of newspapers. Yet the numbers may have a deeper influence. Along with experience and wisdom, it has long been observed that old age brings with it an aversion to risk and change. Cicero put it this way: 'young men for action, old men for counsel'. As people age, moreover, the formative era that shaped their education and outlook becomes ever more remote in time-making them seem, in a changing world, increasingly 'out of date' from the perspective of youth.

E As the entire population of the developed world grows older, the attributes of personal aging may come to define the tone and pace of the culture at large. Part of this tone may be a general slowing down of the pace of social life. As social scientist Andrew Hacker observes, 'Have you noticed how much longer it takes New York buses to get going, since elderly passengers take so much longer boarding and leaving? Or the wait at your bank and post office, when the aged person at the window doesn't understand what he/she is being told?'

F The impact of fewer young people

The shrinking of the average family may reinforce the aging of culture. In a world of steadily falling fertility, a growing share of the population will consist of first born and only children. First born children, many social scientists say, are typically more conservative in their social outlook than later-born siblings. According to historian Frank Holloway, 'First borns are less open to innovation, they tend to be more conforming, more traditional and more closely allied with their parents.'

G Another possibility is that smaller families may make society less willing to put its young at risk in national emergencies such as war. In past generations, families who lost a son in battle could usually take solace in the survival of his brother, and indeed governments have sometimes exempted only sons from war time service. In the coming decades, will developed societies be willing to place their scarce youth in harm's way to defend national interests?

Questions 1-7

Complete the summary of the first two paragraphs of Reading Passage 1.

Choose your answers from the box below the summary and write them in boxes 1-7 on your answer sheet.

NB There are more words / phrases or numbers than you will need to fill in the. gaps. You may use a word or a phrase more than once.

Summary

The ___1___ has always looked towards the future because most people were young. The average age of Americans in 1970 was ___2___ compared to ___3___ in developing countries.

In the future, Americans over 30 will form a ___4___. It is therefore likely that governments will be more concerned with ___5___ In 2030, over 50% of ___6___ of some countries in Europe and 50% of ___7___ in America will be over 50 years old.

developed world	the population	all adults	all adults and children
35	18-20	majority	minority
28	special interest group	the aged	developing world

Questions 8-13

Choose the letter that most closely describes the author's viewpoint A-D for each question and then write the appropriate letter in boxes 8-13 on your answer sheet

8. The aging population ______
   A. has changed tile face of popular culture.
   B. will change the type of music we listen to.
   C. will mean a rise in pensions.
   D. could change the face of popular culture.

9. An aging population may make society ______
   A. out of touch.
   B. risky and changeable.
   C. more cultured.
   D. remote.

10. According to the author the pace of future society is likely to ______
   A. speed up.
   B. remain the same.
   C. become slower.
   D. be difficult to predict.

11. The other factor which may age culture is ______
   A. reduced fertility.
   B. the length of time needed to perform simple tasks.
   C. more wisdom.
   D. an old fashioned education system.

12. First born children are ______
    A. less willing to take risks in time of national emergency.
    B. likely to support their parents views.
    C. always more conservative than their siblings.
    D. unlikely to be asked to fight in future wars.

13. An aging society is likely to happen ______
    A. in America.
    B. in America and Europe.
    C. everywhere.
    D. in developing countries

READING PASSAGE 2

You should spend about 20 minutes on Questions 14-27, which are based on Reading Passage 2.

Questions 14-20

Reading Passage 2 gives 8 realities to refute 8 myths A-H. Choose the most suitable myth for each reality from the list of myths below. Write the appropriate numbers (i-ix) in boxe 14-20 on your answer sheet.

NB There are more myths than realities so you will not use all of them. You may use any of the myths more than once.

MYTHS

i Current solar devices aren't effective; a breakthrough is needed.
ii Solar energy is too expensive.
iii More energy is needed to manufacture a piece of solar equipment than is saved in its lifetime.
iv Solar energy can only heat water.
v To collect enough solar energy requires large arrays of collectors tying up a vast land area.
vi Ordinary homes cannot be designed to use energy efficiently.
vii Solar energy can't be used at night.
viii There isn't enough solar energy to maintain our current lifestyle.
ix Solar doesn't yet supply much energy on a national orglobal scale.

Example	*Answer*
Myth **H**	iii

14. Myth A
15. Myth B
16. Myth C
17. Myth D
18. Myth E
19. Myth F
20. Myth G

Solar Energy: the Myths? the Facts!

Solar and other, renewable energy supply options have the capability to supply a large proportion of our energy requirements. The increased use of renewable energy technologies will reduce pollutants and greenhouse-gas emissions as the energy is derived from the natural source of sun, wind, water and biomass.

Renewable energy technologies already exist in a wide range of forms suitable for satisfying energy demands for many end uses. However, the implementation of these technologies is hampered by myths and misinterpretations.

This information has been produced by the Australian and New Zealand Solar Energy Society to clarify the issues and to dispel some of the more commonly held misconcep tions.

MYTHA

REALITY:

Solar (renewable) energy includes the production of electricity and heat directly from solar radiation for many applications. Designing your house to use solar energy passively can provide 60%-100% of your heating and cooking requirements. Photovoltaics (solar cells), wind generators and hydro can supply electricity for any use. Biomass fuels include wood, alcohol, and methane for heating, electricity generation or transportation.

MYTH B

REALITY:

Solar heat can be stored in thermal mass or thermochemical reactions so it is available on demand at any time. In a solar efficient designed house, the buliding elements themselves store the energy in their thermal mass for nighttime comfort and for cloudy days. Electricity from photovoltaics can be stored in batteries.

Wind generators run day and night. Hydropower, derived from the solar evaporation of the oceans can be used at any time, with water storage buffering the effect of river flow variations.

Solid fuel crops, biogas (methane) and alcohol fuels can be stored and used when needed.

MYTH C

REALITY:

Some solar technologies require no additional. costs, e.g., houses designed to make use of natural energy flows employ 'design', not devices or additional equipment.

Some solar equipment costs less than conventional alternatives to buy and install and also has lower running costs, e.g., solar pool heaters compared with gas heaters; solar clothes lines compared with electric dryers: and photovoltaic. panels for lighting or power supplies in areas too costly to connect to power from the grid.

Some solar equipment costs more up front, but is cheaper overall due to lower running and environmental costs, e.g., water heaters for domestic, commercial and industrial purposes; wind turbines for electricity generation and pumping.

Also, many costings are distorted to solar's disadvantage, e.g., solar water heaters would be even more attractive if you could get the same loan terms that the utility gets to build a power station. Remember, consumers don't have to pay for the power station when they buy their electric water heater.

MYTH D

REALITY:

While researchers continue to produce further improvement in a wide range of renewable energy technologies, the big breakthrough needed is equality of financing terms with conventional energy, e.g., Australia leads the way in solar pool heating. There is a wide range of Australian and New Zealand solar water heaters which are amongst the best in the world.

MYTH E

REALITY:

There is 25 times the yearly energy needs of Australia and New Zealand falling on those land areas on an average day.

The southern coastline of Australia and New Zealand is in the 'Roaring Forties', one of the best wind regimes in the world.

Biomass resources (fuel crops) could supply all of Australia and New Zealand's liquid fuels from crops covering 2% of the land area.

MYTH F

REALITY:

There is sufficient roof space on homes alone to produce the total electricity

requirements of Australia and New Zealand using existing photovoltaic technology.
Wind generators occupy only a small space for the tower with the rest of the land area being available for agricultural uses.
Solar supply allows decentralisation and the use of small modules which can be accurately matched to the load and which minimise electricity distribution.

MYTH G
REALITY:
Energy statistics tend to be biased e.g., they include energy used in drying food by oil fired driers, but ignore energy used in drying food in the sun. Even ignoring the bias in the statistics, solar (renewable) energy supplies 28% of the world's energy now, made up of 14.4% biomass and 7.5% hydro. In comparison nuclear supplies 4.4%.
Solar supplies all the energy used to grow plants, to evaporate water for rain and to maintain the temperature of the planet, all necessary for human life.
Hydro and geothermal power stations already supply 30% of Australia and New Zealand's electricity requirements.

MYTH H
REALITY:
A solar water heater will repay its energy 'debt' in only 6 to 18 months, depending on the location, and will last well in excess of fifteen years.
A photovoltaic module will collect over its operating life four times the energy used in its production.
A wind generator will produce the energy used in its manufacture in 1 to 4 years, depending on the wind regime.

Questions 21-23

Complete the sentences below with words taken from Reading Passage 2. Use **NO MORE THAN THREE WORDS** *for each answer. Write your answers in boxes 21-23 on your answer sheet.*

Using renewable energy can help reduce ___21___.
To reduce costs and conserve energy, houses should be designed to make use of ___22___.
The article suggests energy statistics are ___23___.

Questions 24-25

Using **A NUMBER OR NO MORE THAN THREE WORDS**, *answer the following* *questions. Write your answers in boxes 24-25 on your answer sheet.*

24. What are ***TWO*** natural sources of renewable energy named in the reading?
25. What percentage of the world's energy is presently supplied by solar energy?

Questions 26-27

Choose the appropriate letters A-D for each question and write them in boxes 26-27 on your answer sheet.

26. The central reason for using renewable energy sources is to ________.
    A. reduce the cost of electricity to consumers
    B. assist the industry to develop its technologies
    C. reduce pollution and greenhouse gases
    D. make use of available land
27. The purpose of this text is to ________.
    A. advertise available products sold by the Australian and New Zealand Solar Energy Society
    B. provide factual information about renewable sources of energy
    C. highlight the benefits of changing from electric hot water systems to solar hot water systems
    D. encourage Australians and New Zealanders to use less electricity

READING PASSAGE 3

You should spend about 20 minutes on Questions 28-40, which are based on Reading Passage 3.

What's at Issue Now?

Preface—What to Expect

Students, exposure to many contemporary social, political and moral issues occurs principally, if not exclusively, by way of the electronic and print media. Students often learn of and about these issues through newspapers, radio, television and now the Internet. Even if we put aside such problems as media sensationalism, ratings wars, certain dubious journalistic practices and the need to present information in short grabs of time, the media's role in the presentation of contemporary issues still creates problems for students, particularly when they come to think about issues more critically, as they are required to do as part of their studies.

Thinking about Issues

Thinking more critically about an issue involves thinking about the problems or kinds of problems that the issue is thought to raise, hence its status as an issue. For example, organ donation is a contemporary issue of moral and social import. It has been made possible by advances in medical technology. It is enormously beneficial for those whose lives can be extended by it. But it is also thought to raise a number of problems or questions. Should organs be donated to individuals who are suffering from self-inflicted illnesses? Should individuals be able to sell their organs? Should animals be cultivated for their organs? These are considered problems because they challenge accepted practices, values and beliefs. We don't think people should conceive of themselves as means for another person's ends. We don't think that people should conceive of their bodies—themselves—as a collection of essentially expendable and replaceable parts.

Second, thinking, about an issue involves tracing the arguments that are and can be formulated in response to the problems that the issue is thought to raise. These arguments are often extremely complex, involving lots of interconnecting reasons, assumed principles and theories, as well as detailed information.

Third, thinking critically about an issue involves evaluating these different arguments as either good or bad. This involves determining whether the conclusion is adequately supported by the premises—is the argument valid? —and whether the premises, are true.

Problems for Students

The principal problem that students encounter has two aspects. Students often find that an individual in the media appears to be arguing a point when it turns out that the person is just reiterating the same claim in slightly different ways. Conversely, when an argument is being presented, students find it difficult to identify it as an argument; they find it difficult to distinguish the premise from the conclusion and to trace the interconnections between them. Thinking occurs in language but not all language expresses thought—language can be used to persuade, motivate or inspire a reaction, for example—so there is often a gap between an argument and how that argument is represented in language. We find this each time we read a newspaper article or listen to someone speak, for only rarely does the structure of what an individual writes or speaks imitate the structure of their argument. The premises and conclusion can appear in any order, which makes it difficult for students to discern the structure of the argument. This is further complicated by the fact that not all premises of the argument are stated all the time. The premises that we do not state are the values, concepts and explanations that we take for granted as universally accepted or true. We assume that we all share the same values and so neglect to state that lying and killing are morally wrong. For example: in discussing gambling or retirement we assume that everyone knows what gambling is and what retirement is, and so neglect to define the sorts of activities that they are; it is possible to favour one view of punishment over another on the basis of an assumption about how criminality is caused.

How the Book Helps

Being able to identify an argument in a newspaper article, or what an individual says, is an extremely important skill for students to learn. The primary aim of *What's at Issue Now?* is to help students to recognise arguments about moral, political and social issues. This involves students being able to distinguish a conclusion from the reasons given in support of that conclusion. It involves them understanding the different sorts of reasons and how they operate in the overall argument. Some refer to expert opinion whereas others refer to statistical averages; some refer to moral principles or codes of conduct whereas others refer to human nature; some refer to analogous situations, and so the list goes on. It also involves students identifying the reasons that are assumed and therefore not stated. *What's at Issue Now?* teaches these, skills in three ways. First, the contributors provide simple and succinct summaries of the arguments connected to a particular issue. Familiarisation with these arguments enables students to recognise them as they appear in the electronic and print media. Second, the contributors critically discuss and evaluate the structure of these arguments. They define the terms of the debate, they identify assumptions and fallacious reasoning and so on. Third, they demonstrate the crucial role that our theories and principles play in our reflections on, and discussions of, moral, political and social issues. Students are able to see that although an argument might not be at fault the theory or principle that informs it may be.

Once students can successfully identify arguments they can begin to:

- Evaluate the argument. Is it a good argument or is it a faulty argument? Are all the premises of the argument true? Are all the premises relevant to the conclusion? Does the conclusion follow from the premises?
- Formulate arguments of their own. Do I have a view on this issue? What exactly is my view? What is the clearest way to state my view? What reasons can I give in support of my view? How does my view correspond with what

the experts say, or the information currently available? What objections can I imagine others making in response to my view?

- Think about the relationship between the language in which the argument was or is to be presented and the argument itself. What would be the most persuasive way to present my argument? What emotions should I be appealing to?

Questions 28 and 29

*Choose the appropriate letters **A-D** for each question and write them in boxes 28-29 on your answer sheet.*

28. Which of the following is NOT given as one of the problems with media?

A. Competition for audience B. Time limits on presentation
C. Questions of journalists D. Method of presentation

29. According to the passage, which of the following is NOT an issue of organ donation?

A. animals are raised just for their organs
B. lives can be saved
C. some people sell organs
D. some individuals have caused damage to their own organs

Questions 30-34

*Choose **ONE** phrase **A-H** from the box below to complete each key point below. Write the appropriate letters **A-H** in boxes 30-34 on your answer sheet.*
The information in the completed sentences should be an accuratesummary of points made by. the writer.
You may use any phrase more than once.

Example	*Answer*
A student is most likely to become aware of an issue when	**G**

A. he / she thinks it applies universally
B. the premises are not clearly laid out
C. it is not true
D. he / she can recognise and evaluate the arguments
E. it raises questions
F. students think critically about it
G. it is reported in the media
H. it appears he/she is presenting a new point

30. A topic becomes an issue when ________.
31. A student is beginning to think critically about issues when ________.
32. Sometimes a journalist may be repeating a point when ________.
33. A student will find it difficult to follow an argument when ________.
34. A person may not state a premise when ________.

Questions 35 and 36

Choose the appropriate letters ***A-D*** *for each question and write them in boxes 36-37 on your answer sheet.*

35. Which of the following is NOT mentioned as being one of the types of supporting evidence?

A. personal experience
B. expert opinion
C. human nature
D. statistical averages

36. Which of the following is NOT mentioned as being one of the teaching methods used in this book?

A. demonstration
B. exercises
C. summary
D. discussion

Questions 37-40

Complete the summary of the points made about language in Reading Passage 3. Choose ***ONE*** *word from the passage for each answer. Write them in boxes 38-40 on your answer sheet.*

SUMMARY

As well as expressing ideas, language can be used to ___37___ or ___38___.

Once students can identify an argument it will be easier to ___39___ it, and as they prepare to present their own arguments they will be able to express them in appropriate ___40___.

Answer Sheet

Module taken:

Academic○ General Training○

Version number:

Please enter the number in the boxes and shade the number in the grid.

00	10	20	30	40	50	60	70	80	90
□	□	□	□	□	□	□	□	□	□
0	1	2	3	4	5	6	7	8	9
□	□	□	□	□	□	□	□	□	□

		√ ×			√ ×
1		○ 1 ○	21		○ 21 ○
2		○ 2 ○	22		○ 22 ○
3		○ 3 ○	23		○ 23 ○
4		○ 4 ○	24		○ 24 ○
5		○ 5 ○	25		○ 25 ○
6		○ 6 ○	26		○ 26 ○
7		○ 7 ○	27		○ 27 ○
8		○ 8 ○	28		○ 28 ○
9		○ 9 ○	29		○ 29 ○
10		○ 10 ○	30		○ 30 ○
11		○ 11 ○	31		○ 31 ○
12		○ 12 ○	32		○ 32 ○
13		○ 13 ○	33		○ 33 ○
14		○ 14 ○	34		○ 34 ○
15		○ 15 ○	35		○ 35 ○
16		○ 16 ○	36		○ 36 ○
17		○ 17 ○	37		○ 37 ○
18		○ 18 ○	38		○ 38 ○
19		○ 19 ○	39		○ 39 ○
20		○ 20 ○	40		○ 40 ○

Band Score		Reading Total	

Part 3
Mock Reading Test 3
模拟试题 3

INTERNATIONAL ENGLISH LANGUAGE TESTING SYSTEM

GENERAL TRAINING READING

TIME ALLOWED：1 hour

NUMBER OF QUESTIONS：40

Instructions

ALL ANSWERS MUST BE WRITTEN ON THE ANSWER SHEET

The test is in divided as follows：

Section 1	Questions 1–14
Section 2	Questions 15–28
Section 3	Questions 29–40

Start at the beginning of the test and work through it. You should answer all the questions. If you cannot do a particular question, leave it and go on to the next. You can return to it later.

SECTION1

You should spend about 20 minutes on Questions 1-14.

Questions 1-4

The following table gives information about immunisation.

IMMUNISATION CALENDAR		
AGE	DISEASE	VACCINE
2 months	Diphtheria, Tetanus, Pertussis	DTPw*
	Poliomyelitis	OPV-Sabin vaccine
	Hib	Hib vaccine (HbOC or PRP-OMP)**
4 months	Diphtheria, Tetanus, Pertussis	DTPw*
	Poliomyelitis	OPV-Sabin vaccine
	Hib	Hib vaccine (HbOC or PRP-OMP)**
6 months	Diphtheria, Tetanus, Pertussis	DTPw*
	Poliomyelitis	OPV-Sabin vaccine
	Hib (HbOC schedule only)	Hib vaccine (HbOC)
12 months	Measles, Mumps, Rubella	MMR
	Hib (PRP-OMP schedule only)	Hib vaccine (PRP-OMP)
18 months	Diphtheria, Tetanus, Pertussis,	DTPa or DTPw
	Hib (HbOC schedul only)	Hib vaccine(HbOC)
Prior to school—4-5 years+	Diphtheria, Tetanus, Pertussis	DTPa or DTPw
	Poliomyelitis	OPV-Sabin vaccine

+*Attendance for these booster in jetions is essential.*

**DTP is the abbreviation for diphtheria-tetanus-pertussis vaccine, commonly referred to by the trade name 'Triple Antigen'.*

***Abbreviations for haemophilus influenzae Type b (Hib) vaccines: HbOC is 'HibTITER'; PRP-OMP is 'PedvaxHIB'. HbOC ('Hib TITER') is given at two, four, six and 18 months, PRP-OMP (Pedvax HIB) is given at two, four and 12 months.*

Questions 1-2

Using ***NO MORE THAN THREE WORDS*** *taken from the table, answer the following questions. Write your answers in boxes 1-2 on your answer sheet.*

1. What is a common name for the diphtheria-tetanus-pertussis combination vaccine?
2. What does the abbreviation HbOC stand for?

Questions 3-4

Answer the questions by choosing the appropriate letters A-D and writing them in boxes 3-4 on your answer sheet.

3. Which of the following would be an appropriate schedule for Type b influenza?
   A. 2, 4 and 6 months
   B. 2, 4, 6 and 18 months
   C. 2, 4, 8 and 12 months
   D. 4, 6 and 12 months
4. The symbol "+" indicates
   A. abbreviations for haemophilus influenzae
   B. pre-school children
   C. booster injections are necessary
   D. the information has been adapted from *The Australian Immunisation Handbook*

Questions 5-14

The following reading passage about immunisation gives the answers to questions commonly asked by parents.

Questions and Answers about Immunisation

A For polio, Sabin oral vaccine is given by mouth—a few drops of pleasantly flavoured syrup on a spoon. For diphtheria, tetanus and whooping cough a combined vaccine (triple antigen) is given by injection—a quick prick from the needle, over in a few seconds. Measles and rubella vaccine are also given by injection.

B There are sometimes mild side effects to the triple antigen vaccine. These may include some local redness, tenderness and swelling at the site of the injection during the 48-hour period which follows it. There may also be slight nausea, fretfulness and feverishness. Major reactions are extremely rare. Possible reactions to measles immunisation include fever, rash and a stuffy nose about 5-12 days after the injection. These symptoms last about 2-3 days, do not cause much discomfort and normally do not require treatment. The child is not infective to others.

C A full course of immunisation will still give protection when completed, even if it does not strictly follow the Health Commission's recommended schedule.

D Although two months is the recommended starting age, immunisation will be equally effective if commenced in older children. The early start is advised because whooping cough is most serious in young babies. Immunisation can still ensure protection for children over eight years and adults, provided the vaccine appropriate to their age is used.

E If a child has diarrhoea, Sabin oral vaccine should not be given. If a child vomits within two hours of taking Sabin oral vaccine, the dose should be repeated.

Before you have your child immunised, please tell the doctor if your child:

- Is suffering from any sickness or allergy;
- Has had a severe reaction to a previous immunisation such as persistent screaming or persistent vomiting, or collapse, or convulsions, or fever exceeding 29.5℃;
- Has ever had fits, or if other members of the family have had an illness of the nervous system or convulsions;
- Has had a blood transfusion or an injection of gamma globulin in the last three months;
- Is under treatment with a cortisone-like drug.

F For some children the Hepatitis B vaccine may also be recommended. Please consult your doctor for advice.

G

- Your doctor, or
- Your local council, or
- Community Health Centres in some Health Regions

There are 7 sections A-G.

Choose the most suitable heading for each section from the list below. Write the appropriate numbers (i-x) in boxes 5-10 on your answer sheet.

NB There are more headings than sections so you will not use all of them. You may use any of the headings more than once.

HEADINGS

i What if the course is interrupted?

ii Special note

iii	How is immunisation done?
iv	Who should be immunised?
v	Are there any special precautions to take when immunising?
vi	What if the child is older?
vii	How to treat reactions to immunisation
viii	Will baby have a reaction to the injection?
ix	Where to go for immunisation?
x	Why should children be immunised?

Questions 5-10

Example	*Answer*
Section **F**	ii

5. Section A
6. Section B
7. Section C
8. Section D
9. Section E
10. Section G

Questions 11-12

Choose the appropriate letters A-D and write them in boxes 11-12 on your answer sheet.

11. The vaccine for which illness comes in the form of a syrup?
   A. tetanus B. diphtheria
   C. poliomyelitis D. measles

12. Which of the following is NOT mentioned as a possible side effect of the DTP vaccine?
   A. redness B. nausea
   C. fever D. rash

Questions 13-14

Complete the sentences below with words taken from the Reading Passage 'Questions and Answers about Immunisation'. Use **NO MORE THAN THREE WORDS** *for each answer. Write your answers in boxes 13-14 on your answer sheet.*

13. You must tell the doctor if your child is being treated with a ________ drug.
14. You must tell the doctor if your child has previously had a reaction such as ________.

Section 2

Questions 15-21

Read passage below and answer the questions that follow.

Canadian College

CONDITIONS

Canadian College is a leading provider of acting, film making, English (ESL/EFL), business, computer, and language training in Victoria, British Columbia, Canada. Canadian College is the only private training institution in Victoria, offering Acting, Filmmaking and ESL programs, that is registered and accredited with the Private Post-Secondary Education Commission of British Columbia.

A team of dedicated professionals who are highly respected by government officials, other businesses and the community leads Canadian College. Our mission is to help learners achieve their goals by offering quality educational programs, facilities and services, in a caring, culturally diverse environment.

TERMS AND CONDITIONS OF ENROLMENT

TUITION AND FEES

All tuition and fees must be paid by the due dates specified on the enrolment application (or registration invoice, if applicable). Letters of acceptance, homestay information, diplomas, certificates, transcripts and reports will not be issued unless all required tuition and fees have been paid.

ENROLMENT

Enrolment may be subject to the applicant following with the admission policies for their program of study as well as undergoing an assessment. The college reserves the right to modify programs, materials, schedules, rules, regulations and policies as required. All programs are subject to sufficient enrolment and maybe postponed or canceled at the discretion of the college. In the event a program is canceled, a full refund or credit would be given.

REFUND POLICY

If a student wishes to cancel or withdraw from a program and wishes to be considered for a refund, written notice must be submitted to the Admissions Office. The amount of the refund, depends on when the notice of cancellation or withdrawal is received, type of student and the program duration. An international student is a person who is not a Canadian Citizen or landed immigrant. The program duration is determined by the start and end dates on the enrolment application form.

PLEASE NOTE: Registering for a program duration of three months or more is not the same as registering for a series of individual one month terms. By registering for a program duration of three months or more, a student is committing to attend for one long term, not a series of short one month terms. For this long-term commitment, the student receives a lower tuition fee and their refund is calculated on the registration as one long term, not individual one month terms. Students who are not sure of their future plans and who do not wish to commit to long terms of study are advised to register for individual one month terms.

TUITION REFUND

	International Student	Canadian Citizen
NOTICE RECEIVED	REFUND %	REFUND %
>= 30 days before program start date	75%	90%
< 30 days before program start date	60%	80%
Within 10% of program completed	50%	70%
Within 30% of program completed	30%	50%
After 30% of program completed	0%	0%
* includes books and materials		

HOMESTAY REFUND

Monthly and daily homestay fees are refunded, if notice of cancellation is received 30 days or more before the homestay start date.

BOOKS & MATERIALS REFUND

Books and materials are included in the tuition refund, if notice of cancellation is received before the program start date. Once the program has started, books and materials are non-refundable.

NON-REFUNDABLE ITEMS

No refund or credit will be given for student absences from scheduled classes or tests. Registration fees, TOEIC Testing fees, and Homestay Placement fees are non-refundable.

Canadian College reserves the right to suspend or dismiss a student for disciplinary reasons, if the student acts in contravention to the instructions of college staff or breaches college rules, regulations, or policies. Students are responsible to obtain and abide by the college rules, regulations and policies.

Students participate in college activities at their own risk and by making application to the college, do hereby release Canadian College of Business & Language Inc., its employees, agents, assigns and volunteers from any and all liability for any loss, damage, injury or expenses suffered due to any cause whatsoever.

Questions 15-21

Answer these questions in **NO MORE THAN THREE WORDS**. *Write your answers in boxes 15-21 on your answer sheet.*

15. What kind of institution is Canadian College?
16. In addition to following registration procedures according to admission policies, what else does a student have to take part in?
17. If you don't want to attend the whole year or even for a three month program, how long can you also attend for?
18. What type of student receives a 70% refund if they cancel with 90% of the program still left?
19. If you notify the program after it has started that you are not attending, what will you not get money back for other than tuition?
20. What do students participate in at their own risk?
21. If you skip a class, what can you not receive?

Questions 22-28

Here and on the next page are several passages giving information for exchange students in the Essex Rotary Exchange Program.

The Essex Rotary Exchange Program

INTRODUCTION

In the Essex Program, U.S.A outbound or foreign inbound students spend a full academic year with one or more host families of the visiting country beginning in late summer. Host parents provide room and meals as well as support and guidance. The host Rotary Club provides a limited monthly spending allowance, counseling, and supervision.

IN GOOD COMPANY!

Every year, almost 10,000 young people from 66 countries see the world the way it is best seen—from the inside out—through Rotary's Youth Exchange program. As a Rotary Exchange student, you may learn a new language but you will certainly learn a new way of living—and a great deal about yourself. The people you meet will learn too—about your country, and your culture and ideas. As an unofficial ambassador you will bring the world closer together and make new friends in theprocess.

READY FOR ADVENTURE?

You can make a difference—a world of difference. When you step off the airplane as an exchange student in another country, you have the opportunity to:

- Become part of another culture
- Learn another language
- Gain confidence and maturity
- Broaden your view of the world
- Learn about yourself
- Meet people, make new friends
- Experience new places and cultures
- Be a youth ambassador

GUIDELINES AND CONDITIONS

By participating in a Rotary Exchange program through ESSEX, students and theirparents agree to comply with all rules and conditions of ESSEX's exchange program. Students and the parents of outbound exchange students must read and sign the rules plus submit a signed copy of the rules with the student's application.

AGE—You must be in high school at the time of application, and should be in the age range of 15 to 18 when you will be leaving the country.

EXCHANGE YEAR—This is a school year program. School years vary from country to country.

ESCHOOL—This is a high school (pre-university) program. You will be attending high school in your host country. Requests for instruction at a higher academic institution cannot and will not be accommodated.

SCHOOL CREDIT—You must not expect to receive a diploma or to graduate from high school in your host country. Credits for course work taken in another country cannot be assured. Transferring of course credits will depend on the policies of your home high school and the foreign high school you will be attending.

COSTS—You and / or your parents are financially responsible for:

1) All necessary documents (passport, visa, translation fees, etc.),

2) All round trip transportation (obtained through the official ESSEX approved travel agency, Bokoff-Kaplan),

3) All insurance (the ESSEX approved AIG policy and any policy required by your host Rotary District),

4) Any necessary or required language training or camps (required in some countries),

5) All appropriate clothing, toiletries, and other personal items,

6) Reasonable spending money,

7) Costs of any trips, activities, and events in which you participate,

8) Any required "emergency fund",

9) All phone/computer/intemet charges,

10) Orientation fees (in your sponsoring and in your host Rotary Districts), and

11) All other sponsoring or hosting Rotary District fees.

VACCINATIONS—Check with your doctor, local county or state health department, or the official ESSEX approved travel agency, Bokoff-Kaplan, concerning any necessary vaccinations for your host country. Get those vaccinations in a timely manner.

INSURANCE—The completed application form must be received by your sponsoring District Rotary Youth Exchange Chair prior to your departure. This insurance is mandatory.

DURING THE EXCHANGE YEAR

TRAVEL—This is a cultural exchange NOT a travel exchange. All travel in the host country is subject to the rules of the hosting Rotary District and Multi-District Group.

REGULAR REPORTS—You are required to submit regular reports on your exchange to your sponsoring District Rotary Youth Exchange Chair during your exchange year.

ROLE AS AN AMBASSADOR—You are expected to do your best to maintain a positive attitude throughout the exchange year, and act appropriately as an ambassador for Rotary. You must do your best to adjust to your host family and friends.

VISITS—If your natural parents or other relatives plan to visit you during the exchange year, they should make this visit only during your last two months, and then only with the advance approval of your host District Rotary Youth Exchange Chair, host Rotary Club, and host family.

Questions 22-28

Complete the sentences below with words taken from 'The Essex Rotary Exchange Program' on the previous pages. Use NO MORE THAN THREE WORDS for each answer.

22. When you are part of the program each student lives with a______.
23. Each student is an unofficial ______ in their visiting country.
24. This program is only for ______ students.
25. For transportation you need to deal with the programs official ______.
26. You might have to pay additional fees in your host ______.
27. Students are in this program to learn about cultures, not ______.
28. While in the program you should always keep a ______.

SECTION 3

You should spend about 20 minutes on Questions 29-40 which are based on the reading passage in Section 3.

Vision of Lifelong Learning Put at the Heart of OECD Target

Governments must step up their efforts to encourage lifelong learning, according to a report by the Organisation for Economic Cooperation and Development.

The conclusions of the latest edition of the organisation's Education Policy Analysis were on the agenda at this week's meeting of OECD education ministers, for discussions on how citizens could benefit from opportunities to upgrade education and skills throughout their lives.

The report reviews the achievements of OECD member states—the world's 30 richest countries—since 1996, when ministers committed themselves to a 'cradle-to-grave' vision of lifelong learning.

John Martin, director for education, employment, labour and social affairs, said investment in lifelong learning 'must be a top priority for OECD countries in the years ahead.'

The consensus on education and training 'shared by politicians from George W. Bush to Tony Blair' was based on 'a belief that investing in high-quality education and training is the key determinant in an increasingly globalised world economy, that education has a key role to play in fostering citizenship and social cohesion; and, in the context of ageing populations, there is growing pressure on individuals and firms to upgrade their competencies and skills'.

Reviewing progress, the report finds 'grounds for optimism and grounds for caution'. Though 'many pieces of the lifelong learning jigsaw can already be widely observed in OECD countries... no country has yet put them together to complete the jigsaw', it says.

It identifies education inequalities that are 'compounded by inferior access among traditionally disadvantaged groups to computers and the Internet, especially at home,' though schools play an important part in reducing the digital divide.

Increased public spending does not always produce good education systems, it says, though countries with strong all-round performances—in particular Denmark, Finland, Norway and Sweden—are high spenders.

Spending trends in tertiary education from 1990 to 1996 show that only Australia and Spain increased expenditure per student by more than 10 percent in the face of substantial student expansion. Extra students elsewhere were financed through flexible, cheaper options such as part-time courses, distance learning or private colleges.

The report presents six scenarios for the school of the future, setting out the policy issues and strategic choices that face ministers for shaping schooling in the long term. It places the possibilities in three categories:

- Status quo-schools continue as they are, possibly with greater reliance on market approaches that could have positive effects by introducing innovation, or negative results such as increased risks of exclusion.
- Re-schooling-development of social links and community leadership could strengthen public recognition, support and autonomy of schools, which could become 'learning organisation' with a strong focus on knowledge and highly motivated teachers.
- De-schooling-dismantling school institutions and systems and replacing them with non-formal learning networks driven by information and communications technologies. In the worst case, policies would fail to prevent severe teacher shortages (faced by many OECD countries), and retrenchment, conflict and falling standards would lead to more or less extensive 'meltdown'.

Questions 29-33

Choose the appropriate letters A-D for each question and write them in boxes 29-33 on your answer sheet.

29. OECD stands for
    A. Overseas Education for Community Development
    B. Organisation for Economic Cooperation and Development
    C. Organisation for Education Cooperation and Development
    D. Overseas Economic Community Development

30. Which of the following is NOT given as one of the reasons for encouraging lifelong learning?
    A. The puzzle urgently needs to be solved.
    B. Work skills need to be continually improved.
    C. The world economy is globalising.
    D. It contributes to good citizenship.

31. The digital divide means differences in
    A. mathematical ability
    B. quality of computers available in schools
    C. ability to use the Internet
    D. opportunity to access information technology

32. Four Scandinavian countries are mentioned as examples of countries that
    A. spend a lot on education
    B. continually increase public spending
    C. provide modern technology in schools
    D. have poor education systems

33. Australia and Spain are mentioned as countries that
    A. provide part-time courses for extra students
    B. spent 10% more in 1996 than in 1990
    C. increased funding per student by more than 10%
    D. reduced tertiary education spending

Questions 34-35

Using ***NO MORE THAN THREE WORDS****, name TWO ways that are mentioned in the passage for governments to provide education more cheaply. Write your answers in boxes 34-35 on your answer sheet.*

34. ____________________

35. ____________________

Questions 36-40

Three categories for shaping schooling for the future are given in the reading passage 'Vision of Lifelong Learning Put at the Heart of OECD Target'. With which category is each of the following associated?

SQ *Status Quo*

RS *Re-Schooling*

DS *De-Schooling*

Write the appropriate letters in boxes 36-40 on your answer sheet.

36. New ideas and methods
37. Shortage of teachers
38. Learning networks
39. Greater independence of institution
40. Greater dependence on IT

Answer Sheet

Module taken:

Academic○ General Training○

Version number:

Please enter the number in the boxes and shade the number in the grid.

00	10	20	30	40	50	60	70	80	90
□	□	□	□	□	□	□	□	□	□
0	1	2	3	4	5	6	7	8	9
□	□	□	□	□	□	□	□	□	□

		√ ✕			√ ✕
1		○ 1 ○	21		○ 21 ○
2		○ 2 ○	22		○ 22 ○
3		○ 3 ○	23		○ 23 ○
4		○ 4 ○	24		○ 24 ○
5		○ 5 ○	25		○ 25 ○
6		○ 6 ○	26		○ 26 ○
7		○ 7 ○	27		○ 27 ○
8		○ 8 ○	28		○ 28 ○
9		○ 9 ○	29		○ 29 ○
10		○ 10 ○	30		○ 30 ○
11		○ 11 ○	31		○ 31 ○
12		○ 12 ○	32		○ 32 ○
13		○ 13 ○	33		○ 33 ○
14		○ 14 ○	34		○ 34 ○
15		○ 15 ○	35		○ 35 ○
16		○ 16 ○	36		○ 36 ○
17		○ 17 ○	37		○ 37 ○
18		○ 18 ○	38		○ 38 ○
19		○ 19 ○	39		○ 39 ○
20		○ 20 ○	40		○ 40 ○

Band Score		Reading Total	

Keys to Exercises 参考答案

Chapter Three

part 3

Reading Passage 1

1. ⅳ 2. ⅷ 3. ⅴ 4. ⅲ 5. ⅰ

Reading Passage 2

1. ⅹ 2. ⅲ 3. ⅵ 4. ⅳ 5. ⅴ

Reading Passage 3

1. ⅲ 2. ⅹ 3. ⅴ 4. ⅶ 5. ⅱ

Reading Passage 4

1. G 2. H 3. I 4. E 5. A 6. C

Reading Passage 5

1. ⅱ 2. ⅷ 3. ⅲ 4. ⅴ 5. ⅵ 6. ⅶ 7. ⅳ

Reading Passage 6

1. ⅸ 2. ⅱ 3. ⅳ 4. ⅴ 5. ⅰ

Chapter Four

Part 3

Reading Passage 1

1. YES 2. NOT GIVEN 3. NOT GIVEN 4. NOT GIVEN 5. NO 6. YES

Reading Passage 2

1. No 2. Yes 3. Not Given 4. Yes 5. Not Given

Reading Passage 3

1. Yes 2. Not Given 3. Yes 4. Not Given 5. Not Given 6. No 7. No

Chapter Five

Part 3

Reading Passage 1

1. utilize 2. alleviate 3. landscapes 4. remedies
5. harvested 6. educated 7. parking lots

Reading Passage 2

1. biometrics 2. fingerprinting 3. commercial
4. finger scanning 5. iris 6. retina

Reding Passage 3

1. gains 2. paid labour force 3. participation
4. informal labour sector 5. bargaining power 6. furthermore 7. domestic

Reding Passage 4

1. freedom 2. organised 3. Sports grounds / sports halls
4. intensive 5. one 6. assessments / criticism
7. fun 8. pressure

Reading Passage 5

1. (south) England 2. (high-pitched, warbling) noises / sounds
3. animals / insects / wild creatures 4. avoid

Chapter Six

Part 3

Reading Passage 1

1. B 2. G 3. E 4. D 5. F 6. C

Reading Passage 2

1. C 2. G 3. A 4. F 5. D 6. B or E

Reading Passage 3

1. E 2. B 3. F 4. D

Reading Passage 4

1. pollutants / greenhouse-gas emission 2. natural energy flows 3. biased

Reading Passage 5

1. a threatened species 2. cubs 3. salmon trees 4. Rocky Mountains

Chapter Seven

Part 3

Reading Passage 1

1. C 2. A 3. D 4. A

Reading Passage 2

1. D 2. A 3. B 4. C 5. C 6. A

Reading Passage 3

1. C 2. A 3. D 4. B 5. A

Chapter Eight

Part 3

Reading Passage 1

1. C 2. B 3. A 4. C 5. A

Reading Passage 2

1. AH 2. TM 3. ChD 4. DM 5. TM 6. DM

Reading Passage 3

1. B 2. C 3. A / B 4. D 5. A

Chapter Nine

Part 3

Reading Passage 1

1. low quality 2. (virtually) no THC

Reading Passage 2

1. tree 2. flat 3. slender / curved
4. crow 5. in their wings 6. shallow marine seediments

Reading Passuge 3

1. tea 2. waterborne diseases / dysentery
3. tax / tax on malt / malt tax 4. boiled

Chapter Ten

Part 3

Reading Passage 1

1. USI / Universal Salt Indisation 2. Pakistan (and) Indonesia

3. technical monograph 4. sugar

Reading Passage 2

1. (by) spreading seeds 2. restoring connections
3. connectine (all) (the) wild areas

Chapter Eleven

Part 3

Reading Passage 1

1. offices 2. sorted 3. repulped 4. deink 5. refined

Readin passage 2

1. Cro-Magnons 2. (the) solar 3. (the) ancient Egyptians
4. (the) year 5. 362.242,199

Readin passage 3

1. F 2. A 3. E 4. B 5. D

Chapter Twelve

Mock Reading Test 1

1. ii 2. vi 3. ix 4. v 5. i
6. x 7. iv 8. NO 9. NOT GIVEN 10. YES
11. YES 12. NOT GIVEN 13. NOT GIVEN
14. UM 15. VC 16. TC
17. UM 18. UC 19. NO
20. NOT GIVEN 21. NO 22. NOT GIVEN
23. NO 24. NOT GIVEN 25. pay
26. plagiarism / detection system / device / cheat detector
27. electronic translator
28. A 29. F 30. N 31. A 32. A 33. YES 34. NOT GIVEN 35. NO
36. NO 37. yields 38. England and Europe 39. labelled 40. increased supply

Mock Reading Test 2

1. developed world 2. 28 3. 18-20 4. majority 5. the aged 6. the population
7. all adults 8. D 9. A 10. C 11. A 12. B 13. B 14. iv 15. vii
16. ii 17. i 18. v iii 19. v 20. ix
21. pollutants / greenhouse-gas emissions
22. natural energy flows 23. biased

24. sun / wind / water / biomass (any two of the four)
25. 28% 26. C 27. B 28. C 29. B 30. E 31. D 32. H 33. B 34. A
35. A 36. B 37. persuade / motivate / inspire 38. persuade / motivate / inspire
39. evaluate 40. language

Mock Reading Test 3

1. Triple Antigen 2. HibTITER 3. B 4. C 5. iii 6. viii 7. i 8. vi
9. v 10. ix 11. C 12. D 13. cortisone-like
14. persistent screaming / persistent vomiting / collapse / convulsions / fever exceeding 29.5℃
15. private 16. an assessment 17. one month 18. Canadian citizen
19. books and meterials 20. college activities 21. refund or credit 22. host family
23. ambassador 24. hihg school 25. travel agency 26. rotary district 27. travel
28. positive attitude 29. B 30. A 31. D 32. A 33. C
34. part-time courses / distant learning / private college
35. part-tine courses / distant learning / private cdlege
36. SQ 37. DS 38. DS 39. RS 40. DS